Studies in Social Policy

'Studies in Social Policy' is an important new series of textbooks intended for students of social administration and social welfare at all levels. The books will be directly related to the needs of undergraduate and postgraduate students in universities, polytechnics and similar institutions as well as vocational students preparing for careers in a variety of social and other public services. The series will include the following topics:

the roles of different public and private institutions such as social services departments and building societies in meeting social needs;

introductory guides to new technical and theoretical developments relevant to the analysis of social policy such as political theory and the newly emerging specialism of the economics of social care;

contemporary social policy issues such as the use of charges in the delivery of social welfare or the problem of determining priorities in the health and personal social services.

Studies in Social Policy

Editor: Ken Judge

Published

The Building Societies
Martin Boddy

Pricing the Social Services
Ken Judge (ed.)

Choices for Health Care
Gavin H. Mooney, Elizabeth M. Russell
and Roy D. Weir

Power, Authority and Responsibility in Social
Services: Social work in area teams
Malcolm Payne

Forthcoming

Political Theory and Social Policy
Albert Weale

The Building Societies

Martin Boddy

M

First published 1980 by
THE MACMILLAN PRESS LTD
London and Basingstoke
Associated companies in Delhi Dublin
Hong Kong Johannesburg Lagos Melbourne
New York Singapore and Tokyo

Printed in Great Britain by
A. Wheaton & Co. Ltd., Exeter

British Library Cataloguing in Publication Data

Boddy, Martin
    The building societies. – (Studies in social
    policy).
    1. Building and loan associations –Great
    Britain
    I. Title II. Series
    332.3′2′0941   HG2156.G75

    ISBN 0–333–27150–5
    ISBN 0–333–27151–3 Pbk

Contents

Acknowledgements

Thanks are due to the many people who have contributed to the production of this book by providing information, through discussing their own writing on the subject, or through reading earlier versions of the manuscript. In particular I would like to thank Peter Ambrose, who initially encouraged me to embark on the project; Henry Aughton, Beverley Brown, David Byrne, Simon Duncan, Geoff Green, Ken Judge and Peter Williams for argument and discussion; officials of many building societies, the Building Societies Association and Building Societies Institute for invaluable help, information and explanation; and finally friends at the School for Advanced Urban Studies, Bristol University, in particular Glen Bramley, Alan Murie, Gillian Sawyer and Randall Smith, who straightened out several chapters and produced the final manuscript. Data from HMSO publications are reproduced with the permission of the Controller of Her Majesty's Stationery Office. The book is dedicated with respect to Cris, who died in 1978.

Bristol   MARTIN BODDY
April 1979

Introduction

This book is about building societies, home-ownership and housing policy in Britain. Building societies became in the 1970s a major focus of concern for the public, the press, politicians and policy-makers. The societies have grown from comparative obscurity into one of Britain's largest financial institutions. With collective assets of nearly £40 000 million at the end of 1978 they are second only to the insurance companies, having outgrown the pension funds, high-street banks, savings banks and national savings; 43 per cent of Britain's adult population were investing in a building society in 1978 and over five million people were buying a house with a building-society loan. Snappy advertisements and the mushrooming of prominently placed high-street branches in search of investors have catapulted the societies into the public eye. But the concern of several million existing and aspiring house-buyers has focused more particularly on mortgage availability, house prices, the mortgage rate and building society lending policies. And with this concern has grown the attention of academics, politicians and policy-makers, in the climate of debate fostered by the major government review of housing policy and publication of the Green Paper *Housing Policy: a consultative document*.[1]

The building societies are financial intermediaries channelling money from investors to borrowers. They stand with one foot in the finance market and the other in the housing market directing personal savings and investment into private house purchase. As financial institutions they compete for a share of personal savings with a wide range of public and private institutions. But in the housing market they dominate the supply of mortgage finance almost completely, having provided over 85 per cent of institutional funds for house purchase over the last decade. Over 80 per cent of their total funds on average are loaned out to private households buying houses for owner-occupation and the rest is largely 'liquid assets', cash and investments.

It is above all building-society lending which has enabled and encouraged the massive expansion of home-ownership in Britain since the First World War. In 1919 fewer than one in ten householders owned the house in which they lived. Most rented from a private landlord. By 1979, however, 54 per cent were home-owners, 32 per cent rented public housing and around 10 per cent rented private housing. Owner-occupiers now outnumber quite considerably households in all the other tenure groups. And since the building societies are the major source of finance for house purchase, their performance in the housing market and their detailed lending policies are crucially important to the housing system. Their success in attracting investment largely governs the availability of mortgages; this in turn is a major influence on housing demand and therefore on house prices, land prices and the house-building industry. Who the societies lend to, and on what terms, affect which families get what housing and how much it costs them; the sort of housing which they will grant loans on influences the rate of urban decay and the success of policies to revitalise the inner city.

But the expansion of loan-financed house purchase is more than simply a way of obtaining housing. It is also a form of investment and wealth-accumulation, since owner-occupiers, unlike tenants, acquire a substantial and appreciating capital asset. And home-ownership also represents ownership of private property; the coming of mass home-ownership in Britain is the realisation of the 'property-owning democracy', with widespread social, political and ideological implications.

Support for home-ownership and for its continued expansion has become a central element of government housing policy, and is backed by both major political parties. The dominant role of the building societies in financing home-ownership thus places their operations at the centre of housing policy. Since the early 1970s a new relationship of co-operation has been fostered between building societies and central and local government, within the framework of national housing policy. Government policy has endeavoured to ensure an adequate and stable supply of mortgage funds, to keep down the cost of house-buying, to widen access to home-ownership, and to encourage building societies to finance extension of owner-occupation to lower-income households and those buying older housing. This has, inevitably, raised the question of the impact of the expansion of home-ownership on the housing system as a whole – its impact on the distribution of housing resources and wealth to those who cannot buy and on poorer households who may be forced by lack of alternatives to become mortgaged to the hilt to buy decaying inner-city housing. Thus discussion of building societies and home-ownership necessarily leads one to consider housing policy and the housing system as a whole.

This book starts in the past and finishes by discussing policies for the future. Between the two, it is to be hoped, lies the basis for better understanding of the place of building societies and home-ownership in the finance market, the housing system and society at large. The aim, however, is not simply understanding but change, and this book is offered as a modest step in the right direction. The first two chapters are historical and the third is an account of building societies today. Chapter 1 describes the origin and evolution of the building societies before the First World War, the period during which the foundations were laid for their massive twentieth-century growth and for the expansion of home-ownership. Chapter 2 maps out societies' development since the First World War, their role in the fundamental transformation of housing tenure in the context of national housing policy, and considers the social impact of these changes. Chapter 3 then analyses the present-day financial and organisational structure of the building-society movement, breaking down the aggregate structure into its component parts – societies, branches and agents – and describing societies' policy and control, their legal framework and the influential Building Societies Association.

The next four chapters pivot around the building societies' dual role as financial intermediaries, first at the level of individual investors and borrowers and then at the aggregate level of the finance market and the housing market. Chapter 4 explains the different types of building society investment account and summarises the characteristics of investors. Chapter 5 explains different types of mortgage and analyses building-society mortgage-lending procedures and allocation criteria in detail, contrasting them with lending by local authorities, banks and insurance companies. Chapter 6 considers societies' performance in the finance market, government measures which shelter and advantage their operations, the debate on building societies, monetary policy and the use of resources within the economy, and finally instability of investment in the societies and of mortgage-lending. Chapter 7 then considers the impact of the volume and stability of mortgage-lending on house-building, house prices, land prices and the absorption of funds in the private housing sector.

The last two chapters focus specifically on housing policy and the housing system. Given the strong emphasis in national housing policy on the expansion of home-ownership and on specific measures to achieve this aim, Chapter 8 considers the adequacy of the overall supply of mortgage funds, the terms on which these funds are made available to individual borrowers and the impact of mortgage-lending on older inner-city housing areas, assessing the likely success of the policy objectives. Chapter 9 then examines the overall structure of housing taxation and subsidy in which such policies are set and considers the impact of such policies, should they succeed, on the housing system as a whole and on lower-income households in particular.

1

The origins and evolution of building societies up to 1919

Today's building societies are firmly rooted in the past. Their corporate status as friendly societies distinct from commercial banks and companies, the legal framework within which they operate and many features of their function and practice were largely established before the First World War. Their ideology still draws on the Victorian virtues of thrift and mutual self-help and, beyond this, on their origins in eighteenth-century co-operative and friendly societies. An account of the societies' origins and evolution is thus an essential element in understanding their character today.

The first building societies emerged out of the variety of co-operative and friendly societies which arose in the eighteenth century supporting the uprooted migrants to the new industrial urban areas. The influx of population to the towns in the last half of the eighteenth and early nineteenth centuries produced very rapid urbanisation. In the first 30 years of the nineteenth century cities like Birmingham, Leeds and Manchester more than doubled in size. The lack of social provision and housing for the urban immigrants who had left behind the supports of the rural community was the spur to the foundation of a variety of mutual, self-help organisations to fill the gap, most commonly among the better-off working class with some capacity for saving.

The first society for which records exist was founded in the Golden Cross Inn in Birmingham in 1775, soon followed by others in the Midlands and North. According to the 1836 Building Societies Act:

a building society is established for the purpose of raising, by monthly or other subscriptions of the several members of such societies, shares not exceeding the value of £150 for each share, such subscriptions not to exceed in the whole 20s. per month for each share, a stock or fund for the purpose of enabling each member thereof to receive out of the funds of such society the amount or value of his or her share or shares therein, to erect or purchase one or more dwelling house or dwelling houses, or other real or leasehold estate, to be secured by way of a mortgage to such society until the amount or value of his or her shares shall have been fully repaid to such society, with interest thereon, and all fines.[1]

Members paid their subscription throughout the life of the society. When the joint subscriptions of the various members led to the accumulation of funds equal to one share, this sum of money was allocated to one member by some form of selection procedure, the member continuing to subscribe until the society terminated. By termination every member should in turn have received the amount of their share.

These early societies operated in a variety of ways. Some had houses built while others allocated money rather than houses. Allocation systems also varied, some societies using a ballot, others an auction. In some cases members successful in a ballot would sell their right to money or a house to the highest bidder. A system of fines encouraged members and officers (the latter elected from the members) to maintain payments and fulfil their duties. Usually the rules provided for standard payments for drink to be consumed at societies' regular meetings in inns – the first 50 years of society history reveal no society unattached to licensed premises. This emphasises the genuine working-class basis of the earliest societies, although the level of subscriptions indicates that members were from the more prosperous fractions. The Longridge Society, for example, founded near Preston in 1793, listed among its members weavers, yeomen, stonemasons, a carpenter and a cotton spinner. Initially, societies usually registered under the 1793 Friendly Societies Act and they are still, today, administered by the Registry of Friendly Societies. Their actual legality remained in doubt until upheld in the courts in 1812, and specific legal recognition came with the 1836 Act. These early societies were, however, small and had little impact – Price has estimated that, in the first 50 years up to 1825, 250 societies were involved in the building or buying of only 2000 houses, these mainly in the Midlands and the North.[2]

The major change in the way societies operated and the key to the massive growth of individual societies was the development from the mid-nineteenth century of permanent societies. Previously societies terminated when each member had been allocated a share. Their financial structure discouraged members joining after the initial foundation, since back-payments would be required, and their capacity to accumulate funds was severely limited. Societies tended, therefore, increasingly to take in deposits from investors seeking interest rather than loans or houses, to increase the funds available for members wishing to borrow. Later subscriptions from borrowers repaid investors with interest.

The first recorded permanent society dates from 1845 but according to Cleary there were 540 by 1873, compared with 959 terminating societies.[3] Furthermore the permanent societies rapidly grew into much larger financial institutions than their forerunners. In terminating societies investors and borrowers were one and the same group of people. But in permanent societies the rigid tie between investors and borrowers, loosened by the deposit-taking of terminating societies, was broken. Investors could join at any time and withdraw their money at will; borrowers received loans which they repaid over a fixed number of years. Permanent societies became increasingly attractive to investors. The 1872 Royal Commission report noted that 'a building society, with its money secured on freehold land and leasehold property, and a constant incoming of repayments by monthly instalments may fairly be preferred . . . to a bank',[4] and suggested that permanent societies often appeared to be 'mainly agencies for the investment of capital, rather than for enabling the industrious to provide dwellings for themselves'.[5]

Permanent societies founded in the mid-nineteenth century have in many cases survived to the present day. But as the financial structure of the societies evolved, so their roots in the working class were shaken loose. In 1872 the Commissioners noted the opinion that the growth of permanent societies had 'altogether changed the character and altered the sphere of the building society movement',[6] concluding that:

It appears, indeed, unquestionable that whilst the smaller, terminating societies remain very often still under the management of the working classes, or of persons very near to them in point of station, the larger permanent societies at least are almost invariably under the direction of the middle class. . . . it is safe to say that the English middle class now enters into the building society movement . . . in much larger numbers, take a much larger share in its direction, and derive much greater benefit from it, than they did 30 or 35 years ago.[7]

Permanent societies rapidly became substantial financial institutions, needing skilled management rather than administration on an amateur basis by officers elected from the members. The new type of members wanted little involvement in running the societies, and the changing requirements of management were met by the influx of the educated bourgeoisie, whether socially, religiously or commercially minded. The involvement of the Aykroyd and Crossley families (religiously minded and leading manufacturers) in the Halifax building societies is typical. It was at this time that many societies became dissociated from the demon drink and met in the more spiritual atmosphere of non-conformist schoolrooms or temperance halls, while others, such as the Halifax, acquired office premises in urban business districts. Increasingly towards the end of the century the leaders of the movement had Liberal and non-conformist connections. The *Building Societies Gazette*, founded in 1869 and still the main publication devoted to the movement, received early finance from the non-conformist journal *Christian World*.

The term 'building' society was a misnomer over 100 years ago for, as the Royal Commission reported:

'building societies do not build they simply make advances on building.' They are in fact investment associations, mainly confining themselves to real securities. . . . It must indeed be observed that this was the older practice, of which the present title of 'benefit building society' is a relic.[8]

Although much of their lending was to individuals buying speculatively built houses for owner-occupation, loans to house-builders and to landlords buying houses to let were a significant part of their business. Some societies also, at this time, made loans often of substantial amounts to industrialists and landowners. The Commissioners, however, saw no reason to restrict loans to individual house-buyers.

Corporate status and the 1874 Building Societies Act

Commercial enterprises evolved, in the mid-nineteenth century, into legally constituted corporate bodies. Companies could be incorporated under the 1844 Joint Stock Companies Act and shareholders gained limited liability. Banks could acquire corporate status under the 1855 Bank Act. Corporate status separates individuals from the enterprise, which thereby becomes a legally recognised and responsible body. The continuity through time of the enterprise is established independently of its promoters or members, being managed by persons without, necessarily, any direct financial interest in it. It was against this background that the 1872 Commission considered whether societies should be incorporated under the existing legislation as companies or banks; for the term 'building society' had come to embrace institutions whose activities made them virtually indistinguishable from banks, and others which were in effect commercial companies. The boundaries marking off the field of building-society activity from banks and companies remained blurred, in practice, right up to the First World War.

The Royal Commission considered that societies were marked off from banks because their investment was, usually, mainly confined to property. The resulting security of investment enabled societies to lend for terms much longer than banks felt prudent, given the banks' more varied and generally inferior security. The societies specialised in this field of investment to the exclusion of banks and other institutions. The possibility of societies registering under company legislation was considered at greater length, though strongly resisted by the societies themselves. Finally, however, the Commission concluded that building societies were, like other friendly societies, founded on membership rather than, like companies, on capital. Societies' share capital grows gradually, membership is always open, the number of shares remains indefinite and shares can be redeemed at will, eliminating the need for a secondary market like the stock exchange. As the Commissioners bluntly concluded, recommending the continuation of societies as a distinct corporate form: 'The two forms of undertaking . . . have an equal right to subsist, the one for the use of those who seek to make capital, the other for those who seek, having made it, to use it'.[9]

Corporate status was provided for by the 1874 Building Societies Act, which drew on the recommendations of the Royal Commission. Under this Act members gained limited liability while the society itself, rather than trustees, could now hold mortgage deeds and stand security for loans. Permanent societies were permitted to issue small denomination 'paid up' shares akin to modern ordinary shares rather than only subscription shares involving long-term saving, and could borrow from depositors up to two-thirds of the sum secured by mortgages. Investment of surplus funds was restricted to mortgages or securities carrying a government guarantee, thus prohibiting direct investment in land or other property, companies etc. A number of other rules limited the operations of societies incorporated under the Act and gave the government regulatory powers. A hundred years later the Chief Registrar of Friendly Societies wrote that the 1874 Act 'provided the legal framework within the broad scope of which building societies have operated ever since . . . The sound basis of this Act is illustrated not only by its survival in modern building society legislation but also in the undoubted confidence which its creatures, the building societies, have been able to inspire'.[10]

This 'undoubted confidence' was, however, severely tested in the period up to the First World War, certainly the most testing in the societies' history. The 20 years after 1874 were a period of economic depression generally, an era of falling prices and interest rates and also falling property values. Building societies, by maintaining their mortgage rates, were able to attract an increasing volume of savings, but falling property values and the rising volume of surplus funds meant that demand for loans backed by adequate mortgage security was inadequate to absorb the societies' funds. Societies with surplus funds extended their business into increasingly risky areas and many got into difficulties. Competition between societies, many not incorporated under or restricted by the 1874 Act, took the form of more generous advances against poorer security, an extension into increased finance of commercial enterprises and an increase in more purely banking business.

The difficulties of individual societies, whether creatures of the 1874 Act or not, shook investors' confidence in the movement as a whole. Two major crashes which in particular reverberated through the movement and checked its expansion were those of the Liberator, which went under in 1892, and the Birkbeck, in 1911. Both failures in a sense tested the boundaries of building-society business and demonstrated the dangers of overstepping them. The Liberator had grown to twice the size of its nearest rival by 1892, becoming in the process increasingly involved in financing the property and industrial companies which were its downfall. The assets of the movement as a whole actually fell by £10 million to £42 million by 1894, when a further Building Societies Act was passed, requiring wider disclosure of information and extending the Registrar's powers. Mortgage arrears and property taken into possession by societies now had to be declared, and societies could not accept property which was already mortgaged to another party as security. The brief calm following the 1894 Act was shattered in 1911 by the failure of the Birkbeck, which had narrowly stayed afloat in the wake of the Liberator crash. The Birkbeck had in effect become a bank, with most of its assets in government gilt-edged securities. It was the decline in their market value and the directors' inexperience in banking business which was the society's undoing. The assets of the building-society movement again fell – by almost £20 million to £58 million. But by the First World War the movement had partially recovered and, surviving intact, its membership by 1919 was back to the 1892 level. Societies were then poised for their major inter-war growth, funding the expansion of home-ownership, with which the next chapter is concerned.

2

The silent revolution: home-ownership and housing policy since 1919

In 1919 fewer than one in ten of British households owned the house in which they lived; 80 per cent rented housing from private landlords, and building societies were, relatively, still only minor financial institutions. But the foundations had been laid for their expansion into a massive financial structure, dominating the supply of loans for house-purchase (Figures 2.1 and 2.2 in the Appendix, and see Chapter 3). It was this massive growth of the building societies which both enabled and encouraged the revolution in housing tenure that has taken place since 1919. By 1979 54 per cent of households were owner-occupiers, 32 per cent rented from local authorities or new towns and only about one in ten rented from private landlords. The historical development of tenure structure and of housing policy can only be understood as an effect of the socio-economic structure as a whole; for political and ideological influences have played a major part in combination with economic factors. This chapter presents an account of the growth of home-ownership in the context of national housing policy and of the crucial role of the building societies in this process; it concludes by considering briefly the social impact of the radical restructuring of housing tenure which has taken place.

The inter-war rise of home-ownership

From the start of this century the return on investment in housing to let has been seriously eroded by a combination of increased housing costs and rent control. Alternative forms of capital investment have become relatively more attractive. The consequent decline of the private rented sector has been continuous, though varying in pace: by the mid-thirties there was a partial revival in investment in rented housing, but strict rent control and rising house prices after the Second World War finally relegated the sector to its relatively minor role.[1] Much rented housing was sold for owner-occupation, contributing directly to the latter's expansion, while many small landlords transferred their capital to the building societies, where the return compared favourably with that on investment in housing to let.

Although private house-building was encouraged by subsidies equivalent to those for local-authority housing under the 1919 Housing and Town Planning etc. Act and 1923 Housing Act, the real boom in private building for owner-occupation took place in the thirties (Figure 2.3 in the Appendix). Labour governments had emphasised public housing for general needs in the 1924 Housing (Financial Provisions) Act (the 'Wheatley Act') and slum clearance in the 1930 Housing Act (the 'Greenwood Act'). Labour was, however, replaced in 1931 by MacDonald's Tory-dominated National Government. In 1933 subsidies to local authorities to build housing for general needs were abolished and the role of public housing confined to slum clearance and rehousing. No numerical increase in the public housing stock was envisaged – working-class housing need was to be met by the private sector. The Health Minister argued that abolishing subsidies to the public sector would, by reducing competition, allow private enterprise to meet general housing need with housing to let. But the private building boom of the thirties produced mainly housing for owner-occupation; the rents of houses which *were* built to let largely excluded the working class.

The building societies' role in the building boom was crucial. Unlike many financial institutions they survived the economic crisis of the early thirties virtually unscathed, the slump merely checking their rapid growth (Figures 2.2 and 2.4 in the Appendix). Their funds were maintained by the flow of repayments and interest from borrowers. But new investment also continued to flow into the societies, which became increasingly attractive owing to the liquidity and secure capital value of investment and relatively high rate of return on building society shares, compared with company shares and securities or government stock. The real incomes of those in employment were actually rising, as prices in general tended to fall, and, coupled with a rise in the proportion of incomes devoted to saving, this swelled the tide of investment flowing into the societies. And the same rise in real incomes increased, in turn, the demand for loans from building societies.

It was the combination of a spectacular intake of investment, rising real incomes and static or falling house-prices which fuelled the building boom. The boom itself has been ascribed considerable importance in Britain's relatively early recovery from the depression of 1931–2 and, as Harold Bellman observed, 'The institutional medium which gave the boom reality was the building societies movement'.[2] As a key industry generating a large proportion of the total national product, the influence of the building boom spread; it revived confidence and generated demand not only for building materials but also for physical and social infrastructure, and household goods and furnishings. In a wider sense the individualistic, automotive-oriented suburban life-style and the 'age of high mass consumption' was born in the thirties' building boom. Mortgage-financed individual home-ownership has remained, since then, a major factor in the maintenance of effective demand in the post-war economy.

In the thirties building societies were desperate to lend out as mortgages the massive funds they had attracted, since alternative investments for their funds gave both a low and uncertain return. One MP commented in 1939 that the 1933 Housing Act was

> . . . placed on the Statute Book simply because the building societies were absolutely bursting with money for which they had no outlet, and it compelled local authorities to cease to build houses for the ordinary applicants, for one purpose only, namely in order that people might be driven into the hands of the building societies and called upon to purchase houses for themselves.[3]

This need to lend out money prompted changes in societies' lending practices. Mortgage terms were extended from the customary 16–20 years to 21–5 years by 1934, and some societies gave loans over 30 or more years, reducing the monthly payments entailed by a given loan and thus encouraging borrowing.

Societies also developed ways of lending more than the customary 70–75 per cent of the value of the house being bought by accepting additional forms of security covering larger than normal loans, such as insurance policies or money deposited with the society. This reduced the amount house-buyers had to find from elsewhere. Two schemes in particular were important. Firstly, there were insurance company guarantees covering the amount in excess of what a society would normally lend, in return for a single premium paid by the borrower to the insurance company. The company compensated the society for any loss resulting from the excess loan. Insurance companies were keen to expand this scheme, which represented valuable business, and it survives today in the commonly used Building Societies Indemnity Scheme. Secondly, the 'builder's pool' developed and became widespread in the thirties. House-builders eager to sell houses deposited cash with societies equivalent to the excess loans on a batch of new houses (say 15–20 per cent of their value) on which the society could draw if borrowers defaulted before reducing their outstanding debt to the amount they would normally lend. 'Pool' business possibly accounted for as much as half the total lending by some larger societies.[4]

The societies' desire to lend was a major force in the expansion of owner-occupation at this time. Competition between societies to obtain mortgage business became severe at times, putting builders in a strong position to dictate terms to them. In 1933 Walter Harvey, who became chairman of the BSA, commented that 'The profits of housebuilders and landowners are in many instances unconscionable and responsibility attaches to societies which make them possible',[5] and later, when reviewing the inter-war years, Harvey maintained that the societies 'were drawn off financing the building of houses to let by the . . . much more profitable business of financing house purchase at scarcity prices, mainly for the benefit of the builder-seller'[6] and, consequently, 'The new owner-occupiers were so by necessity rather than choice . . . The main source of the increased demand for building society mortgages came from people forced to become owner-occupiers because there were no houses to let'.[7] The societies, which had previously been providing loans on a significant scale to private landlords, came by the end of the thirties to concentrate more on financing owner-occupation.

The quality of housing at this time fell markedly as speculative builders sought to maximise profits and extend housing for sale as far down the income scale as possible, and societies were forced to lend on shaky security in which borrowers might have a minimal cash stake. In many cases the determining factor in selling a new house became 'not the quality of the house, but the terms on which it can be bought'.[8] The legality of the builder's pool was in fact challenged (and upheld) in the case of a Mrs Elsie Borders, who refused payment to the Bradford 3rd Equitable, alleging it had lent money on a badly built house. Increasing concern over the effects of inter-society competition led to the 1939 Building Societies Act, defining acceptable forms of collateral, whose stringent conditions effectively killed off the builder's pool.

Post-war: the triumph of the owner-occupier

Falling demand for loans, coupled with the continuing flow of repayments and interest, meant that building societies emerged from the war with massive surplus funds (25 per cent of which were invested in government stock), and with financial potential to support the continued expansion of home-ownership. Initially this potential was held back by the Labour government elected in 1945, which aimed to meet general housing needs with public housing, for which subsidies to local authorities were increased. This served only to bring the subsidy to council tenants into line with the subsidy to owner-occupiers via tax concessions,[9] but building for the private sector was restricted by the retention of the war-time licensing system for new construction. Labour's post-war housing policy paralleled its massive programme of nationalisation, social insurance, health and education provision. However, devaluation and the sterling convertibility crisis in 1947, coupled with pressure from the Marshall Aid commissioners to cut welfare expenditure and expand directly productive investment, brought Labour's programme to a halt. Most local authorities were for a time forbidden to sign new housing contracts as Labour embarked on the 'austerity programme', closely watched by the United States, which had appointed an overseer to review in detail Britain's internal policies under Labour. As David Coates comments, 'Aid continued only because the Chief of the Special Mission was able to reassure the Congressmen that the Labour Government . . . was not on the slippery slope to communist takeover'. The overseer's report spoke of an 'improvement' since 1947: 'the housing programme has been quite seriously cut back. So has the health programme, and so has the programme for education'.[10]

Meanwhile the building societies had largely been financing sales of existing houses. Many landlords took advantage of the strong market in housing to sell off property, the extension of war-time rent controls accelerating this trend. Surprisingly, perhaps, there is little evidence that the societies themselves were ever seriously considered as candidates for nationalisation, given their massive financial resources within the housing system, which might have been channelled into Labour's general housing programme rather than being seen strictly as integral to the owner-occupied sector.

The return of the Conservatives unleashed the potential for expansion in owner-occupation and the pent-up funds of the building societies, and was to confirm owner-occupation as the dominant form of housing tenure in Britain. Private construction was effectively unfettered by December 1952, though in Macmillan's initial housing drive subsidies to local authorities for building housing to rent were actually raised in an attempt to achieve the target of 300 000 new houses built per annum – a target which was met in 1953 and exceeded in 1954. Council building, however, fell rapidly once it had helped achieve the level of new building promised in the election manifesto, and there was a massive reversal in housing policy. Subsidies to public housing for general needs were progressively cut back to zero by 1956, and policy swung firmly behind the expansion of owner-occupation (see Figure 2.3 in the Appendix). Michael Pinto-Dushinsky suggests that the Conservatives sacrificed the long-term well-being of the country in favour of palliatives bringing an immediate political return. On social grounds housing policy in general would have been directed at slum clearance. In fact more slums were probably *created* in the early 1950s by neglect leading to dilapidation than were removed by slum clearance, while the cost-cutting and poor design standards of the council housing built in the earliest years of the Macmillan drive have today left many councils with their worst 'problem estates'. According to Pinto-Dushinsky:

Although there were complex economic and social arguments for and against the housing drive, the decisive factor was political (one might even use the word 'ideological'). Tory leaders were convinced that home ownership eroded socialist zeal and led to wider electoral support for the Conservative cause. The Socialist answer to the problem of the uneven distribution of property was common ownership. By contrast the Conservatives sought to defend the property system by giving as many people as possible a stake in it . . . The housing programme benefited the upper-echelons of the working class and middle classes – Conservative voters or potential supporters.[11]

As Anthony Eden had claimed at the 1946 Party conference, the Conservatives' objective was 'a nation-wide property-owning democracy'.

The proportion of new houses built for owner-occupation increased under the Conservatives from 12 per cent of total output in 1951 to 56 per cent by 1959, supported by building-society lending, which expanded steadily through the decade. The post-war growth of owner-occupation initiated under the Conservatives was stimulated by a long series of measures which both lowered the cost of ownership relative to other tenures and sustained and encouraged the expansion of the building societies. In addition, changing building-society practices put house-purchase within reach of an increasing number of households.

In 1953 the cost of new building was reduced by the abolition of development charges on new building under the 1947 Town & Country Planning Act. In 1954 a new scheme guaranteeing excess advances was introduced by the government with considerable success until curtailed by monetary policy in 1957. From the 1957 Rent Act decontrol of private sector rents was initiated, the rise in rents encouraging the transfer to owner-occupation. In 1958 stamp duty on the transfer of houses priced under £3000 was reduced. From 1959 to 1962 the government lent the building societies £100 million to encourage lending on pre-1919 houses, generally at the cheaper end of the market. Finally, in 1962, owner-occupiers were exempted from income tax under schedule 'A' (see Chapter 9).

By 1964, when Labour returned to office under Wilson, 46 per cent of householders – and voters – were home-owners. Whereas the thirties' boom had been mainly a middle-class phenomenon, by the sixties owner-occupation had been extended to a significant proportion of the upper working class. It is, perhaps, not surprising then that the 1964 Labour government continued the drive towards what had previously been the essentially Tory ideal of a property-owning democracy:

> It is this conversion of the Labour Party to his cause which really marks the triumph of the owner occupier, By 1964 the Labour Party at the national level, pre-occupied with its electoral concerns, had adopted Tory policy lock, stock and barrel . . . If Tories could win elections on Tory Policy, then Wilson showed that Labour could too.[12]

As Richard Crossman, housing minister 1964–6, commented, 'Of course we wooed the owner-occupier during the general election'.[13] In September 1965 he wrote:

My plan . . . is primarily concerned to increase the production of owner-occupied houses; we only build council houses where it is clear they are needed . . . My aim is to make owner-occupation a possibility for a whole group of average and below-average workers at present excluded because they can't afford the current mortgage rates . . .[14] [and later he said of this 'new philosophy of owner-occupation'] I hope it will swing the Party into a new line which will help us in the general election.[15]

To Crossman's assertion in July 1966 that 'We came into office as socialists and the essence of a socialist policy is a shift from private to public expenditure',[16] we can only add that so far as housing policies are concerned they went out of office as Conservatives. The Option Mortgage and Guarantee Scheme introduced in 1967 was specifically designed to reduce the mortgage rate for the lower-income workers of Crossman's 'plan'. The scheme introduced subsidies equivalent to tax relief on mortgage interest for borrowers with incomes too low to pay income tax (see Chapter 5) and guarantees allowing loans up to the full value of the house being purchased, thus minimising the deposit to be found from elsewhere.

The Conservative government returned in 1970 under Heath consolidated the strength of owner-occupation and lent support to the building societies through the financial upheavals of 1973–4. In 1974 the societies received a three-month government bridging grant intended to enable them to keep the mortgage rate down to $9\frac{1}{2}$ per cent against the rising trend in interest rates which was draining away funds, and the rate on bank deposits under £10 000 was limited to $9\frac{1}{2}$ per cent in an attempt to reduce the volume of funds siphoned off from the societies. The societies were simultaneously encouraged to limit large loans and concentrate on lending to first-time buyers, and the house-price limit for 100 per cent option mortgages was raised from £5000 to £7500 to increase access to ownership for lower-income households seen as 'Conservative voters or potential supporters'. The flow of funds for house-purchase from the societies was supplemented by the removal of the ceiling which restricted the volume of lending by the local authorities.

The government's 1971 White Paper, *Fair Deal for Housing*, claimed increasing home-ownership was 'a sign of social advance':

Home ownership is the most rewarding form of house tenure. It satisfies a deep and natural desire on the part of the householder to have independent control of the house that shelters him and his family. It gives him greatest possible security against the loss of his home; and particularly against price changes that may threaten his ability to keep it. If the householder buys his house on mortgage, he builds up by steady saving a capital asset for him and his dependants. In this country the existence of a strong building society movement helps him to realise these advantages.[17]

This supposed innate and natural desire for private property and the security and independence derived from living in a capital investment are the essentials of the ideology of owner-occupation and the property-owning democracy developed in opposition to social, public housing. The White Paper was the prelude to the 1972 Housing Finance Act, implemented against massive countrywide opposition from tenants and Labour councils. The Act aimed to phase out direct exchequer subsidies to council housing, make better-off tenants subsidise those with lower incomes, and, by raising the real cost of council housing to the better-off, encourage the latter to become owner-occupiers. Simultaneously, local authorities were encouraged to sell council houses to tenants and to build new housing for sale to owner-occupiers. The 1973 White Paper, *Widening the Choice: the Next Step in Housing*,[18] asserted that 'most people want to own their own home' and declared the government's determination to 'reinforce the momentum towards home ownership' by achieving a high and stable output of houses to buy, an adequate supply of mortgage funds, increasing the supply of building land and encouraging local authorities to sell off rented housing and build for sale.

The next steps in housing were, however, taken by the Labour government returned to office in 1974; but Labour continued along the same path, starting with a £500 million loan to the building societies (under an arrangement made by the outgoing government) to help them maintain the level of lending without pushing the mortgage rate up beyond $9\frac{1}{2}$ per cent. More recently Labour has shown itself as firmly committed to home-ownership as were the Conservatives in *Fair Deal for Housing*. According to *Housing Policy*, the 1977 consultative document, 'An increasing number of people want to own their own home. The government welcome this trend and intend to continue to support home ownership',[19] and, echoing the ideology of the Conservative White Paper it was argued that: 'A preference for home ownership is sometimes explained on the grounds that potential home owners believe that it will bring them financial advantage. A far more likely reason for the secular trend towards home ownership is the sense of greater personal independence that it brings. For most people owning one's own home is a basic and natural desire.'[20]

The central role of the building societies was explicitly recognised in the government's hope and expectation that societies would 'be ready to shoulder still greater responsibility and to extend their voluntary co-operation . . . in the expansion of home-ownership'.[21] Finally, in December 1978 the government 'Homeloan' scheme for first-time house-buyers, first outlined in *Housing Policy*, was launched under the Home Purchase Assistance and Housing Corporation Guarantee Act. This offers house-buyers who qualify by saving a specified amount for at least two years a £600 extra loan interest-free for five years and a tax-free bonus of up to £110 (see Chapter 8).

The Conservative government elected in May 1979 indicated that it intended to outdo Labour's efforts to expand home-ownership by increasing aid to first-time buyers. It has also taken steps to increase sales of council houses to sitting tenants by allowing local authorities to offer them for sale at discounts of up to 50 per cent of their market value, and intends introducing legislation giving tenants the statutory right to buy their homes.

The spread of owner-occupation into the lower-income groups from which, traditionally, Labour draws much of its electoral support, set against the long-term decline of its social programmes into 'Labourism' has left the Labour Party firmly wedded to the expansion of home-ownership. It remains, however, more committed to the continuing role of the public sector than the Conservative government, which made its plans to sell off local authority housing a major element of its successful election campaign in 1979.

Tenure change and social class

The coming of mass home-ownership is commonly seen as the realisation in Britain of the 'property-owning democracy', recognising that the structure of housing tenure has a particular social impact and definite political and ideological implications. This final section sketches in the structure of housing tenure and considers alternative accounts of its social impact.

Between the wars the proportion of households in both owner-occupied and public rented housing showed a marked increase. By 1938 a quarter of householders were home-owners and 10 per cent rented local-authority housing (Figure 2.5 in the Appendix). The proportion in private rented housing, however, declined rapidly from 80 per cent in 1914 to 56 per cent in 1938. After the war the private rented sector continued to contract, particularly in the 1950s and early 1960s. In the early post-war years the public rented sector grew strongly, almost doubling from 12 per cent of the housing stock in 1945 to 23 per cent by 1956, but increasing more slowly thereafter. Home-ownership expanded rapidly from the early 1950s, and by 1970 more households were in the owner-occupied sector than all other tenures together. By the end of 1978 54 per cent of householders were home-owners, and 32 per cent lived in public rented and 14 per cent in private rented or other housing. The proportion of owner-occupied houses owned outright, without a mortgage, was 43.6 per cent in 1978, having fallen almost continually from around 50 per cent in 1966; the proportion owned with a building society mortgage rose from 35.4 per cent in 1966 to 44.8 per cent in 1978, while the proportion owned with any other mortgage fell from 14.7 per cent to 11.6 per cent.

The national pattern of housing tenure, however, conceals significant regional variation (Figure 2.6 in the Appendix): home-ownership is lower than elsewhere (though increasing faster) both in Scotland and Northern England, where a large proportion of the stock is rented from local authorities, and also in Greater London, where private renting remains important. In the Northern region large-scale slum clearance and redevelopment with public housing led to a rapid decline in the private rented sector. Home-ownership is particularly strong in the South-East and South-West regions, which have about the average proportion of private rented housing but a relatively small volume of public rented accommodation. Variations in tenure structure, however, tend to be much greater within regions than between them, particularly the contrast between rural and urban, and between inner-urban and suburban districts.

There is also a strong variation in the tenure pattern of different socio-economic groups, but with a considerable overlap in the middle ranges (Figure 2.7 in the Appendix). In 1977 83 per cent of home-owners with a mortgage earned £3000 or more per annum, compared with only a third of local-authority and private tenants. Only 62 per cent of outright owners earned £3000 or more, since many were retired and living on pensions. In 1977 24 per cent of all householders were outright owners and 30 per cent mortgagors. In 1977 34 per cent of mortgagors were in the professional and managerial group and only 9 per cent in semi-skilled and unskilled manual groups. However, only 6 per cent of local-authority and 17 per cent of all private tenants were in the upper group, with 32 per cent of local-authority and 26 per cent of private tenants in the semi-skilled and unskilled manual groups. But although there remain considerable contrasts in the tenure structure of different socio-economic groups, and home-ownership is far from being a general tenure form, in its long-term expansion it has extended down the socio-economic scale. Thus 42 per cent of manual workers, the traditional working class, are now home-owners.

It has often been argued that the diffusion of home-ownership, specifically among the 'working class', increases support for the ownership of private property in general and anaesthetises housing as a field of social conflict, serving to stabilise the existing social structure founded on capitalist private enterprise. Harold Bellman, chairman of the BSA and the Abbey Road (later Abbey National), wrote around the time of the general strike (1926): 'These young men had been fighting overseas for their homes and were ready to fight for them in England if need be . . . The stage was set for a great national tragedy. The Red Harvest of Russia had – not unintentionally – broadcasts its seeds across the world'.[22] But any revolutionary seizure of power was averted by *The Silent Revolution* (the title of Bellman's book), in which the 'Building Society movement provided a good deal of the ballast that kept the ship of state on an even keel'.[23] He had said in an earlier book:

The man who has something to protect and improve – a stake of some sort in the country – naturally turns his thoughts in the direction of sane, ordered, and perforce economical government. The thrifty man is seldom or never an extremist agitator. To him revolution is anathema; and, as in the earliest days Building Societies acted as a stabilising force, so to-day they stand, in the words of the Rt. Hon. G. N. Barnes, as 'a bulwark against Bolshevism and all that Bolshevism stands for'.[24]

Neville Chamberlain spoke similarly of home-ownership as 'a revolution which of necessity enlisted all those who were affected by it on the side of law and order and enrolled them in a great army of good citizens';[25] and Lord Alness wrote in a special issue of *The*

Times on home-ownership in 1938 that 'It is the antidote to all disease that threatens the body politic. Bad houses breed Bolshevism: good houses make for civil content and peace . . . Building societies are rendering untold service in this direction'.[26] In the thirties 'The Building Society Movement, which had always had official blessing, was publicised and elevated into a sort of crusade for good against evil'.[27] More recently, in 1976, a BSA official observed: 'The point where more than half the houses in the country have become owner-occupied was a significant milestone because even a small stake in the country does affect political attitudes. The greater the proportion of owner-occupiers the less likely were extreme measures to prevail'.[28]

More specifically, at the level of political struggle, home-ownership eliminates both the overtly antagonistic class relations of tenant versus profit-seeking private landlords and the equally conflict-ridden relationship of council tenants to local authorities. Both forms of rented housing have periodically been a focus for political action in the form of rent strikes. In Glasgow in 1915 private tenants withheld rents in protest at landlords who had taken advantage of the acute housing shortage, created by the influx of thousands of munitions workers into the city, by raising rents. Following walkouts in a number of works and shipyards, and the threat of a general strike by Clyde munitions workers, which seriously threatened the government's war effort, Lloyd George, the munitions minister, ordered legal action against the strikers to be dropped, and an Act restricting rent and mortgage payments was rapidly pushed through Parliament. In Birmingham in 1939 14 000 local-authority tenants voted for a rent strike against the introduction of higher rents and means-tested rent rebates by the council. Local-authority tenants also went on strike in St Pancras in 1959 and East London in 1968–70, while in 1972 there were strikes in over 60 local authorities against the rent increases and cuts in direct exchequer subsidies brought about by the Housing Finance Act.[29] In contrast, the only recorded mortgage strikes are those in the thirties in protest at the low quality of houses on which building societies were granting loans. Home-owners have no obvious opponent against which to struggle.[30] Outright owners have no payments to withhold. Mortgagors are, according to the building societies' ideology, individual members of a mutual, non-profit-making movement, drawing its funds from millions of small savers who include the borrowers' workmates, neighbours and friends. 'Self-help', the motto of the movement, privatises the provision of housing and of housing finance.

These political effects of home-ownership have frequently been promoted by invoking the individual's innate desire for private ownership of property. *The Times* claimed in 1938 that 'There is in human nature a natural law of possession';[31] a book approved by the BSA asserted, in 1964, that owner-occupation 'satisfies a basic human need' and 'reflects the independence of the British and their desire for privacy';[32] and in 1975 the BSA stated that 'The desire for a home of one's own and the need for a profitable home for one's savings – these are the two basic human needs which the building societies exist to serve'.[33] Similarly, in government policy, *Fair Deal for Housing* claimed home-ownership 'satisfies a deep and natural desire on the part of the householder to have independent control of the house that shelters him and his family'; and *Housing Policy* stated, 'For most people owning one's own home is a basic and natural desire'.[34]

The myth of an innate desire for private property functions by projecting on to *individuals* the characteristics of the particular socio-economic system in which they are located – a system largely founded on private ownership of property. The 'desire' for private property springs not from individuals but from the socio-economic system – the way in which economic production is organised and the particular political, legal and ideological forms which combine in the system as a whole. Bellman himself observed that building-society members had 'consciously or unconsciously' been taught the virtues of thrift and home-ownership, which would 'pass gradually into the mental and moral heritage of the race'.[35]

However, despite the undoubted political and ideological impact of the spread of home-ownership, it does not represent the simple diffusion of capitalist property ownership or the basis for the expansion of the dominant capitalist class. From a Marxist perspective classes arise from the contradiction between wage-labour and capital and the expropriation of surplus value by capital in the production process – possession of and separation from the means of production is the crucial property relation. Home-ownership and tenure categories are therefore no basis for class-formation.[36] From this perspective Rex and Moore's thesis of class-formation and struggle on the basis of 'housing classes' is invalid.[37] It is argued, instead, that increasing working-class home-ownership – the explicit aims of the Conservative and, after Crossman, Labour parties –

operates at the ideological level to obscure the fundamental class conflict between wage-labour and capital and to fragment the working class; for, even though home-ownership is not equivalent to ownership by private capital of the means of production, home-owners may *identify* with the interests of capital without precisely *sharing* them. *Any* threat to private property may then be seen as a threat to home-ownership. Thus the *Daily Telegraph* in the thirties spoke of home-ownership 'spreading from the individual to the community and linking up all classes'.[38] But the non-ideological basis for conflict over housing is between users and those who finance its purchase, own or supply it – 'I rent, you buy, we lose, they profit'.[39] Harvey, however, has also emphasised the role of debt-encumbrance and the need to maintain mortgage repayments as a factor promoting social docility.[40]

Arguing from a Weberian rather than Marxist perspective, Saunders also rejects Rex and Moore's notion of 'housing class'.[41] Criticising the Marxist perspective which sees only the ideological effect of home-ownership he argues that the real financial gains from home-ownership (see Chapter 9) make it, in a Weberian sense, property usable for real returns. He argues, therefore, following Carchedi,[42] that home-ownership forms a basis for identifying a middle, intermediate class between non-owners and private capital. Politically, home-owners may form temporary alliances with non-owners or private capital. Thus, while from a Marxist perspective tenure groups may reflect real divisions of political interest, recognising the 'necessary non-correspondence' between economic classes and political struggles,[43] from a Weberian perspective they can form a basis also, for class-formation. The political and ideological impact of increasing home-ownership is thus generally acknowledged from a variety of standpoints but the precise nature of its long-term effects on Britain's socio-economic and political structure is a matter of debate.

3

The financial and organisational structure of the building societies

Financial institutions and finance for house purchase

Building societies, collectively, are the second largest financial institution in Britain, their assets at the end of 1978 of nearly £40 thousand million being topped only by the insurance companies (Figure 3.1 in the Appendix). In the 1970s the societies have captured on average over 30 per cent of total personal savings in the main institutions (Figure 3.2 in the Appendix).[1] The societies are thus a major element of the country's financial structure, their competitive strength and stability both influencing that structure and affecting their own performance. They are financial intermediaries, standing between the finance market and the housing system and channelling funds from investors to borrowers. Their role and function in the housing system is thus strongly linked to their role as financial institutions. As financial institutions they are, however, unique in their degree of involvement with the personal sector as both source *and* destination of funds. At the end of 1978 over 95 per cent of their funds had originated in the personal sector and nearly 80 per cent of their assets were mortgage loans to this sector, the remainder being mainly 'liquid assets' (described below).

Building societies are the main source of finance for house-purchase in Britain. Since the mid-sixties they have accounted for over 80 per cent of lending by the four main institutions – local authorities provided 8 per cent, and insurance companies and banks about 4 per cent each (Figure 3.3 in the Appendix). Insurance companies were in second place in the fifties but declined in importance thereafter. Local-authority lending, which peaked at nearly a quarter of net lending in 1965, fell sharply when monetary restrictions were introduced from the late sixties, expanded rapidly in

1973–5 when the restrictions were lifted, but was again cut back by government controls from mid-1975. The clearing banks, which had a significant share of total lending in the fifties, found lending for house-purchase relatively unattractive in the sixties but expanded lending sharply in the 1972–3 credit boom. Bank, and to a lesser degree insurance-company, lending expanded in parallel with and reinforced the boom in building-society lending in 1972–3 and contracted in unison again; the expansion of local-authority lending, however, acted to a certain extent in a counter-cyclical fashion. At the end of 1978 loans for house-purchase outstanding to these four institutions totalled £38 029 million, of which building societies accounted for 83 per cent, local authorities 8 per cent and insurance companies and banks 4 per cent each.[2] In terms of number rather than value of loans the societies' share is about the same, local authorities' larger and banks' and insurance companies' smaller, owing to differences in average loan size between the institutions.

Information about total flows of lending is only available for the main institutions. One must therefore rely on household sample surveys to indicate the relative importance of the full range of sources. The most comprehensive of these was the National Movers Survey conducted in 1973 (Figure 3.4 in the Appendix), which shows the main source of finance used by buyers. This indicates that the importance of different sources of finance varies significantly for first-time and existing owners: 94 per cent of first-time buyers borrowed in order to buy and 90 per cent borrowed from one of the four main institutions, compared with 76 per cent and 74 per cent respectively of existing owners. Private loans were a major source of finance before the First World War, were still significant between the wars but have declined rapidly as alternative institutionalised investment opportunities have developed, and are now of minor importance. A significant proportion of buyers – nearly a quarter of existing owners with cash from selling a previous house – relied primarily on ready money rather than borrowing; and 12 per cent of first-time buyers borrowed from local authorities but only 2 per cent of existing owners had done so. The survey also indicated that the importance of building societies and insurance companies increases with borrowers' incomes, and that of local authorities, banks and private loans decreases.

The societies thus dominate the supply of finance for house-purchase as a whole, and their performance in the finance market is the single major influence on the supply of funds to the housing market. This dominance makes their lending policies and procedures of crucial importance in structuring the owner-occupied sector of the housing system. But whereas in the finance market the societies meet strong competition in raising funds, in the housing market they have to ration their lending as demand for mortgage loans outstrips supply. The alternative sources of finance are thus complementary to rather than competitive with the societies'.

Financial structure

The balance sheet for all building societies taken together (Figure 3.5 in the Appendix) describes the assets owned by the societies and how these are financed by their liabilities at a point in time.[3] The societies' funds or liabilities consist of money invested as 'shares and deposits'. The 'taxation' item is funds set aside to pay corporation tax and basic-rate income tax on behalf of investors at the end of the year. The societies' main assets are mortgage loans, primarily to individuals buying houses for owner-occupation. A significant proportion of their funds are, however, held as liquid assets, which include investment and cash. The bulk of the societies' liquid assets is invested in the short-term money market and in longer-term local-authority and central-government securities. By law societies are limited to prescribed, highly secure forms of investment. Building-society legislation also defines investments in three bands of decreasing 'liquidity' – roughly the time within which investment can be turned into cash. This requires societies to have $7\frac{1}{2}$ per cent of their assets in the most liquid group before investing in 'band two' investments, and $7\frac{1}{2}$ per cent in 'band two' before moving into 'band three', thus enforcing a certain degree of liquidity in all societies.

The function of liquid assets is twofold. First, they are intended to absorb any increase in withdrawals over receipts. Cash and current bank accounts cover day to day variations while invested liquid assets meet larger-scale fluctuations. Second, they act as a reservoir to stabilise the flow of lending, being built up when funds are flowing strongly into the societies and released to supplement the level of lending when the intake of new money is lower, thus insulating the level of lending to some extent from the wider repercussions of the finance market. A ratio of liquid to total assets of at least $7\frac{1}{2}$ per cent is one requirement for a society to be granted 'trustee status' by the Registrar, enabling the society to receive funds invested by trustees on behalf of other individuals or organisations and taken as a hallmark of respectability. In practice society 'liquidity ratios' are normally at least twice this prescribed minimum. Office premises are a small proportion of total assets although large in terms of absolute value, but they are widely considered to be considerably undervalued in balance sheets. Societies are not allowed to hold or invest in property in their own right, but may rent off premises surplus to their immediate requirements.

The value of the societies' total assets exceeds that of their liabilities by the value of their reserves – a safety margin ensuring that ultimately their liabilities, mainly money invested as shares and deposits, could be repaid in full by realising their assets and thus maintaining investors' confidence. Reserves are not separately identifiable funds or assets but rather the difference in value between total assets and liabilities. A minimum reserve ranging from $2\frac{1}{2}$ per cent of total assets for smaller societies to under 2 per cent for larger is a second requirement for trustee status (the third being total assets of at least £$2\frac{1}{2}$ million).

The flow of societies' funds over a period of time (Figure 3.6 in the Appendix) indicates best how they actually operate. The main sources are net investment (receipts minus withdrawals); repayment of existing loans, including both regular monthly repayments and premature redemption, generally when a house is sold; and mortgage interest. Investment interest, primarily on liquid assets, is a significant source of funds. In addition, insurance companies pay commission for house-insurance business introduced by societies. The major use of funds is new mortgage loans, though many borrowers will have redeemed an existing loan. Taxation is the amount actually paid in the year, both corporation and on behalf of investors (out of funds earmarked in the balance sheet). The main management expenses are wages and salaries, office rents and running costs, which accounted for 77 per cent of expenses in 1978. A further 6 per cent was spent advertising for funds, and 9 per cent was paid to 'agents' who channelled investment to the societies.

Finally, the pattern of income generated and expenditure entailed by this flow of funds (Figure 3.7 in the Appendix) completes the financial picture. Mortgage interest obviously accounts for the major part of income, but investment interest also makes a substantial contribution – £661 million in 1978. Interest paid to investors is the main item of expenditure – nearly 65 per cent in 1977. Taxation accounted for a further 23 per cent, mainly income tax paid on behalf of investors rather than corporation tax. Income minus expenditure, taking into account exceptional items, leaves the net surplus, which contributes to the societies' reserves by swelling their total assets. An expanding society will obviously have to generate a surplus in order to maintain the ratio of its reserves to the increasing value of its assets. The 'exceptional' item in 1977 was mainly profit from sales of investments.

Organisational structure

Societies

At the end of 1978 there were 316 building societies in Britain, ranging from massive national organisations like the Halifax with assets of £7603 million (19 per cent of the movement's total) to small local societies run on a part-time basis.[4] The assets of the movement are strongly concentrated in the large societies, the 36 largest accounting for over 90 per cent of the total in 1978; at the other end of the scale the 232 societies with assets of no more than £25 million accounted for 2.9 per cent of the total (Figure 3.8 in the Appendix). Policy and procedures of a relatively small number of societies are thus of major significance for the supply of finance for house-purchase, and lending policy in particular.

The number of societies has declined continuously from an estimated peak of 3500 in the 1890s,[5] initially reflecting particularly the winding-up of terminating societies, which accounted for 50 per cent of the total number in 1912 and 16 per cent in 1932 (see Figures 2.2 and 3.9 in the Appendix). From the 1930s, however, the decline reflects primarily the amalgamation of permanent societies to form larger units. Mergers take the form of 'transfers of engagements' or, more rarely and usually where the societies are roughly the same size, unions. In the period 1953–78 the number of societies declined by 466 from 782 to 316: 441 societies transferred their engagements, 37 were dissolved and 50 united. The unions produced 24 new societies but only 90 entirely new societies were formed – over 60 of these before the legal requirements were tightened in 1961. The process of amalgamation has polarised the movement around a few major societies, many of which gained their initial stature through a major merger. The outstanding example was the union in 1928 of the Halifax Permanent (assets £33 million) and Halifax Equitable (£14 million), then ranked first and second in terms of assets. More recently, for example, the Bradford Equitable (£57 million) and the

Bingley (£47 million) merged in 1964 to form the Bradford and Bingley, now in tenth place. Other societies have grown by absorbing a series of smaller societies: for example, the Nationwide, now ranked third, was founded in 1884 as the Southern Co-operative Permanent, and had acquired 22 smaller societies by 1975.

The Registrar has approved the general trend of amalgamation, since it reduces duplication of branch offices in particular areas; absorbs smaller, less profitable societies, thus stabilising the movement as a whole; and generally increases the standard of management.[6] A society in financial difficulty is usually swiftly rescued by absorption into a larger stable society for the good of its own members and the stability of the movement as a whole. For example, in 1975 the Bournemouth and Christchurch transferred its engagements to the Portman because of its serious lack of reserves and liquid assets, and in 1978 the assets of the Grays were transferred to the Woolwich following the misappropriation of £8 million, BSA member societies contributing to a compensation fund.

The assets of the movement as a whole have become increasingly concentrated in the larger societies, owing both to mergers and to the tendency of larger societies to grow faster than smaller ones. The largest five societies increased their share of the total from 39 per cent in 1930 to over 54 per cent by 1978 (Figure 3.10 in the Appendix), and the share of the top twenty rose from 65 per cent to over 84 per cent. The decline in the number of societies and increasing concentration of assets mirror progressive concentration of capital into larger financial and commercial enterprises typical of the development of western economies. For example, the number of joint-stock banks in Britain fell from 104 in 1890 to 25 in 1942, and by 1973 only 13 clearing banks remained. The largest five banks held 27 per cent of British bank deposits in 1900 and 79 per cent in 1953; by 1973 the 'Big Four' plus two smaller London Clearing Banks accounted for 86 per cent of British current and deposit accounts by value.

Branches and agents

Most national and larger regional societies have developed extensive networks of branch offices, which have played a major role in their expansion through attracting new investment. The number of branches more than doubled in the decade to 1978 (Figure 3.9 in the Appendix) but their distribution among societies remains very uneven. In 1978 the largest five societies accounted for 41 per cent of all branches and the largest thirty-six for 89 per cent. Most societies with assets over £10 million have branches, but few of those with under £2 million have. The motive for branch extension is to attract new investment. The demand for loans is such that societies have no need to attract in borrowers. Centrally located offices obviously pull in more money than obscurely sited premises but the rush of high-street premises and the duplication of facilities by different societies is often criticised. The value of societies' assets tied up in offices is, however, relatively low; if realised, it would produce only a small, once and for all increase in money available for new lending, and the saving in running costs would be marginal. But the planning issue is increasingly recognised by those local authorities who adopt a more critical attitude to planning applications for additional branch offices in shopping areas. From the societies' point of view new branches are only opened after detailed research suggests that the likely intake of new investment warrants expansion.

Below the level of branches is an important tier of 'agents', whose primary function is to channel investment to the societies. In return, agents may receive commission from societies and/or a quota of mortgage funds earmarked for borrowers nominated by the agents. 'Official' agents are commonly paid retainers, provided with pro-motional material, and display the society's name. Commission is paid pro rata for investment introduced to the society, often at a rate of £1 per £100, subject to the money staying in the society for a minimum of, say, six months. Accountants, solicitors, estate agents and insurance brokers are the usual professionals who act as agents, channelling funds to the societies in their capacities as financial advisers and holders of trust money. Accountants are usually the most productive; solicitors also advise on investment, particularly of inherited money, and act as trustees; estate agents will suggest that clients selling houses (again often inherited) invest the proceeds in a particular society but are generally less productive than other agents. Mortgage quotas are related to investment received on, say, a £1 for £1 basis. Agents nominate borrowers, who automatically receive a loan, provided the societies' usual lending criteria are met (see Chapter 5). Agents use quotas to further their own business: solicitors and accountants attract clients, the former particularly conveyancing business; estate agents sell houses more easily with mortgages available; and insurance brokers link loans to insurance policies to form endowment mortgages (see Chapter 5). It has been estimated that societies may receive up to 40 per cent of their total new investment via agents, and that the proportion of mortgage lending arranged through agents may be even higher.[7] Societies use quotas as a way of procuring investment and often speak of using mortgage funds for 'development purposes'.

Major national societies generally have a head office in the town of origin, a set of regional offices, branches throughout the country and a larger lower tier of agents. For example, in 1975 the Leeds Permanent's head office was in Leeds, where the society was founded in 1848; there were ten regional offices controlled from head office; 177 branches, including seven in Central and 32 in Greater London; and 1487 appointed agents throughout the country. Regional societies are more restricted but may have a scatter of branches and, particularly, agents outside their main territory, including usually a London office. Many local societies have only a single office plus a few agencies. The smallest societies are frequently linked with other enterprises, often sharing office accommodation with their directors' or officers' other interests. The 1969 Registrar's Report noted that, of societies with assets under £½ million, 'at least 155 of the 216 societies (75 per cent) are known to be managed in close association with professional firms or businesses'.[8]

Policy and control

Societies generally display relatively strong hierarchical control and policy formation from head office via regional offices to branches. Branches are usually, in turn, responsible for agents, though some societies set agents' quotas at regional or head office. Policy-making rests with the boards of directors of the individual societies, who, in smaller societies, may be involved in day to day business; in others, directors consider only 'special advances', and in the major societies may have little to do with the routine running of the society. Non-executive directors are commonly occupied in related businesses such as finance, property or building, but the trend is towards increased representation of managers and executives on boards, linking the operational level to that of control and policy-making. Policy is largely concerned with interest rates, (though most follow the BSA's recommendations), branch development and attraction of investment, rather than the details of lending policy.

In theory all loans are approved by a society's board of directors, but in practice a large proportion of loans are granted at branch level and automatically approved. Practice varies among societies, but the larger the loan the higher up the hierarchy it tends to pass for approval. In some societies loans above say £10 000 require regional-office approval and in many societies 'special advances' (loans to individuals or to corporate bodies of over £20 000) require head-office approval. Investment targets and mortgage quotas for individual branches are usually set by head and regional offices.

Branch managers ostensibly have considerable power over the detailed allocation of their mortgage quota, but are in practice subject to strong constraints and influences. First, they are subject to head-office guidance and expectation. Head offices commonly issue lending manuals or guidelines to branches, supplemented by periodic circulars. Societies generally appear to emphasise the attraction of investment and minimising mortgage default as the main aims of branch managers. Indeed, one manager interviewed by the author stressed the need to avoid drawing regional- or head-office attention by taking on 'bad payers'; another claimed it was 'impossible to make a name for yourself through mortgage business' and 'what counted was how much investment you pull in while keeping your nose clean on the mortgage side'. Second, managers are influenced by their own socialisation into 'sound building-society practice', in terms of attitudes to risk, security, borrowers' characteristics etc., reinforced by the emphasis on internal promotion and career structures within individual societies. Societies' internal training courses, Building Societies Institute courses and professional examinations contribute to this. Third, managers are constrained by their relations with agents. Since mortgage quotas must be used to attract investment, detailed control of a significant part of societies' total lending lies outside branch managers' hands, provided agents' nominees meet the usual lending criteria.

Individual societies are usually strongly growth-orientated, emphasising the attraction of new investment, branch extension and merger. In many respects they act like any other commercially orientated financial institution: for example, a general manager of the Bristol and West Building Society has been quoted as saying 'societies are run as commercial enterprises and not as extensions of the welfare state',[9] and Williams has suggested 'investment has become the primary concern with lending on mortgages being an outcome of it'.[10] Being 'mutual' institutions societies do not distribute profits, nor do they need to demonstrate growth in order to attract subscribers to new share issues. They do, however, strive for commercial efficiency, minimising the operating margin between mortgage and share rates in order to offer investors the maximum return and thus to attract investment: 'the time honoured concept of building societies as part of the self-help movement is steadily giving way to more businesslike consideration'.[11] Social functions remain, however, at least an element of societies' ideology: 'Although building societies compete with each other and strive for commercial efficiency, they conceive of their function as partly a social service',[12] and their motivation is related in part to belief in the promotion of thrift and home-ownership. The societies have a strong vested interest in the maintenance and extension of the private housing market, since this now represents their field of investment and is reinforced by their strong political and ideological commitment to private home-ownership in the tradition of Samuel Smiles. To quote one society: 'We believe profoundly in the ideal of a property-owning democracy, and it is our purpose to play a part in translating the ideal into a reality'.[13]

The relationship of building societies to other sectors of the economy – property, finance and commerce – is illustrated by the interests of their directors.[14] The late Sir Stanley Morton, when Chairman of the Abbey National, was also a director of the London Brick Company, Lloyds Bank, and Legal and General Insurance; a member of the Housing Corporation, National Housebuilding Council and Milton Keynes New Town Development Corporation; and sat on the management committee of the London Quadrant Housing Trust. In 1978 nine directors of the Halifax held at least 76 company directorships, including at least 17 of property and investment companies, while five Nationwide directors had 37 company directorships between them, including 18 of building or property companies (Figure 3.11 in the Appendix).

Directors of smaller societies are commonly 'exchange professionals', and property managers such as estate agents, solicitors, accountants and are often more closely involved in the actual running of societies. For example, in North Shields (Tyne–Wear) in 1975 the Tynemouth, Tynemouth Victoria, Standard and Mercantile societies, with assets of £22½ million, between them included in their 30 directors five solicitors, two estate agents, two builders and five accountants, and a significant volume of their funds was lent on mortgage to property companies in which the societies' directors had some interest (see Figure 3.12 in the Appendix).[15] At a local level interlinked directorships and interests appear to overlay functional linkages in the form of flows of finance or the channelling of business between the agencies involved. In the larger societies they indicate more a general complicity of interests and ideology between the societies and the commercial world of house-building, property and finance.

The legal framework

Societies operate within a common legal framework largely defined by the 1962 Building Societies Act and administered by the Chief Registrar of Friendly Societies. Societies must have first claim on the mortgaged property and cannot lend more than the market value of the property mortgaged as security. They are not obliged to lend solely to individuals buying houses for owner-occupation. However, lending in the 'special advance' category, which includes all loans to corporate bodies, loans for investment purposes (including loans to landlords) or loans to individuals over £20 000 (in 1979), may not exceed 10 per cent of a society's lending in any year. As well as providing for incorporation and limited liability, the 1962 Act restricts societies' powers of borrowing, lending and investing; provides for annual audit and publication of accounts; and establishes the regulatory powers of the Registrar.

The Registrar's function is to ensure societies operate in the best interests of their members and the public at large. The Registrar scrutinises societies' annual returns, and can request information, conduct investigations and, with Treasury approval, can prohibit or restrict societies taking or advertising for new investment. New practices are monitored and are likely to cease if the Registrar comments adversely. In 1974 the Registrar warned societies of the danger to their margins inherent in increasing the volume of high interest rate fixed-term shares and recommended they should not exceed 10 per cent of total shares. The Registrar hears disputes involving building-society law, authorises banks to hold building-society money and grants societies trustee status.

The Registrar thus has considerable powers of intervention and control. But the Registrar's terms of reference and the 1962 Act in general are primarily orientated towards ensuring the soundness of societies as *financial* institutions and protecting investors' money. The legal framework is not concerned with the social or housing-policy aspects of lending; it is concerned with lending only in so far as this affects the security of funds invested. Thus, for example, the special advance regulations were introduced in 1960 to curb practices which threatened the financial stability of the societies and caused the collapse of the State Building Society in 1959.

The societies' legal framework does not as yet allow them to operate outside this country, but the societies have been actively seeking powers to operate in Europe.[16] A proposed special EEC directive for housing-finance organisations must be issued before societies could operate across frontiers. But the British government has opted to defer the immediate application of a general EEC directive issued in December 1977 requiring member states to set up procedures co-ordinating laws, regulations and procedures of credit institutions. In particular the BSA has expressed concern lest the Bausparkassen, the German equivalent of the building societies, be allowed to operate in Britain but the societies be excluded from Germany, since the German government has not deferred applying the general 1977 directive. The BSA has worked to establish European contacts and to investigate the legal, financial and marketing conditions which building societies would face. The first two countries which seem to offer the greatest scope are Belgium and West Germany. In Belgium it is the size of the British expatriate colony associated particularly with the EEC and NATO which attracts the societies. In Germany it is the level of domestic prosperity and well established thrift habits, together with the flexible, simple structure of building societies, which would allow them to compete successfully with the rigid, complex German system. Given the necessary legislation, societies consider they can emulate the success of British banks and insurance companies in Europe.

The Building Societies Association

The BSA is the societies' national trade association.[17] It is their collective voice and also concerns itself with the internal functioning of the movement. About 70 per cent of building societies are members of the Association, but these account for about 99.9 per cent of the movement's total assets. Members' reserve and liquidity ratios must qualify for trustee status, though societies may be excluded or expelled by the BSA. Societies pay subscriptions related to the size of their assets. The Association has no formal powers, operating instead by advice and recommendation. Its governing body, the BSA Council, is composed of nominated representatives of the largest ten societies and the ten regional associations affiliated to the national association, fifteen representatives elected from societies on a national basis and up to four members co-opted by the Council. Societies represented on the Council account for about 90 per cent of the movement's total assets. The main aims of the Association are:

1. to promote the interests of and co-operation amongst building societies and to foster a high standard of prudence and practice in their management;
2. to formulate and to promote the adoption and observance by building societies of regulations for the carrying on of their business;
3. to encourage the practices of savings and investment, to promote home ownership and to assist in raising housing standards;
4. to advocate and promote such legislation, practice and reforms as may be conducive to any of the objectives of the Association.

The Association's functions may be summarised as follows: information and advice to member societies; a forum for discussion and policy formulation; informing outside bodies and members of the public about building societies; acting on behalf of member societies in discussions with other representative bodies, e.g. insurance companies and builders; undertaking research and producing statistics on relevant matters; and acting on behalf of societies in discussions with government and the Bank of England. One of the Association's major functions is to recommend to members a maximum share rate and minimum mortgage rate. This practice was developed in the 1930s when competition between societies was strong, threatening the movement's stability and giving rise, amid great dispute, to a 'Code of Ethics'. Most members follow the recommended rates, though smaller societies often operate higher rates. The last major disagreement contributed to the withdrawal of the Halifax from the BSA from 1956 to 1964. More recently, however, several societies, including the Abbey National, Leeds Permanent and Britannia, broke ranks, choosing to ignore the reductions in the ordinary share rate recommended by the BSA in September 1977 and January 1978. Normally about 86 per cent of the value of the largest twenty societies' shares pay the recommended rate, though at the end of 1977 this dropped to 62 per cent. The BSA also promotes sound practice by issuing circulars and advice on innovatory practices, the effects of changing legislation or economic circumstances and financial and taxation issues. Finally, it promotes the image of the movement and encourages public support for increasing home-ownership through advertising campaigns.

The Joint Advisory Committee

A Memorandum of Agreement was drawn up by the Building Societies Association and the government in October 1973 with the following agreed objectives:

1. to continue to support the growth of owner-occupation;
2. to produce and maintain a flow of mortgage funds to enable the house-building industry to plan for a high and stable level of house-building for sale;
3. to contribute towards the stabilisation of house prices;
4. to maintain an orderly housing market in which, subject to point 3, above, sufficient mortgage funds are available to allow purchasers a reasonable choice of owning the sort of house they want.[18]

The Joint Advisory Committee on Building Society Mortgage Finance was set up to further the agreed objectives. Composed of government and building-society representatives, the Committee meets periodically, acting as a forum for debate. The societies are represented by the BSA; representatives from the Department of the Environment and the Treasury are joined by delegates from the Bank of England. Despite the Committee's avowed aims, house-builders are not represented, although the BSA maintains contact with the House-Builders Federation and is represented on the National House-building Council.

The JAC in turn set up a Technical Sub-committee to consider forecasts and analyses of the housing market and to improve on information-gathering. In 1975 a further agreement was negotiated on arrangements to stabilise mortgage finance, whereby the JAC assesses the amount of mortgage lending needed to maintain a healthy housing market while avoiding undue price increases. In 1978 the societies agreed to limit the level of lending (see Chapters 7 and 8). The building-society 'support scheme' for local-authority lending (see Chapter 5) was similarly negotiated through the JAC. The JAC is thus a forum for discussion and promotion of co-operation between government departments, the Bank and the Registry of Friendly Societies.

The Building Societies Institute

The BSI is the professional association for building-society personnel. Its main function is to organise training and education through courses, summer schools and texts on building-society management, and by setting examinations. Members are, however, a minority of society employees and most 'fellows' (senior members) and associates achieved their status before the introduction of qualifying examinations. The BSI also fulfils a social and representative function for employees at local, national and international levels. Its role is somewhat ambiguous, however, given the much stronger organisational focus of the regional and national associations, and because of the conflict between 'in-house' training, particularly in the larger societies, and the Institute's own educational role.

4

Shares and investors

By 1979 43 per cent of the adult population in Britain had money invested in a building society. There were over 25 million share and deposit accounts – four and a half times the number of people borrowing from the societies. Though much attention focuses on the societies' role in the housing system, they are obviously major savings institutions. This chapter looks at the different types of building-society accounts and the characteristics of investors.

Shares and deposits

There are several different types of building-society investment account but by far the commonest is the *ordinary share* account, which at the end of 1977 accounted for over 83 per cent of funds invested in the societies (Figure 4.1 in the Appendix). Any amount can be invested from £1 up to the effective £15 000 limit created by taxation arrangements (see below), and, in practice, money can be withdrawn on demand or at very short notice. Building-society shares yield a fixed rate of interest, the level being set periodically by the directors, taking account of other interest rates in the economy and mainly following the recommendations of the BSA. Interest, usually credited half-yearly, may be withdrawn, but many investors choose to add it to their accounts. Interest is an important source of new investment, representing 31 per cent of the net increase (receipts less withdrawals) in shares and deposits in 1978. Many societies also offer 'monthly income' shares on which interest is paid monthly, but on which a month's notice is required for withdrawal. The interest rate on ordinary shares recommended by the BSA in early 1979 was 8 per cent free of any liability to income tax at the basic rate – equivalent for an investor paying the basic 33 per cent rate of tax to a gross (pre-tax) interest rate of 11.94 per cent (see Figure 4.2 in the Appendix, and note 4 to this chapter). Many smaller societies offered slightly higher rates, generally 8.25 per cent.

Although shareholders generally treat building societies like any other investment institution, they are in fact 'members' of their society; they receive annual accounts and directors' reports, have the right to attend and vote at general meetings, and are bound by the societies' rules. However, building-society shares have little in common with company shares, since they have a fixed capital value, can be turned into cash by withdrawing money from the society and pay a set interest rate.

Many investors will use building-society share accounts in order to qualify for government assistance to first-time house-buyers under the 'Homeloan' scheme launched in December 1978 (described in detail in Chapter 8). Purchasers must save for two years in a participating institution (including most societies), accumulate at least £600 and keep at least £300 in their account for the second 12 months.

Many societies offer $1-1\frac{1}{2}$ per cent above the ordinary share rate on money invested for a fixed period, usually two, three or four years, in the form of *term shares*. Schemes vary between societies but normally at least £500 must be invested, sometimes in multiples of £100, and larger amounts (over £5000) may attract higher interest rates. Withdrawals may be prohibited, or penalised by reduced interest payments. Term shares are mainly intended to tie down investment which is likely to flow out of the societies when their interest rates are temporarily less attractive than their competitors'. Investment in term shares grew rapidly from spring 1974 as the societies faced a serious outflow of funds. The Registrar commented in his report on 1974 that societies had in recent years attracted increasingly large individual investments and it was this type of money which was most likely to be withdrawn to take advantage of better interest rates elsewhere. To offer a slightly higher rate for term shares is therefore now accepted by many societies as sound business sense.[1] The proportion of funds invested in the societies as term shares increased from 2.4 per cent in May 1974 to 9.4 per cent at the end of 1977. According to the Registrar's report, 'it is clear that much of the increase in this type of business in 1974 stemmed from money being transferred from existing share accounts or from a society not offering term shares', the extent to which *new* funds were attracted being limited. The effectiveness of term shares has not been really proven as yet, and, as the Registrar warned, their higher interest rates eat into the societies' operating margin. For the foreseeable future, however, the societies' funds will remain mainly as short-term ordinary shares.

Higher interest rates are also paid on *regular savings* accounts. A fixed sum is invested every month, between £1 and a specified maximum (£30–£50 usually). No fixed term is normally specified and cash can often be withdrawn without forgoing interest, but interest is all credited to the account. Rates can be as high or higher than those on the most attractive term shares, and the regular savings account has frequently been termed a 'loss-leader', a marketing gambit to attract young savers who, it is hoped, will later save substantial amounts in ordinary shares. Societies often encourage prospective house-buyers to save for a deposit by regular saving, giving the societies a steady inflow of funds and also demonstrating the prospective borrowers' thrifty habits. About 2.5 per cent of funds invested in the societies at the end of 1977 were in regular savings accounts, but this percentage shows no signs of significant increase in the future.

Since October 1969 societies have also participated in the government's *Save As You Earn* (SAYE) scheme, which offers substantial tax-free bonuses for long-term regular saving. SAYE provides societies with a very regular, stable inflow of funds, but it can prove costly and inflexible. The bonuses are equivalent to a high interest rate; furthermore they are fixed at the outset, whereas other interest rates, including that received by societies on mortgages, vary through time. The share of total investment in the societies in SAYE accounts has been falling, and represented under 1 per cent by 1978.

About 100 societies operate *life assurance linked investment* schemes with insurance companies. Monthly premiums are paid to the insurance company, which retains a proportion (depending on the investor's age) to provide life-cover, then invests the remainder in the building society. Contracts are usually for ten years, after which the investor receives the accumulated building-society investment with interest and usually a bonus. 'Life-linked' investment is attractive because income used to pay life-assurance premiums is taxed at only half the basic rate, so that the investor gains tax relief on the capital built up in the building society as well as receiving the interest basic rate income tax paid. Insurance companies had invested £26 million with building societies by the end of 1977, an insignificant proportion of total shares and deposits.

Deposits are formally distinguished from *shares*, since depositors are creditors of a society rather than members; they have a claim to the society's assets prior to shareholders. In the past, when the possibility of a society going bankrupt or being wound up at a loss was not entirely remote, deposits were more secure than shares, and, accordingly, attracted a lower interest rate. As the security of share accounts has become assured, so the share of deposits in total investment has fallen – from 25 per cent in 1910 to 7.5 per cent by 1960 and 3.9 per cent by the end of 1977 – and the customary differential below the ordinary share rate has shrunk progressively from 1 per cent in 1910 to, currently, $\frac{1}{4}$ per cent. Few individuals now have money on deposit. Deposits are largely held by limited companies and other institutions on terms and interest rates negotiated with societies on an individual basis, some being held by societies as additional collateral for mortgage loans.

Different societies offer different versions of the main types of investment outlined above and many smaller societies offer slightly higher rates on equivalent investment accounts. Figure 4.2 in the Appendix summarises a typical structure of interest rates for a large national society in early 1979. Though the interest rates in general may vary quite often, the differentials between the different types of investment are usually preserved.

As societies have grown, and as conditions in the market for personal savings have changed, they have tended to develop in recent years a more flexible and sophisticated structure of investment rates. Term shares are an important aspect of this process. Small ordinary share accounts have frequently been criticised: they are costly to administer, generating many transactions as investors use them almost like current bank accounts; they fail to justify their relatively high interest rate; and often they are opened by those who save in order to qualify subsequently for a mortgage. Rather than helping to meet increased demand for loans, they actually increase it in the long run. According to one commentator, 'It is becoming increasingly obvious that the value of these accounts is minimal. . . . we must recognise that only by attracting an increasing number of accounts for larger sums, are we likely to have any effect at all upon the mortgage demand'.[2] Greater use of term shares was advocated. It was further suggested that ordinary share accounts of under £500 be treated as 'current accounts' and paid a relatively low interest rate; ordinary shares could then be divided into two classes, £500–£5000 and over £5000, the latter attracting a higher interest rate. A move in this direction seems quite likely to evolve, possibly coupled with an extension of societies' other facilities, such as credit cards, standing-order payments, cheque facilities etc.

Building-society investors pay no basic rate income tax on share and deposit interest.[3] The societies pay tax in lieu of investors' basic-rate tax liability direct to the Inland Revenue under a special arrangement. This arrangement yields roughly the same tax revenue as if the normal taxation system had been used and repayment claims from investors not liable to tax had been met. Deducting tax at source has the advantage of eliminating the bureaucratic cost of individual assessment on millions of accounts and preventing tax evasion through non-declaration of interest received.

Tax is paid by societies at a special 'composite rate' rather than the basic rate. This is roughly the average rate at which investors are liable to pay tax, excluding higher than basic rates (thus it is an average of zero and basic rates only), weighted by the amounts held in individual accounts and thereby taking account of the amount of interest received by taxpayers and non-taxpayers. The rate is fixed annually after negotiation between the Inland Revenue and the BSA and is an estimate, based on a sample of investors conducted every three or four years by the Inland Revenue, and adjusted between samples to take account of changes in the tax rate and income trends. From a sample in 1976–7, for example, it was estimated that 79.3 per cent of interest was paid to investors liable to at least the basic rate of tax, so the composite rate was set at 79.3 per cent of the basic rate (then 35 per cent), i.e. 27.75 per cent. Since a significant proportion of interest goes to non-taxpayers, the composite rate is thus less than the basic rate – 22.25 per cent in 1978–9 as against 33 per cent basic rate. The gap has, however, narrowed considerably over the years as rising incomes and the lowering of tax thresholds have reduced the proportion of interest paid to non-taxpayers. The 25 per cent tax band introduced in 1978–9 has complicated the calculation and changes in personal allowances and in the basic tax rate following the June 1979 budget have altered the precise figures, but the principle remains the same.

Investors who pay no tax cannot reclaim tax paid on their behalf at the composite rate by the societies, and therefore they gain no benefit from the scheme. Investors liable to basic-rate income tax benefit in that they receive interest free of liability to tax. Societies normally quote both net and gross interest rates. The gross rate indicates the pre-tax rate of interest on alternative investment such as a bank deposit would have to offer to give a return equivalent to that on building-society shares. Thus, for example, the gross equivalent of an 8 per cent ordinary share rate for a basic-rate taxpayer is 8 per cent $\times (100/100 - 33) = 11.94$ per cent[4]. According to the BSA, 'to say that only net rates should be advertised would be merely giving ground to the societies' competitors'.[5] Higher-rate taxpayers pay tax at their particular tax rate on interest grossed up at the basic rate – thus, for example, to a 55 per cent taxpayer an 8 per cent ordinary share rate is worth 11.94 per cent $- (11.94 \times 55/100) = 5.37$ per cent. Thus the rate of return on building-society investment falls as the borrower's tax rate increases. The composite tax arrangement applies to interest paid to individuals with up to £15 000 in any society and to certain non-profit-making bodies. Societies have to pay tax at the basic rather than composite rate on interest paid on the whole amount of individual holdings in excess of £15 000 in any one society and on investments of any size by companies, so they normally limit individual investment to less than £15 000 and negotiate rates with corporate bodies. However, an individual investor can place up to £15 000 in as many different societies as they choose and each society will only pay tax at the composite rate. Though building-society interest is free of basic-rate tax liability, the tax authorities take into account gross interest received in assessing investors' tax bracket.

In discussing the societies' special tax arrangement Revell observed: 'Since the authorities lose no tax from the composite tax arrangement it is a tax subsidy of a peculiar kind – from one group of persons to another'.[6] This is because investors with incomes too low to bring them into the tax net – the young, the low-income investors and the elderly retired – cannot reclaim tax paid on their behalf. If such investors were allowed to reclaim income tax, thus putting building-society interest on an equivalent basis to earned income for taxpayers and non-taxpayers alike, the societies would have to pay tax at the full basic rate in lieu of individual investors' liability in order to maintain the Revenue's tax income. The 8 per cent share rate in early 1979 worth 11.94 per cent gross to basic-rate taxpayers cost societies only 10.32 per cent gross, since they paid tax at the 22.5 per cent composite rate rather than the full 33 per cent basic rate (8 per cent $\times [100/100 - 22.5] = 10.32$ per cent). This difference of over $1\frac{1}{2}$ per cent is paid for by the non-taxpaying investors who cannot reclaim income tax. For a given mortgage rate the special tax arrangement therefore gives the societies a significant competitive edge over their rivals such as the clearing banks.

If investors were allowed to reclaim tax and societies paid the full basic rate on behalf of taxpaying investors, to maintain the same yield as before to taxpaying investors the mortgage rate would have to be put up by about $1\frac{1}{2}$ per cent in order to maintain the societies' operating margin. If the mortgage rate were not raised, then the rate paid to investors would have to fall by an equivalent amount, making the societies less competitive and leading to loss of funds (which would only partly be counteracted by the increased attractiveness of the societies to non-taxpayers able to reclaim tax). Thus non-taxpaying investors are effectively subsidising the mortgage rate, currently to the tune of about $1\frac{1}{2}$ per cent. Though developing with the tax system, intended to simplify tax collection and involving no tax concession to the societies, the arrangement nevertheless gives them a significant competitive advantage.

Investors

The number of building-society share accounts increased by a factor of ten between 1950 and 1977, more than doubling in the seventies alone to reach over $22\frac{1}{2}$ million by 1977. Since, however, many individuals hold more than one account, a more accurate picture of the extent of investment in the societies is provided by various market research surveys. These indicate that the proportion of the adult population holding building-society accounts rose from 11 per cent in 1965 to 21 per cent in 1970, and reached 36 per cent by 1977.[7] In comparison with other savings institutions the societies have significantly increased their 'market penetration' (Figure 4.3 in the Appendix). Only the clearing bank current accounts, which are not primarily a form of saving, also showed any significant increase in recent years. Building-society investors do tend to use other savings institutions as well. In 1974, for example, about half also had current bank accounts, 22 per cent had bank savings or deposit accounts, 48 per cent held premium bonds, 9 per cent had stocks and shares, and 3 per cent gilt-edged securities.[8] Not surprisingly building-society investment accounts form a considerable proportion of total household wealth (Figure 4.4 in the Appendix). By the end of 1976 shares and deposits represented nearly 18 per cent of households' financial assets compared with 8 per cent in 1966; their share of more closely comparable short-term financial assets rose from 24 per cent in 1966 to over 40 per cent in 1976, and their share of *total* household wealth of all kinds rose from 5.2 per cent to 8 per cent over this period.[9]

Though it follows that a wide range of people invest in the societies, the proportion investing increases markedly with socio-economic status. In 1974 over 40 per cent of those in higher and intermediate managerial and professional occupations (social classes A and B) had building-society accounts, compared with 12 per cent of those (classes D and E) in semi-skilled and unskilled manual occupations (Figure 4.5 in the Appendix). The societies' expansion has, however, taken in an increasing volume of money from those lower down the scale of income and occupational status, notably those largely excluded by societies' lending criteria from obtaining a mortgage loan. As would be expected, the proportion of building-society investors in the population similarly increases with income and wealth. In 1974 52 per cent of those with incomes over £5000 had building-society accounts, compared with 17 per cent of those whose income was under £1000; 61 per cent of those with total savings over £5000 held money in a society, compared with 40 per cent of those whose savings were no more than £2000. These figures are backed up by the Royal Commission on the Distribution of Income and Wealth (1975), which found that 70 per cent by value of individuals' investment in the societies was held by those whose total wealth exceeded £10 000 and only 14 per cent by individuals whose wealth was under £5000. In 1974 20 per cent of women but 26 per cent of men were building-society investors. There was also significant regional variation in the proportion of the population who were investors – from 29 per cent in the South East to 22 per cent in the North, and only 9 per cent in Scotland, where the savings banks remain strong.

Traditionally the societies cater for the small saver, an image they actively cultivate to distinguish themselves from 'high-finance' and justify their advantage from their special tax treatment. Over 93 per cent of share and deposit accounts did in fact contain under £5000 at the end of 1977, and 'small-savers' undoubtedly get a good deal out of the societies in terms of interest; but this is a rather misleading picture because the larger accounts represented a much higher proportion of societies' total funds (Figure 4.6 in the Appendix). At the end of 1977 42 per cent of total funds was held in amounts over £5000, in only 6.8 per cent of accounts by number.[10] Conversely, the 53 per cent of accounts with no more than £500 accounted for only 5 per cent of societies' total funds – the societies, therefore, can hardly be said to rely on the small savers! By way of contrast, in 1974 45 per cent of bank-deposit accounts held under £100, compared with 24 per cent of building-society accounts, and only 7.6 per cent held over £1000, compared with 23.2 per cent for the societies. Though the societies are important to the small saver, it is those with higher incomes and relatively substantial sums to invest that are of major importance to the societies' funds. The societies are based on *investment* rather than on *savings*, money on which the return obtained is at least as important as the aim of accumulating and preserving savings for future consumption.

Societies also receive investment from companies, pension funds and insurance companies. This money, usually invested in relatively large sums, tends to be more volatile than normal building-society money, but the total amount is relatively small. At the end of 1978 societies held £421 million invested by industrial and commercial companies, 1.4 per cent of total shares and deposits, and £34 million invested by insurance companies and pension funds.[11] Societies generally try and tie down corporate money for fixed terms or by requiring long notice of withdrawals, though in 1977 some societies were waiving these restrictions. A proportion of corporate investment in building societies is, however, invested in return for societies providing mortgage funds to the employees of a company. Banks and other institutions also place relatively large sums in societies, made up of the investment of many individual clients' money. Like corporate money, this also tends to be volatile.

Much of the societies' past success can be attributed to their ability to offer in the finance market an investment that has qualities which appeal to the sophisticated investor with considerable funds to invest, rather than to any special orientation towards the small saver. But because a large proportion of the societies' funds is drawn from the more sophisticated investor (whose money is often professionally managed), and is switched between different investment media according to the relative returns they offer, there is a considerable degree of volatility in them. As the societies have expanded, they have increasingly come to rely on larger, more volatile investments, in the context of a finance market in which competition based on frequently changing interest rates has increased in recent years. This has important implications for the societies' financial performance and lending activities, which are explored more closely in Chapters 6 and 7.

5
Mortgages and borrowers

At the end of 1978 building-society mortgage-lending amounted to £31.6 million, 80 per cent of the societies' total assets, and building-society borrowers numbered 5.1 million. Although societies make some loans to landlords, house-builders, housing associations and other bodies, about 99 per cent of their mortgage funds are loaned to private households buying dwellings for owner-occupation. This chapter describes the main types of mortgage, the mortgage allocation process, societies' lending criteria and the pattern of mortgage allocation, and finally the societies' role in the supply of mortgages in comparison with other sources of loans.

Mortgage mechanisms

Few householders can afford to buy a house outright from income or savings, since house prices are generally several times their annual income. For example, the average house price in 1978 (£15 674) was 3.3 times average earnings (£4770). Loan-financed house-purchase, like renting, enables households to obtain housing now but spreads out through time their contribution to its capital cost in keeping with their income. The seller thus receives the capital value of the house in a lump sum; so an existing owner selling has the cash to redeem an outstanding loan and/or put it to buying a subsequent house, and a builder recovers capital invested in house-building and can start another production cycle.

In the case of rented housing a landlord (private investor or public authority) assembles capital, buys a house and sells the use of the house for regular payments of rent. In the case of loan-financed house-purchase a person borrows capital, buys a house and occupies it while repaying the loan, with interest, over an extended period of time. The occupier acquires a legal title to the property as well as the right to use it but the title is usually qualified in that the loan is 'secured' by way of a 'mortgage' on the property. This is a legal agreement giving the lender rights over the property if the borrower defaults on the loan. Repayment must generally be spread over a long period for the level of payments entailed by typical loans to be commensurate with household incomes. When a loan is fully repaid, the purchaser acquires full legal title to the property. It is the duration of the useful life of housing and retention of market value that facilitates long-term mortgage finance; for it is because of lenders' confidence, the confidence of building-society investors in particular, that property represents adequate security throughout the life of the loan, and that the flow of long-term loans to individual households with generally little in the way of personal financial assets is maintained. A mortgage loan is thus 'a device for spreading out the high capital cost of house purchase in a way that avoids undue burdens on the purchaser while providing the lender with an adequate rate of return on the money advanced combined with security for eventual repayment of the principal'.[1]

The commonest form of repayment mechanism is the *capital repayment mortgage*, which accounted for 66 per cent of new loans in 1978. Regular monthly payments are made to the society throughout the life of the loan. Part of each payment represents interest on the amount still owed and the rest goes towards repaying the loan. Early on, the amount still owed is large, so most of the payment represents interest, but as the debt falls, so also does the interest component, and the amount of the loan repaid each month rises (Figure 5.1 in the Appendix).

Borrowers claim tax relief on the interest component of their monthly payments, i.e. they pay no tax on income used to pay mortgage interest. This effectively cuts the mortgage rate, the BSA recommended rate in early 1979 of 11.75 per cent dropping to 7.87 per cent for a basic (33 per cent) taxpayer. Higher-rate taxpayers derive greater benefit from tax relief, the 11.75 per cent mortgage rate dropping to 6.46 per cent for borrowers paying tax at 45 per cent and 4.7 per cent for a 60 per cent taxpayer [net mortgage rate = quoted mortgage rate $\times (100 -$ borrower's tax rate$/100)$]. Since 1974, tax relief has been limited to loans for house-purchase or improvement not exceeding £25 000, and relating only to an individual's first or principal residence (or one occupied by a dependent relative). Unless the mortgage rate changes, monthly payments before tax relief are constant over the life of the mortgage. But since the interest component of payments falls over the mortgage life, so too does the benefit derived from tax relief, and the level of payment in money terms therefore declines. Monthly payments on a loan of given size increase with the mortgage rate and decrease with the repayment term (Figure 5.2 in the Appendix).

Borrowers with incomes too low to benefit fully from tax relief can obtain assistance roughly equivalent to tax relief at the basic rate by taking out an *option mortgage*. The government's option-mortgage scheme was introduced in the 1967 Housing Subsidies Act, coming into effect in April 1968. The borrower forgoes any claim to tax relief but pays less than the normal mortgage rate. With a mortgage rate of 11.75 per cent the option mortgage rate is 7.95 per cent. The government reimburses the society the difference between the option and normal mortgage rates. The percentage of all loans accounted for by option mortgages rose to over 20 per cent in 1972 but declined thereafter to 11 per cent in 1978, owing to the increasing number of borrowers who became liable to income tax as the tax threshold fell. Monthly payments on an option mortgage are constant unless the mortgage or subsidy rate changes. Early on, they are higher than on an ordinary mortgage with basic-rate tax relief, the position being reversed later as tax relief declines. An option mortgage can be changed to a tax-relief mortgage after four years, and a tax-relief mortgage into an option mortgage at any time if the borrower proves financial hardship. Local authorities and most insurance companies also provide option mortgages.

The second main type of repayment mechanism is the *endowment mortgage*. The borrower pays only interest to the building society. To pay off the capital, regular payments are made to an insurance company for an endowment insurance policy running for the term of the mortgage, which, on maturity, yields a lump sum out of which the capital debt is repaid. The combined cost of interest and insurance premiums generally makes endowment mortgages more expensive than repayment loans, but they usually yield a substantial capital sum after repaying the outstanding debt, in effect combining saving with house-purchase. Furthermore tax relief is obtained at half the basic rate on the insurance premiums as well as on interest paid. The percentage of all mortgages repaid by the endowment method rose from around 8 per cent in the late sixties to over 23 per cent in 1978. 'Combination' loans, which are part endowment, part repayment and cost less than a full endowment loan, have also increased their share of all mortgages recently. Loans to building-society borrowers nominated by insurance companies acting as agents for the society (Chapter 3) are generally all endowment mortgages. Option and endowment mortgages can be combined, but most option mortgages are of the cheaper repayment type.

The mortgage rate on all mortgages, existing as well as new, can be altered to keep it in line with what societies are paying investors. For a given size and term of loan, the higher the interest rate the higher the level of monthly payments. When rates rise, however, existing borrowers are often allowed to extend their mortgage term rather than pay out more each month, a process which absorbs the increase by spreading payments over a longer period. However, with interest rates already high, the effect on monthly payments of lengthening the term is limited, while recent increases in the mortgage rate have been too large to absorb in this way. Many borrowers have thus found their outgoings increased in the seventies. Terms on endowment loans cannot usually be extended, so that higher rates are reflected in borrowers' outgoings.

Most societies charge the BSA-recommended mortgage rate, though some smaller societies charge more. Endowment loans generally cost $\frac{1}{4}$ per cent or $\frac{1}{2}$ per cent more. 'Special advances' to corporate bodies may cost up to 2 per cent more and those to owner-occupiers (i.e. loans over £20 000) at least $\frac{1}{4}$ per cent more. During 1975 most larger societies started charging differential mortgage rates, related to loan size, starting at £13 000 and rising to over $1\frac{1}{2}$ per cent on amounts over £20 000. These higher rates increase the societies' income, paralleling higher rates paid on, particularly, term shares. At the end of 1977 the BSA-recommended rate of 9.5 per cent was being charged on 68.6 per cent of outstanding mortgage balances, up to $\frac{1}{4}$ per cent more on 22.7 per cent, and over $\frac{1}{2}$ per cent more on 3.8 per cent.[2]

To complete the picture we must note the impact of inflation on the real burden of mortgage payments. If incomes rise, then the *real* cost of monthly mortgage payments will fall, unless offset by rising interest rates. Mortgage payments take a progressively smaller cut of the borrower's current income. Even low rates of increase in income cause a fairly rapid reduction in the burden of mortgage payments: 5 per cent income inflation would halve the proportion of an average borrower's income taken by payments on a typical mortgage within 15 years while higher rates of inflation rapidly reduce the burden to an insignificant level (Figure 5.3 in the Appendix). Although interest rates have tended to rise, the effect of this has been far outweighed by rising incomes. A typical borrower who took out a mortgage in 1963 would have devoted 21 per cent of their income to payments in the first year. By 1976 they would be paying only 7 per cent of their income, despite intervening increases in the mortgage rate (Figure 5.4 in the Appendix). Income inflation cuts borrowers' costs because the capital sum originally borrowed remains fixed in money terms whereas money incomes rise. Borrowers repay the historic cost of loans out of current income levels. The length of time different borrowers have had a loan thus strongly affects their housing costs. In 1972 the median mortgage payment of borrowers with loans less than a year old was £397 p.a. and for those with mortgages 11–20 years old £152 (50 per cent pay more and 50 per cent less than the 'median').[3] Variation between mortgage payments associated with the age of the mortgage is at least as great as that associated with differences in income. Borrowers with identical houses can have very different mortgage outgoings, depending on when they took out their mortgage.

Rapid increases in money incomes combined with high interest rates lead to bunching of repayments in real terms in the early years of a loan. This has come to be known as 'front loading' of mortgage payments. In the example illustrated in Figure 5.5 in the Appendix a 3 per cent interest rate with no income inflation gives total mortgage payments equal to 14 per cent of the borrower's income throughout the loan. With an interest rate of 11 per cent, accompanied by 8 per cent income inflation (representing a real interest rate of 3 per cent as before) total mortgage payments take 30 per cent of the borrower's income in the first year, falling to 5 per cent after 25 years. Front loading raises the initial barrier to owner-occupation while rapidly reducing the burden on those who overcome it.

The application process

The initial filter societies apply to potential borrowers is their system of priority categories, which gives first place in the mortgage queue to applicants who have invested a substantial amount for some length of time in the society and to borrowers introduced by agents. Next in line are generally existing borrowers moving house because they have changed jobs, then existing borrowers who are simply changing houses, and lastly applicants with no previous connection with the society, who do not generally get a look in. First-time buyers may get some measure of priority, and from 1975 applicants nominated by local authorities under the 'support scheme' (discussed later) have, to a certain extent, been treated as special cases.

In 1972, when funds were plentiful, it was possible to borrow from some societies without previous connection, but in the depths of the mortgage slump in 1974 even substantial investors were being turned away. The situation eased later, but societies have generally continued to require that at least £500 or in some cases 10 per cent of the purchase price be invested for six months or more before a loan is granted, the requirement varying with the availability of funds. Applicants nominated by agents, however, gain priority not because of their own links with the society but because of the agent's; nominated applicants have to meet the societies' usual lending criteria regarding property and borrower, but can often jump the mortgage queue. Many societies also make quotas available to house-building companies, who can then offer their new housing for sale with a mortgage to suitable applicants. Large companies may employ their own mortgage broker to raise funds from societies. The building companies can sell much more readily in this way, especially if funds in general are short, and societies welcome the convenient, regular flow of good mortgage business secured against new housing.

Having passed the initial hurdle of priority categories, a prospective borrower's application form will be considered by the society. The form requests a wide range of information about the property to be purchased; the applicant's income, occupation, financial track record and family status; and the loan requested and how the rest of the purchase price is being raised. If the borrower appears to have the financial capability to meet the payment entailed by the loan requested, and the property seems suitable as security, the society does two things. First, it requests a surveyor to inspect and value the property and report on its suitability as loan security, at the applicant's expense. Societies generally follow closely their surveyor's recommendation in deciding whether to grant a loan and, if so, how much to lend and whether they should, for example, require repairs to be carried out to the property. Surveyors, legally, need only be 'competent and prudent', submit a written report, and have no interest in the transaction. Most surveys are in fact carried out by qualified surveyors, about 85 per cent of whom are private practitioners usually employed by estate agencies rather than building societies.[4] Second, the applicant's financial status is checked: employers are usually asked to confirm applicants' occupation, income and prospects; and bankers, landlords, or other societies which have made loans to the applicants may be consulted and the applicant's creditworthiness investigated.

If property and borrower are still acceptable, a loan will be offered. The offer may be less than the amount requested, be for a shorter term or be conditional on, for example, repairs being effected, and may cause the applicant to withdraw. Finally, having made an offer, the society will instruct its solicitors to investigate the 'title' to the property to ascertain legal ownership and any claims to the property, and also investigate whether any planning schemes are likely to affect it. If all that is satisfactory, the mortgage agreement will be signed and a cheque issued.

The mortgage agreement sets out the terms on which the loan is to be repaid and gives the society a legal claim over the property that can be exercised if the borrower fails to repay on the agreed terms. Ultimately, if a borrower gets into serious arrears with the payments, a society will usually obtain a possession order through the county courts, sell the property, and take what is owed, including costs, out of the proceeds, leaving any remainder for the borrower. In practice, however, it is usually possible to negotiate a less drastic solution. Apart from financial mismanagement or refusal to pay, serious arrears usually arise from borrowing too much to start with, borrowing from a fringe bank or other source at high interest rates to meet the deposit or cost of furniture etc., or failing to maintain household income through unemployment or illness. Marital breakdown is a frequent source of problems, particularly when a wife, often with dependent children, is left in the mortgaged home and the husband does not continue to meet the mortgage payments.[5] Early negotiation and action, before arrears become serious, are usually in the best interests of the borrower. The society may agree to the arrears being paid off in a lump sum or over a period of months if the borrower's problems are temporary. The term of the loan may be extended, thus cutting monthly payments, and arrears may be added to the outstanding debt and paid off with the rest of the loan. Most societies will accept interest payments only for a number of months, and where borrowers are unemployed, the Supplementary Benefits Commission is empowered to meet interest charges. Where the borrower *is* taken to court, the judge will often use the court's wide discretionary powers of action and avoid giving the society possession (leading to the borrower being evicted from the house). If the borrower agrees to pay off the arrears on specified terms, subject to a court order, possession is unlikely to be granted.

Mortgage allocation and lending criteria

Building societies' lending policies take into account two sets of factors – the applicant's 'status' and the nature of the house being bought, which will form the security for the loan. Societies attempt to assess applicants' financial capability in terms of the level of mortgage payment they can be expected to maintain, thus minimising the risk of non-payment and arrears requiring action to recover the debt. They also seek to ensure that if the borrower *does* default, then ultimately the mortgaged property could readily be sold on the open market at some future date for an amount which would cover the capital debt, arrears on interest and costs. Security thus means saleability, and relates to a society's estimate of future demand for and market price of the property. The security of their investors' money is the societies' paramount concern; but at the same time societies try and avoid encouraging applicants to borrow more than their income can sustain, or buy housing which may drop in value or prove a financial burden.

Five general points must be considered before looking more closely at lending criteria and allocation. First, societies' lending 'rules' and 'criteria' are an amalgam of relatively ill-defined guidelines and established practice. Although, for example, building-society manuals may recommend maximum ratios of loan size to borrower's income, the actual distribution of mortgage to income ratios cannot simply be read off from the criteria. The criteria are only guidelines; they cannot be rigidly applied to individual cases, and, furthermore, individual managers have considerable discretion.

Second, and related to the previous point, the pattern of allocation will reflect a combination of constraint by rules and criteria and the preference of borrowers. Borrowers vary, for example, as to the amount they want to borrow relative to their income. Thus a lender may stipulate a maximum ratio of loan to income, but a proportion of borrowers will not want the maximum and others will of course want more. Obviously the higher the borrowers' income group, occupational status, savings, etc., the greater the freedom to exercise preference and the less likely they are to be constrained by societies' lending criteria. But whether such constraint is attributable to institutional criteria or to outside factors, particularly the distribution of income, is a matter of interpretation.

Third, since the early fifties demand for mortgages has exceeded supply. There has been no serious competition on the lending side between societies since the thirties, neither have they had to compete for mortgage business with other lending institutions. This has allowed societies to be particularly selective in granting loans. But despite this general 'excess' demand, societies allocate their funds by rationing them according to lending criteria rather than allowing the price of mortgages (the mortgage rate) to be bid up to an equilibrium level at which supply equals demand and the market for loans is 'cleared'. This keeps down the mortgage rate and hence housing costs, and, in theory, lower-income householders are better able to obtain loans than in a free market. It also, however, enables societies to exercise caution in selecting borrowers and property and setting conditions on loans.

Fourth, although different societies' lending policies are generally similar, they do vary to a certain extent and are individually determined. Criteria and lending patterns also vary over time, depending on the availability of funds. When short of funds, societies consciously or unconsciously lend lower multiples of borrowers' incomes, lower proportions of property values and take less account of wives' earnings or overtime. Interviewing estate agents in Birmingham, Lambert was told it was 'normal practice for societies to clamp down on older areas when funds were low and that this was sensible management of the investors' money'.[6] Thus, when funds are short, those with lower incomes buying older and cheaper housing are disproportionately affected, suggesting an inherent conservatism in the management of investors' money.

Finally, the legal framework specifies that societies can only lend on freehold or leasehold land and property ('estate') by way of a mortgage or legal charge, so they cannot lend more than 100 per cent of the value of the land or property, and must have first claim on the security before any third party. It defines what additional forms of security are acceptable, and the duty of directors to satisfy themselves that mortgage security is adequate. It also limits 'special advances' to no more than 10 per cent of a society's annual lending. Beyond this there are no legal constraints on societies' lending criteria and policies.

Characteristics of building-society borrowers

Income

Societies try to ensure that any loan granted is well within the capacity of the borrower to repay, so that there is minimal risk of arrears through overcommitment. Societies often work on the basis that loans must not exceed two and a half or three times a borrower's gross annual income, or that a borrower's monthly mortgage payments must not exceed their gross weekly income; interest rate and repayment term, therefore, affect the maximum loan (Figures 5.2 and 5.6 in the Appendix). Societies might be more generous to applicants on rising salary scales or with a large cash stake, and less generous where the property might require more expenditure on maintenance than normal or the applicant has large hire-purchase commitments. 'Income' is usually taken to be gross annual income; where bonus or overtime earnings are regular, 50 per cent may be taken into account. In the case of married partners up to 50 per cent of the wife's income might be taken into account or an amount equal to one year's income added to the loan size, depending on how permanent her employment appeared and whether the husband was on a rising salary scale; if the wife earned more, hers may be taken as the dominant income. Female applicants are treated the same as male applicants, taking into account the societies' estimation of their career and earning prospects. Where households consist of un-married couples or groups of adults, societies normally lend only on the basis of one individual's income, since such groupings are considered unstable. Societies may require existing owners selling a house to plough back a proportion of the net cash proceeds.

In 1978 the average size of loan was 1.82 times the average income of those buying for the first time and 1.64 times that of existing owners. (See Figures 5.7 and 5.8 in the Appendix.)[7] This reflects the fact that many borrowers, particularly existing owners (often with higher incomes and more savings), do not want to borrow up to the maximum. The average income of first-time buyers borrowing from the societies in 1978 was £5283 and of existing owners £6161, compared with average male earnings of about £4770; 22 per cent of all buyers (27 per cent of first-time buyers) earned under £4000; and 58 per cent of all buyers earned £5000 or more.[8] Loan-size relative to income varies with the availability of funds. The average loan to first-time buyers was 2.26 times their average income at the start of 1973 when funds were plentiful then fell back to 1.74 times average income by mid-1977 (partly reflecting the rise of incomes relative to house prices). Underlying this variability, societies have tended to become rather more liberal in terms of loan to income ratios and the proportion of non-basic and wives' earnings taken into account. This has been encouraged by rising incomes, which quickly reduce the burden of loan repayments, and rapidly rising house prices, which open up a large gap between the amount borrowed and the market value of the house as loan security.

Creditworthiness

Societies assess applicants' creditworthiness through a variety of enquiries. Applicants are generally asked whether they (or their wives) have ever been insolvent, bankrupt or in court for debt, and a variety of enquiries may be made at credit agencies, other societies the applicant has borrowed from, banks and former landlords. According to the BSI, 'If the applicant has ever been made bankrupt or made an arrangement with his creditors the value of his covenant is immediately in doubt'.[9] Bankruptcy, adverse county-court judgements or serious arrears with another society were described by one society as 'like a cloud that follows you everywhere' and likely to rule out a loan from any society. Minor misdemeanour might be permissible if far in the past, if the applicant has maintained a good credit and savings record subsequently and built up a substantial deposit; and if the problem was related, for example, to illness rather than wilful refusal to pay or manage finances.

Occupational status

Applicants in non-manual, particularly professional and managerial, employment with regular assured incomes may find it easier to borrow and be able to borrow more for a given income than many manual wage-earners, who are more likely to be hit by temporary unemployment and lay-offs. Since less account is taken of overtime and bonuses in determining loan size, manual workers may be treated less generously than those with equivalent but more regular incomes. Barbolet found 'a subtle form of what might be termed social discrimination' in mortgage allocation, suggesting this 'seems to be directed against manual workers and to involve the use of criteria for home ownership which do not rest on income alone'.[10] A second study found that some societies have a policy of always accepting applications from such people as policemen, journalists or teachers, because they have secure jobs and they hold influential positions in all communities.[11] In Newcastle it was found that semi-skilled and unskilled workers, who made up about 29 per cent of the male workforce, accounted for about 5 per cent of building-society borrowers, reflecting both income and occupational status; nearly 30 per cent of borrowers were in professional and managerial classes, which made up 12 per cent of the male workforce.[12] Skilled manual workers, with generally higher and more stable incomes than the semi-skilled and unskilled, accounted for about 27 per cent of borrowers and 40 per cent of male workers.

Age of borrower

Prospective owners take time to accumulate a deposit, build up a record of saving with a society and reach an income level adequate as a basis for a loan. However, in 1978 a third of first-time buyers were under 25. The proportion of young first-time buyers is considerably higher where houses are relatively cheap, as in the Northern region (45 per cent were under 25 in 1978), than where prices are high, as in London and the South East (21 per cent and 30 per cent under 25). Societies are reluctant to allow the term over which a loan will be repaid to extend beyond the borrower's expected date of retirement. Loan terms are therefore reduced for older borrowers. Taking 65 as the age of retirement, 25-year loans would generally only be available to borrowers aged under 40. The length of repayment term granted reflects societies' criteria regarding the borrower's age, the age and type of property (see below) and the borrower's preferences; 25 years is the customary 'normal' term, accounting for 60 per cent of loans in 1977, when 2 per cent were for over 25 years and 38 per cent for less. Loan term is particularly significant, since, for a given size of loan and mortgage rate, the shorter the term the higher the monthly payments – monthly payments on £10 000 at 11.75 per cent rise from £104.50 over 25 years to £109.90 over 20 years and £146.00 over 10 years (before tax relief).

Previous tenure

The proportion of mortgages to first-time buyers fell progressively from 63 per cent in 1969 to 47 per cent in 1978, largely reflecting the increase in the proportion of existing owners in the total number of households – from 49 per cent in 1969 to 54 per cent by 1978. An increasing proportion of loans are therefore made to existing owners moving house. Of those buying for the first time in 1978, 21 per cent were new households (mainly newly married or previously living with parents), 16 per cent had been in private rented housing and only 7 per cent in local-authority housing.

Characteristics of houses mortgaged to building societies

House price, value and loan size

The average price of houses bought by first-time buyers in 1978 was £12 023 and by existing owners £18 792; average loan size was 80 per cent and 57 per cent respectively of the dwelling price. Of all houses bought, 54 per cent cost £13 000 or more – 72 per cent in the case of existing owners. A comparison can be made between the price distribution of houses sold with a building-society mortgage and the price distribution for all houses sold (based on Inland Revenue data for 1975). For new houses the distributions are virtually identical. But whereas 75 per cent of all sales of secondhand dwellings appear to have been financed by building societies, only about 10 per cent of sales of houses priced under £4000, and about 40 per cent of houses priced between £4000 and £5000 were funded by the societies.[13]

Societies base the amount loaned on their surveyor's estimate of a dwelling's market value for mortgage purposes rather than the price the buyer actually pays. This will often be slightly less than the buying price, particularly on older houses. Societies initially determine a maximum normal loan based on the property only, disregarding additional security, to give the necessary margin for possible depreciation and costs in event of forced sale. This would generally be 80 per cent of the value of the best property, such as sound, conventional post-1930 houses, falling to 70 per cent on such dwellings as the best pre-1918 terrace houses and down to 60 per cent on poorer property (Figure 5.8 in the Appendix describes the characteristics of mortgaged dwellings). Societies will frequently lend an 'excess advance' on top of the normal percentage of valuation, provided this extra is covered by an insurance company guarantee. A standard form of insurance has been agreed between the BSA and the insurance companies under the Building Societies Indemnity Scheme. The borrower pays a single premium and the insurance company covers any loss the society sustains from making the excess loan, if the borrower defaults and the property is sold. With a guarantee, up to 20 per cent extra may be added to the normal loan, but 100 per cent loans are only allowed where valuation or purchase price, whichever is lower, is no greater than £14 000. A special Option Mortgage Guarantee Scheme provides for guarantees of up to 25 per cent of the value of the property and for loans of 100 per cent of values, on loans up to £14 000, the risk being shared equally between the government and the insurance company involved. Societies will in some cases grant excess loans against other forms of additional security, such as claims on insurance policies, or other property.

A house might thus cost £11 000 to buy and be valued at £10 500 by a society's surveyor; a 75 per cent normal loan plus 20 per cent excess loan covered by a guarantee would add up to £9975, leaving the buyer to find a deposit of £1025. The deposit often represents the major barrier to home-ownership facing first-time buyers and low-income households that may have incomes adequate to maintain loan payment but have been unable to accumulate savings. Societies usually prefer that borrowers have demonstrated financial discipline by saving and that they have a significant cash stake in the house from the start to encourage a 'responsible attitude'. Many buyers raise all or part of the deposit in the form of an additional 'topping-up' or 'secondary' loan from an insurance company, fringe bank or finance house, usually at high interest rates, which can seriously strain the financial resources of lower-income borrowers. Societies may, however, refuse or reduce the main loan if it is thought borrowers may get into difficulties by raising a secondary loan. The average deposit paid by first-time buyers in 1978 was £2421 (20 per cent of the average dwelling price) and by existing owners £8181 (44 per cent of average price), emphasising the greater financial re-sources of former owners, particularly the net proceeds from selling an existing house. These averages disguise the fact, however, that 39 per cent of first-time buyers paid deposits under £1000, and in regions with generally lower house prices over half paid under £1000. Of first-time buyers, 27 per cent obtained loans of over 90 per cent of purchase price but only 2 per cent obtained over 95 per cent, indicating that the majority did have to find a significant cash stake.

Dwelling age

Property age indicates to societies a dwelling's present and likely future value, probable rate of deterioration, the likelihood that major repairs will be necessary or structural faults emerge, and, ultimately, the life of the dwelling. Societies give proportionately more loans on newer housing and less on older housing relative to the age distribution of the housing stock; in 1978 18 per cent of loans were on new houses, which accounted for under $1\frac{1}{2}$ per cent of the stock, and 24 per cent were on pre-1919 houses, which represented 32 per cent of the stock in 1975. However, it must be remembered that all new houses come on to the market but only a proportion of existing houses do, so that the pattern of lending is less disproportionate in terms of the age distribution of the flow of dwellings for sale rather than the stock – 28 per cent of *existing* houses on which loans were granted in 1978 were built before 1919, compared with 30 per cent of the stock.

The proportion of loans on new housing fell from 27 per cent in 1970 to 18 per cent in 1978, largely reflecting the fall-off in house building from nearly 200 000 per annum in the early seventies to under 150 000 in 1978 (in Great Britain). The proportion of loans on pre-1919 houses rose from 17 per cent in 1970 to 24 per cent by 1978; this partly reflects the declining proportion of loans on new houses (loans on post-1940 houses also rose, from 34 per cent to 39 per cent), but the figures suggest a significant expansion of lending on older housing, particularly since the cutback in local authority lending in 1975. A large proportion of the pre-1919 houses on which loans are granted are post-1900, societies remaining more reluctant to lend on nineteenth-century houses.

Loans granted on older housing tend to cover less of the purchase price and be for shorter terms; the first leaves buyers more to find as a deposit and the second raises the level of monthly payments on a given size of loan. This particularly affects lower-income buyers, for whom older, cheaper housing is the only way into owner-occupation. The societies' 'normal' loan is often reduced to 70 per cent on older (pre-1919) houses, and they are less likely to grant much of an 'excess'; the total loan may also be limited to 90 per cent of valuation. Valuations of older property are more likely to fall short of purchase price, further raising the deposit barrier.

Loan terms are generally reduced on older property on the assumption that their life and the security they represent is less certain. Whereas 25 years is the norm for recent and new housing and 30 years not uncommon on new housing, terms on pre-1919 housing are often reduced to 20 or 15 years, depending on type, condition etc. A rule of thumb quoted by some societies is that property should have 25–30 years' life left after expiry of the loan terms. In Newcastle at least 25-year terms were found on nearly 90 per cent of loans on post-1965 houses, whereas 70 per cent of loans on pre-1919 houses had terms of 15 years and only 5 per cent more than 20.[14]

House type

The distribution of loans in terms of house type reflects both the make-up of the housing stock and societies' lending criteria.[15] Societies lend on a wide range of types of house; in 1978 roughly a third of loans were on detached houses, a third on semi-detached and the remaining third on terraced houses or flats. This compared with the housing stock of about 16 per cent detached, 33 per cent semi-detached and 49 per cent terraced houses and flats in 1975. The proportion of first-time buyers purchasing terraced houses and flats rose from 32 per cent in 1969 to 51 per cent in 1978, probably reflecting the increased availability of such houses through new building, rehabilitation and transfers from the private rented sector.[16] Demand has also tended to rise, since first-time buyers can increasingly afford only flats or terraced housing, which generally represent the cheapest end of the market.

Within this broad spectrum of lending there is a range of types of housing on which societies *do* lend but much less readily and then only on the best examples of the type, on the grounds that uncertainty as to either future demand or durability makes them less suitable as security. These often include very large houses showing signs of, or easily adaptable for, multiple-occupation; houses with outside toilets, downstairs bathrooms, no garage or parking space or lacking basic amenities; houses in urban areas with no front garden or forecourt and which therefore open straight to the street; back to back houses and old (pre-1919) terraced flats; such unusual or unconventionally constructed houses as timber-framed or prefabs; and former council houses in areas still predominantly council-owned. It is worth emphasising again that societies *do* lend on all these types in *some* particular cases, but proportionately often much less frequently than on other types, and they are much more likely to refuse applications or offer low-percentage loans and shorter terms on these house types.

Societies only lend on leasehold rather than freehold flats, since owners' financial responsibility for and rights over common areas and structures (stairs, roof etc.) need to be laid down in a lease to avoid the possibility of any unreasonable financial burden, which would, in turn, endanger the society's security. Societies prefer modern, purpose-built small flat-blocks under five storeys, though recent good-quality conversions into self-contained units are often acceptable.

Freehold houses are perfectly acceptable. On all leasehold dwellings societies generally require the lease to have at least 50 years left to run and to extend 25 or 30 years beyond the mortgage term, since values drop rapidly towards the end of the lease. This rules out loans on some houses and limits terms to 15 or 20 years on others, affecting particularly older inner-city housing, much of it built prior to 1919 and originally sold on 99-year leases.

House improvement

The *Housing Policy* Green Paper observed:

> There is a range of properties that building societies will rarely accept as security, of which unmodernised 19th century houses appear to be the main group. In 1976 the building society mortgage survey indicates that about 0.4 % of all advances on second hand houses (some 2000 in total) were on houses without a bathroom. But there were some 300,000 owner-occupied houses in total in England and Wales without bathrooms . . .
>
> Owner-occupiers without a fixed bath . . . were numerous in 1971 and widely distributed between regions.[17]

Where a society considers that repairs or improvements are required for a house to represent adequate security, it may require an undertaking from the borrower to effect these within a given time as a condition of the mortgage; it may retain a portion of the loan until repairs, improvement or redecoration are effected to its satisfaction; or it may refuse any loan until the work is done, forcing the applicant to buy the property first, usually with a bank bridging loan, and repair or improve it before the society makes a firm offer. These financial barriers raise the cost and obstacles facing those buying older houses, and will often prevent the purchaser being able to proceed.

Three specific problems arise when applicants are intending obtaining improvement grants through the local authority. First, a loan on unimproved property can only legally be made up to its existing, unimproved value rather than its value after improvement, so that societies cannot in effect finance any part of the improvement. Second, statutory conditions attached to grants under the 1974 Housing Act designed to prevent abuse allow local authorities to reclaim the grant with interest unless the recipient occupies the property for at least one year and keeps it available for letting for a further four years if they move out. The possibility that grants might have to be repaid reduces the value of such property as security and societies are reluctant to lend on property to be improved using grants. Third, local authorities have been unwilling to commit themselves to grants until property is owned, while societies have been unwilling to lend unless assured the property will be improved, for which the buyer would require a grant. Following discussions on Department of the Environment Circular 38/77, issued to local authorities, authorities have been generally willing to indicate grants will be given but less willing to waive the right to reclaim grants. Societies frequently grant additional 'further advances' to existing borrowers for house-improvement, but these are commonly for central heating or double glazing rather than covering owners' contributions to grant-aided basic amenities and improvements.

Property location and 'red lining'

Building societies consider a dwelling's surrounding area, its location, to be one of the attributes affecting demand, and hence the dwelling's value as mortgage security. According to a BSI handbook, 'It may have been decided, for example, to restrict lending in a certain area because of certain disadvantages attached to that area . . .',[18] and the BSI's model of mortgage lending procedure includes in it such questions to the surveyor as the following: 'Is the property suitable to the district . . . Is the district improving, static or deteriorating . . . Is there good demand for this type of property in this district?'[19] And according to the Chief General Manager of the Nationwide in 1977, 'Societies are, moreover, reluctant to lend on properties, which may be acceptable in themselves, if the environment in which houses are situated is declining and the values of the properties are therefore likely to depreciate'.[20]

Societies' lending policies regarding property age, type and location combine to create areas, particularly of older, inner-city housing, in which mortgages will rarely be granted. Evidence of such areas has been assembled in a number of cities.[21]

Societies interviewed in Newcastle in 1974 indicated areas in which they would rarely if ever lend; these contained all but one of the city's General Improvement Areas. In Leeds several societies had reportedly ruled out lending in a considerable part of the central area; applicants were told variously that 'We don't lend in that area', 'You have to draw the line somewhere', and 'The house is mortgageable, the area is not', when trying to raise loans on property in the Hyde Park/South Headingley area. A couple trying to sell a house were told by a firm of estate agents that Leeds 6 'is a dead duck so far as mortgages are concerned . . . you don't stand a chance of selling there, except to coloureds. Between you and me, no matter what they say about "Blue Zones", they do exist – Building Societies won't touch them'.

In Leicester three societies indicated on maps supplied to the local authority areas in which they would rarely lend, and these areas contained 55 per cent of the city's owner-occupiers and half the private tenants in 1971. According to Lambert, who interviewed building society managers in Birmingham:

. . . the building societies either deliberately steered clear of certain older areas . . . or exercised extreme caution, although they usually emphasized that there was no written policy which precluded all houses in those areas. However two or three managers did say that they had marked off areas on a map (in one case we were shown this) and rarely looked at any property falling within these boundaries.

One manager said:

Both individuals and property in the older areas are poorer risks. Ultimately, the solution to not losing money is good property . . . the problem in Birmingham is that here is a modern affluent city with thousands and thousands of houses built since the second world war. Money is always limited – then how much more sense it is to lend it on those modern houses than in the riskier areas.[22]

In Huddersfield Duncan reports:

> Mortgages were most unlikely to be approved for houses in so-called blue zones. A particularly cogent definition of these areas is couched in racist terms. Indeed in questioning the managers about area differences . . . it was immediately assumed that I was talking about race. Particular areas were then mentioned which because of the number of blacks living in them were generally avoided (Figure 5.9 in the Appendix).

Societies consider property located in such areas poor security for their investors' money. Specific features which deter societies from lending include high levels of multiple-occupation, rented housing, students and other transient social groups, immigrants, and municipalised housing. Proximity to redevelopment areas and areas scheduled for clearance particularly discourages lending, and, according to one manager in Newcastle, the clearance programme there had 'cast a big shadow over much of the city'. Societies frequently argued that uncertainty as to central government policy and detailed local-authority plans and their likely success make property in older areas unsuitable as mortgage security. Societies may also feel that the type of borrower attracted to cheaper, older areas increases the risk of arrears, such borrowers being thought more prone to unemployment, domestic trouble or financial mismanagement. But societies have frequently denied accusations of specific 'red lining' practices. The president of the Leeds Permanent stated in 1975 that 'there was no embargo on lending money anywhere in the country', and the chairman of the Nationwide has claimed: 'We do not red line. We look at any property submitted to us and decide on the basis of the individual property whether it is worth lending on'.[23]

Concern with the existence of red lines, managers' real or mental maps, or the fact that some societies may occasionally take short cuts by turning down property solely on the grounds of its location without further investigation – issues on which much of the recent debate has focused – largely misses the point. It must also be recognised that societies' policies vary, that it is not claimed that there are necessarily *no* loans in these areas, nor is the large proportion of building society loans on pre-1919 houses denied. The significant point to be made is that societies' lending policies, aiming to ensure what they consider adequate mortgage security, create areas of older, mainly inner-city housing where they will only rarely lend. As the current chairman of the BSA commented in 1976, 'there must still be areas in our big cities, in particular, where building society loans to individuals would be inappropriate'.[24] This has important implications both for individuals' access to housing and housing costs, and for inner-city decay and the improvement programme, which will be examined in Chapter 8.

Building society loans to house-builders

Building societies tend to see their main role as lending to individuals buying houses for owner-occupation. They do, however, play a limited role in financing the production of housing by providing working capital for house-builders.[25] Building finance has averaged about £7.5 million annually in the 1970s, rising to £10 million in 1972 and 1973. This, however, represents a very small proportion of total lending, at most 0.3 per cent in any year, though the importance of building finance varies greatly between societies. Societies may grant loans on land on which development is about to commence; maximum loans are usually $66\frac{2}{3}$ per cent of the value of the land. More commonly societies provide building finance secured against property under construction or completed but unsold, lending up to 75 per cent of the valuation of the property or selling price of the houses, whichever is lower. For example, the Halifax lent nearly £600 000 to the York-based builder Shepherd Homes Ltd over the period 1971 to 1976; and the Abbey National lent £3.8 million to three company groups from 1970 to 1976, including £1.3 million to Wates Construction Ltd or subsidiaries thereof.[26]

Finance in advance of sales on particular developments is limited in scale, and the terms of the loan depend on the size of the development. A five-year period is common, though in practice societies often accept interest only during development, with capital repayments as and when completed houses are sold. Many societies couple the provision of building finance with the promise of quotas of mortgage funds earmarked for those purchasing the houses on completion. Such arrangements give builders confidence and a secure financial basis. *Housing Policy*, however, concluded, and the building societies generally agree, that the house-builders' main source of loan finance, the banks, should be able to meet most of the demand for building finance.

Institutional roles in the supply of mortgages

Building societies' lending now covers all but the lowest-priced housing sold for owner-occupation. Previously emphasising the middle price-ranges, they have increased lending on more expensive houses where the banks and especially insurance companies have withdrawn. However, under-representation relative to the volume of houses sold remains at the lower end of the market. This final section describes lending by the three main alternatives to the societies – the most important, the local authorities, followed by insurance companies and banks.

Local authorities

Local authorities' powers to lend are largely set out in the 1958 Housing (Financial Provisions) Act as extended by section 37 of the 1974 Local Government Act. There are few statutory conditions governing local-authority lending, but their activity has been subject to monetary constraint and to lending 'guidelines'.

After their powers were consolidated in 1958, net local authority lending rose from £26 million in 1959 to £168 million by 1965, nearly a quarter of lending by the four main institutions (Figure 3.3 in the Appendix). Since then lending, which is accounted as public expenditure, has been subject to various monetary restrictions in line with government macro-economic policy (detailed in Figure 5.10 in the Appendix), which have been strongly reflected in the volume of lending. Lending fell sharply after 1965, rose to a peak of £533 million in 1975 after monetary limits within defined lending categories were lifted in 1971, then fell back sharply when restrictions were reimposed.

Following the introduction of monetary limits, the government indicated in 1966 that 'local authorities should direct their efforts in the current year to supplementing other sources of finance for house purchase, and should concentrate on helping those with housing needs who might not otherwise be provided for'.[27] Priority lending categories were introduced and have continued since with occasional changes. From 1974–5 to 1975–6 the categories were as follows:

1. Existing tenants of any local authority, people who are high on an authority's waiting list for housing, or people displaced by slum clearance or other public-authority development whom a council would otherwise have been obliged to rehouse.
2. Applicants who are homeless or threatened with homelessness, or living conditions that are overcrowded or otherwise detrimental to health.
3. Individual numbers of self-build groups when they are about to occupy the premises as individual mortgagors.
4. Applicants who want to buy older property suitable for single-family occupation and unlikely to attract a commercial mortgage advance; and more particularly persons who want to acquire a house with a view to improving it subsequently for their own occupation with the help of a renovation grant or loan.
5. Applicants who want to buy larger property for only partial occupation by themselves in areas where conditions of over-crowding seem liable to develop.
6. Applicants taking up residence in or around a development or intermediate area or overspill-receiving area.
7. Staff urgently required where the local authority are satisfied that they are needed in the interests of the efficiency of the public service and that they are unlikely to obtain the requisite mortgage advance from another source.

For 1974–5 only, an eighth category was added:

8. Purchasers of newly built houses from builders or developers where the mortgage transactions may reasonably be expected to be completed by the end of 1974.

For 1976–7 to 1978–9, categories 3, 6 and 7 were dropped and category 1 extended to cover new-town tenants.[28]

In 1974–5 an estimated 55 per cent of loans went to applicants wanting older property with a view to improvement, 15 per cent to applicants who were homeless or threatened with homelessness, 15 per cent to existing tenants, and people high on waiting lists or displaced by slum clearance, and 8 per cent to staff urgently required by the local authority.[29] The authorities' role since 1965 has been primarily to complement rather than replicate lending by other institutions, 'the same as the general purposes to which local authorities direct their efforts under the Housing Act; namely to meet housing needs';[30] and the 1976 Public Expenditure White Paper referred to authorities as, specifically, 'lenders of last resort'.[31] In practice, however, local authorities have had considerable freedom to determine their own policies, and, within the general monetary constraint and lending guidelines, have developed schemes varying considerably in scale and scope. According to *Housing Policy*:

> In the past, local authorities have developed to a certain extent their own interpretation of the categories which were applicable. This means there has been a diversity of practice in local authority lending with some authorities taking a wider view than others of their role. Knowledge of this is limited, but it is thought that the result has been that in some areas borrowers were able to turn to the local authority only in special circumstances (e.g. if they were seeking an older property needing improvement), while in other areas local authority lending was widely available and not necessarily only to those who could not obtain a building society loan.[32]

There has always been considerable overlap between the lending patterns of the authorities and building societies, which became especially marked in 1974–5, when the societies were short of funds and unrestricted local-authority lending expanded to fill the gap. However, local authorities tend to lend proportionately more than the societies to those buying older and cheaper housing (Figure 5.11 in the Appendix), to lower-income and age groups and to first-time buyers; they also tend to lend more generously in relation to house-prices and incomes, and grant proportionately more 'option' and 'low start' loans (Figure 5.12 in the Appendix). In 1975 62 per cent of local-authority loans were on pre-1919 property, but only 19 per cent of building-society loans were; 42 per cent of local-authority borrowers earned under £2500, compared with 16 per cent of building-society borrowers, and 57 per cent bought houses for under £6000 as against 7 per cent of building-society borrowers. In 1975 the local authorities may have financed about 30–40 per cent of sales of houses for under £4000, leaving over 50 per cent of such sales to be financed from cash or loans from other than the two main sources. In 1975 11 per cent of all existing houses sold for under £4000.[33] Of local-authority and building-society borrowers, 87 per cent and 47 per cent respectively were first-time buyers; most first-time buyers borrowing from a local authority obtain subsequent loans from building societies, so these figures partly show the complementary role of the two institutions. Borrowing from many local authorities is more expensive than borrowing from the societies, since local authorities' mortgage rates are tied to the rate the authorities themselves have to pay to borrow, and the cost of money to many authorities is considerably higher than to societies.

The Support Lending Scheme Following the cutback in local-authority lending in 1975, the government negotiated a scheme whereby building societies would step in to fill the gap.[34] In July 1975 £100 million was earmarked to be lent under the scheme, £176 million for the financial year 1977–8 and £300 million for 1978–9. Under the scheme people apply to a local authority for a loan, and if the authority considers it would have granted a loan had funds been available, it nominates the applicant to a building society, which treats the application in the normal way.

The scheme was very slow to start, owing primarily to administrative problems and misunderstanding between societies and local authorities. By February 1976 only £18 million had been loaned under the scheme; however, activity picked up subsequently and a total of £160 million had been reached by March 1977, and a further £105 million was loaned in 1977–8.

The volume of 'support lending' is in itself a fairly meaningless index of societies' success in filling the gap left by local authorities. Similarly the rate of refusal of nominees largely tells how far local-authority officers appreciated the societies' lending criteria. Refusal rates thus generally fell through time, in Scotland from 80 per cent in 1975–6 to 40 per cent in 1976–7, for example, as greater understanding developed. Further difficulties arise because some borrowers who might previously have gone to a local authority will have applied directly to a building society.

It seems that societies have increasingly granted loans to those who would previously have obtained local-authority mortgages, expanding lending in that part of the mortgage market where considerable overlap had developed between societies' and authorities' lending patterns, and particularly when the authorities moved up-market in the early seventies. But there is little evidence that societies are now lending on property or to borrowers that previously they would have refused but that local authorities would have accepted. In Leeds, for example, a comparison of support lending with local-authority lending in 1974–5 before the scheme operated indicated that societies had granted loans on property which previously would more likely have been bought with local-authority loans; but that societies were not prepared to lend on back to back terraced houses, which in 1974–5 accounted for nearly 30 per cent of local-authority loans. It is important also to consider the terms on which loans are given – percentage of valuation, repayment period, repairs and retentions etc. – in order to evaluate how far the societies have 'replaced' local-authority lending. The main point seems to be that local authorities were not aware of building-society lending criteria, for 'it has always been axiomatic in the scheme that the societies would apply and preserve the appropriate criteria on the basis of which they would be prepared to lend',[35] and 'The scheme has always operated under societies normal lending criteria'.[36]

Much of the 'replacement' would probably have occurred without the elaborate nomination procedures, as happened when local-authority lending was cut back after 1965. Some degree of greater understanding between building societies, government and local authorities has undoubtedly been generated by the exercise. But its main function seems to have been to facilitate the government cut in local-authority lending and for the societies to generate goodwill by demonstrating their willingness to cooperate with the government, rather than to fill the gap left by local authorities.

Insurance companies

Insurance companies lend mainly as a way of increasing insurance business. In 1978 the average price of houses bought with insurance-company loans was about £21 140 compared with £15 590 for building societies and the average loan £11 876 as against £10 137 for the societies. The average income of those borrowing from insurance companies is considerably higher than that of building society borrowers; hence most are in the professional and managerial classes. Maximum loans are usually less than the societies' norm of two and a half times borrowers' income, terms are shorter and interest rates higher. Nearly a third of insurance-company lending for house purchase (by value) is in the form of secondary 'topping up' loans, where the main loan is from a building society; both main and secondary loans are normally insurance-linked. Insurance companies' main involvement in house-purchase is through endowment mortgages rather than actually lending capital; about £1400 million of building-society lending in 1977 was repayable by endowment policies, compared with £166 million direct lending by insurance companies (gross). Excess loan guarantees, house-insurance and mortgage protection policies also provide considerable insurance business.

Banks

The clearing banks' main involvement in house-purchase, apart from staff loans, is in providing short-term bridging finance, covering the time between a person buying one house before completing the sale of another and needing the sale proceeds to repay an existing mortgage. Longer-term loans are usually granted only to long-standing customers with substantial incomes; loans are usually above, say, £15 000, only up to ten-year terms, and at interest rates considerably above the societies'. Both banks and insurance companies, and indeed building societies, grant staff mortgages at discretionary rates (usually $2\frac{1}{2}$–5 per cent).

The exception to this pattern was the period 1971–7, when clearing banks, particularly Barclays, directly or through subsidiaries were an important source of five- to ten-year loans at relatively high interest rates, funding the purchase mainly of older dwellings at the lower end of the market. In certain inner-urban areas the clearing banks, together with fringe banks and such finance houses as Julian Hodge and Co., became the dominant source of loans, and the usual sources of loans in national terms became relatively unimportant. One survey showed that in Saltley in inner Birmingham, in 1972–4, 50 per cent of loans came from the clearing banks and 11 per cent from fringe banks and finance houses.[37] Local-authority lending was no more than the national average at 8 per cent and building societies supplied only 7 per cent; 22 per cent of houses were bought for cash or with an informal loan. The pattern was repeated in two other areas surveyed, and limited evidence suggests a similar situation in Newcastle, Leeds, Huddersfield and indeed most major cities. Loans from clearing banks and fringe banks bear higher interest charges, terms are short, and option mortgages are unavailable. Average monthly payments to fringe banks in Saltley were more than twice those to building societies and the local authority. In 1974 average costs of loans from the main sources in Saltley were as shown in the table on p. 78. A loan of £3000 over five years at fringe-bank interest rates, such as 24 per cent, would cost over £90 per month. Spread over 15 years it would cost £62 as against £47 at 17 per cent and £35

	Interest rate (%)	*Term (years)*	*Average payment per month (£)*
Building society and local authority	11	15–25	20
Clearing bank	16–18	5–10	34
Fringe bank	17–28	5–10	47

at 11 per cent. Loan costs in these areas, which are often the only areas where many lower-income households can afford to buy, are thus much higher than on conventional loans. Clearing-bank lending in such areas seems to have dropped back since 1974 but, as the societies themselves are aware, banks may be seriously considering a more general expansion of mortgage-lending,[38] and could come to play a more significant role in the future. The more general issue of mortgage-lending and the role of home-ownership in older inner-urban housing areas are taken up in Chapters 8 and 9.

6

Building societies and the finance market

Building societies have become major financial institutions in their own right, competing for investment with a wide range of institutions. As they have grown, they have become increasingly integrated with the rest of the finance market. But though they are now an integral part of the general finance market, societies enjoy special tax treatment and freedom from many of the controls applied to institutions such as banks. The societies' increasing size and integration with the rest of the market has led to criticism of this special treatment, particularly from the banks. It has also raised more fundamental issues relating to monetary policy and to the use of finance and resources in the economy. Finally, it has increased societies' reliance on more volatile investment, causing sharp variations in their receipts, which are in turn reflected in the level of mortgage-lending.

Building societies versus the finance market

The personal-savings market offers the investor a wide range of types of investment of varied characteristics. The return, liquidity and security of the capital invested are the three main aspects of any form of investment; these may be combined also with specific functions such as life assurance and pension schemes. The societies' most direct competitors are institutions offering investments of roughly comparable liquidity and security, such as bank deposit, savings bank and National Savings accounts. Here competition focuses on the interest rate. Less direct competition comes from investments which offer a rather different bundle of characteristics but which investors still consider as alternatives to putting their money in a building society. Thus local-authority securities, gilt-edged (government) securities, unit trusts, life assurance and company stocks and shares all provide a certain amount of competition to the societies by offering higher returns at the expense of liquidity or in some cases security. Building-society shares combine a high degree of security and liquidity with an assured and highly competitive rate of return. They also have the particular attraction of priority access to mortgage loans (see Chapter 5).

Investment in the societies is particularly safe because it is largely secured by mortgages on owner-occupied housing, and could ultimately be recovered by selling the mortgaged property. The effectiveness of mortgage security depends on societies' lending policies. The security of the rest of the societies' funds depends on their skill in investing in liquid assets, though the regulations leave little room for serious loss. Although several societies have experienced financial difficulties since the Second World War, these have mainly related to misconduct by individual officers, as in the recent cases of the Wakefield and the Grays societies, and apparently no investors have suffered any loss since the war. Societies in any difficulty have usually been simply taken over by one of the major societies. For practical purposes the security offered by the societies is effectively equivalent to that of banks, savings banks and National Savings – it would take a financial blizzard of catastrophic dimensions to expose any real differences. It is, however, particularly important for the societies to maintain investors' confidence in the security of their money, since they borrow short and lend long to an exaggerated degree compared with banks and other institutions, so that a run of withdrawals is potentially more serious for the societies.

Building-society shares are highly liquid; most of the societies' funds can be withdrawn with at most a few days' notice. This appeals both to the small saver who wants cash as needs arise and to the more sophisticated investor wanting to switch money rapidly to other institutions when their interest rates are more attractive. By comparison, bank deposits commonly require seven days' notice, National Savings Investment Accounts require a month, while premature redemption of National Savings Certificates or insurance policies, on which terms are measured in years, considerably cuts the return. Building-society shares are of fixed capital value – if £100 is invested £100 can be withdrawn. In contrast, company, government or local-authority securities quoted on the stock exchange, though 'liquid' in the sense that they can be sold at their prevailing price, may, depending on the time when they are sold, produce a capital loss. Strictly speaking, liquidity refers to the time taken to turn investment into cash, taking any loss of capital value or return into account. But although building-society investors *can* withdraw money at short notice, many leave it invested for several years – the average turnover time of shares and deposits is three to four years. So many investors consider investments such as fixed-interest local-authority bonds or National Savings Certificates, nominally of much lower liquidity, as comparable alternatives. The societies also add convenience to liquidity, since, unlike banks, they are open for normal office hours during the week and Saturday morning as well.

Much of the societies' success is attributable to the highly competitive return on share investment. The interest rate on small amounts is particularly attractive, but the societies compete effectively for larger investments, for which the range of alternatives is greater. Figure 6.1 in the Appendix indicates the general structure of investment yields; newspapers and publications such as *Money Management* or *Investors Chronicle* give the up to date picture. Taxpaying investors benefit from the societies' special tax arrangement (Chapter 4), but those paying higher than basic rates do have to pay some tax on share interest and may find it advantageous to hold up to the limit in tax-free investments – for example, national savings, SAYE or low-coupon gilts. Non-taxpayers may find alternatives give a higher return than building-society shares, since they receive interest net of tax which cannot be reclaimed. In recent years local-authority short-term investment, finance-house deposits and national savings have emerged as strong competitors to the societies. Personal bank deposits offer relatively poor returns on small amounts but banks offer progressively higher rates on larger amounts; the top rates may be $3\frac{1}{2}$–4 per cent above the quoted deposit rate, which is a minimum rate only, and the banks constitute a major competitor to the societies for larger amounts. The societies' tendency to loosen up investment rate structures, relating them to size and terms of investment, is partly a competitive response to the banks.

The sheltered circuit of housing finance

House-buyers seeking mortgages face competition in the finance market from industry, the government, local authorities and other bodies, which are generally in a much stronger position to raise funds. In keeping with social and political aims in the housing field, the government has strengthened private households' borrowing power by fostering a special market for house-purchase finance institutionalised in the form of the building societies and sheltered from other sections of the finance market. There are two main elements to this 'sheltered circuit', as Revell has termed it.[1]

First, the special arrangement whereby societies settle investors' basic-rate tax liability at the composite rather than full basic rate gives societies a competitive advantage over such of their competitors as banks. For a given rate charged to borrowers societies can pay investors a more attractive rate than if subject to the same tax arrangements as, for instance, banks, and can attract funds more successfully. This was not originally designed to advantage societies in this way but now has this effect. Societies also pay a lower rate of corporation tax on gross surplus and, like trustee and national savings banks, pay no corporation tax on gains from selling government securities held for at least 12 months.

Second, societies' lending has been specifically excluded from credit restraints applied periodically to lending by banks and other institutions and supported by direct government measures designed to keep down the mortgage rate. Monetary policies built around credit restraint have attempted to curb inflation and/or protect the value of the pound in order to avert balance of payments crises, encourage economic growth and curb the erosion of real wages and the value of savings. After 1965 attempts to control the volume of credit and thus, it is argued by monetarist economists, the rate of inflation via the supply of Treasury Bills were reinforced by direct controls in the form of ceilings imposed on bank-lending. With lending restricted, the banks' demand for funds was cut back, they became less competitive and their rate of growth was restricted. The building societies were able to take advantage of this situation, since they were able to lend as much as they could attract, and they pressed home their advantage by attracting as much as possible. This was reflected in the growth of the societies' assets, which accelerated from the mid-1960s (Figure 2.4 in the Appendix). In 1971 a new credit control regime based more on interest rates than direct control of credit was introduced. Under this regime the societies suffered the effects of changing financial conditions to a greater extent and were singled out for government support, which aimed to help them weather the worst effects of the stormy conditions that typified the early 1970s.

The inflationary boom of 1971–3, resulting from attempts by the

Conservative government to stimulate the economy, was followed in late 1973 to 1974 by credit control and wage and price restraint in an attempt to control the excesses of inflation on which the boom had been founded. The building societies, which had shared in the 1971–2 boom, found their competitive strength severely eroded and receipts slumped dramatically. To freedom from credit constraint the government added a bridging grant in April 1973 and a £500 million loan to the societies in April 1974, to help them maintain lending without raising the mortgage rate, and from September 1973 to February 1975 banks were requested to limit interest on deposits under £10 000 to 9½ per cent, thus curbing one of the societies' main rivals. Societies' freedom from restraint was checked, however, in 1978, when they reluctantly agreed with the government to cut back their lending. But this mortgage squeeze originated from and was calculated in relation to the government's fear of an explosion in house-prices akin to that of 1972 (Chapter 7) rather than from monetary policy – though the effect might be argued as similar to credit restraint.

These two elements of the 'sheltered circuit' give specific support to building societies. Revell suggests that tax relief on mortgage interest and option-mortgage subsidy (Chapter 5), which substantially reduces the cost to borrowers of a given mortgage rate, constitutes a third element. The 11.75 per cent mortgage rate current in the first half of 1979 cost basic-rate taxpayers only 7.87 per cent, but societies, which received the full 11.75 per cent, could offer investors 8 per cent on ordinary shares and even more on term shares. However, since all borrowers for house-purchase benefit from tax relief, not just building-society borrowers, this element of the sheltered circuit is not specific to the societies. It simply puts house-buyers on a par with companies and other institutional borrowers, who can generally deduct loan interest from taxable income. The 'sheltered circuit' of house-purchase finance fostered by the government has significantly encouraged the growth of building societies as financial institutions, increased the volume of funds devoted to house-purchase and reinforced the societies' dominant role in the supply of finance for owner-occupation.

Competition, credit control and industrial investment

Faced with the massive expansion of the building societies, the clearing banks have increasingly criticised the advantage to the societies afforded by the 'sheltered circuit'. The debate was fuelled in particular by the banks' evidence to the 'Wilson Committee' – the 'Committee to Review the Functioning of Financial Institutions' – in 1978. While acknowledging that they have always been in direct competition with the societies, the banks have suggested that societies are beginning to operate more like banks, offering easy withdrawal of cash, making cheque-like payments to third parties on behalf of investors and granting loans for such home-improvements as double glazing and central heating. At the same time, expanding demand for mortgages has caused societies to look beyond their traditional sources of funds, and they have been considering turning to the money market in the future. Personal-sector bank deposits increased only 165 per cent between 1969 and 1978 to £24 490 million, while building-society shares and deposits rose 325 per cent to £39 713 million.[2] The banks have argued that the societies' tax treatment and freedom from monetary control give them a significant and unwarranted competitive advantage, which both increases the funds attracted by the societies and raises the cost of funds for banks and their borrowers.

The building societies argue strongly that the composite-rate tax arrangement be retained, since its removal would either raise the mortgage rate or reduce their ability to attract investment. The banks argue that it is illogical to give special concessions only to the societies, and that if the government wants to cheapen house-purchase finance, then all institutions should be taxed and controlled on an equivalent basis, particularly if the banks were to expand their homeloan business. While acknowledging this argument, the effect, on the one hand, of societies' longer opening hours and increasingly sophisticated investments, and, on the other, banks' relatively high overheads and the competition they face on lending from overseas banks, must also be taken into account.[3]

The banks' arguments raise wider issues of macro-economic policy in relation to the societies. It has been argued that the exclusion of building-society shares and deposits from government control of the money supply and their mortgage-lending from credit control are serious anomalies in macro-economic policy. While banks have undoubtedly lost ground to the societies, the effects of an increase in the societies' funds on the money supply and credit are complex, depending particularly on what would otherwise have been done with investment received, what societies do with this investment (especially what part of liquid assets they put into public-sector debt), and the policy responses of the monetary authorities.[4] As the societies now hold 5 per cent of all government stock and 12 per cent of stock with a maturity under five years, they have also become a significant force in the market for national debt. According to the Governor of the Bank of England in 1978:

> The building societies lend predominantly to a specialised market in which the banks are hardly engaged save as providers of bridging finance. And this traditional demarcation has justified a difference of treatment by the authorities in respect of guidance or other official influence on lending. However, the greater the breaking down of this demarcation as a result of ventures into house lending by the banks or increased use of loans from building societies to finance purchases other than of houses, the stronger the case could be for treating building societies and banks similarly for monetary policy purposes.[5]

It has also been argued that the advantages granted to the societies and their spectacular success in attracting funds may have diverted funds from trade and industry and thereby retarded economic growth. The Labour Party National Executive Committee argued in 1976: 'The heart of Britain's weakness lies in its comparably poor record of investment, especially in manufacturing industry which has grown anaemic as a result and needs a major transfusion amounting to a doubling of the rate of manufacturing investment over the next decade'.[6]

Britain's average annual increase in national output attributable to investment in the period 1967–72, was estimated as 0.33 per cent, compared with 1 per cent in West Germany and 1.9 per cent in France. In the early seventies investments in manufacturing industry represented only 18 per cent of gross domestic product in Britain as against 28 per cent in France and West Germany. According to the National Economic Development Office: 'That part of the capital market which services industry suffers from discrimination against it and in favour of finance for Government and finance for housing. It suffers international comparative disadvantage as other countries offer preferential terms on funds raised for industry.'[7]

Personal holding of shares in Britain has fallen markedly in recent years, whereas institutional holdings have almost doubled. But the proportion of institutional funds (other than banks') used to purchase company shares has also fallen. In the period 1972 to 1977 an average of 31 per cent of the funds of financial institutions (other than banks) were used for house-purchase, but only 13 per cent were used to purchase ordinary company shares.[8] Bank loans to manufacturing industry in 1977 amounted to just over 16 per cent of the value of house-purchase finance. The 'investment diversion' argument parallels criticism of institutional investment in the commercial property boom of the early seventies – 26 per cent of net lending by insurance companies and pension funds between 1972 and 1974 purchased land, property and ground rents, while bank lending to property companies increased by £220 million between 1971 and 1974. Yet the flow of funds through the societies financing house-purchase is on a considerably larger scale and thus demands serious consideration. At the end of 1977 the largest property company – Land Securities Investment Trust – was worth £871 million (total capital employed). The Halifax Building Society had assets of £5411 million, over six times as big. The largest seven building societies were *all* individually bigger than Land Securities.

Investment diversion arguments must be placed in context, for there is little evidence that industry has been suffering from lack of capital in recent years. Low levels of profitability on industrial investment related in part to lack of demand have generated little demand for capital. However, this in no way removes the possibility that a revival in profitability and demand for funds could bring finance for house-purchase and industrial investment into more immediate conflict, raising questions about the use of finance and resources within the economy as a whole and, more specifically, the efficiency of loan-financed house-purchase as a form of housing provision.

Setting interest rates

The volume of funds attracted by the societies is primarily determined by the rate of interest they offer to investors compared with other forms of investment. In simple terms, societies estimate the appropriate level of mortgage-lending and set their share rate to attract the necessary funds, given the prevailing level of interest rates in the market. The mortgage rate is then set by adding on to the share rate the operating margin, i.e. management costs, taxation and a contribution to reserves, sometimes termed the 'cost-plus' model. Societies aim to achieve a level of lending which will maintain a healthy housing market and avoid any shortage of funds, which might cause the building industry to lose confidence, without unduly pushing up house prices. There is also pressure from the government particularly to keep the mortgage rate as low as possible, since it is sensitive in the context of prices and incomes policy, balanced against the desire to maintain the flow of mortgage funds. This contrasts with a 'market-clearing' mortgage rate, whereby societies would allow supply and demand to determine an equilibrium price (mortgage rate) for loans and set the share rate by subtracting the margin from the mortgage rate.

Since 1939 the BSA has recommended share and mortgage rates to its members, taking account of the requirements of the housing market, the general level of interest rates, the conflicting interests of investors and borrowers and the societies' need to maintain adequate operating margins and liquid assets. These rates are not obligatory, but under the 1973 Memorandum of Agreement with the government the eighteen largest societies must generally keep to the recommended rates. On 1 August 1977, 93 of the Association's 243 members were paying above the recommended ordinary share rate and 62 charging more than the recommended mortgage rate.[9] While this 'cartel' arrangement has been criticised, its abandonment could lead to mortgage rates being pushed up, given persisting unmet demand for loans, as societies competed for funds by raising share rates. Desired levels of lending and trends in the housing and finance market are discussed with the government in the Joint Advisory Committee (Chapter 3), particularly when these indicate the need for changes in interest rates.[10]

Most of the societies' funds are withdrawable on demand or at short notice, whereas mortgage loans are made for long periods, generally 25 years. Heavy demand to withdraw cash could not be met because funds are tied up in long-term loans. Societies avoid this problem by the use of variable rate mortgages; interest rates charged to existing borrowers may be raised or lowered subject to a period of notice. So if interest rates in general rise, threatening to attract investment away from the societies, the mortgage rate can be raised, allowing societies to offer a higher rate to investors so as to retain existing funds and continue to attract new funds; alternatively a fall in interest rates can be passed on through a cut in the mortgage rate. Societies' interest rates therefore tend to follow the general level of rates in the market (Figure 6.2 in the Appendix).

Societies' capacity to follow changes in market interest rates is, however, limited, particularly given the size and speed of changes in the 1970s. In autumn 1976, for example, rates rose almost 4 per cent and mortgage rates would have had to rise an unprecedented $4\frac{1}{4}$–$4\frac{1}{2}$ per cent from $10\frac{1}{2}$ per cent to match the market.[11] Societies are reluctant to change rates frequently, since this disrupts household budgets; there are also time-lags in making changes and inevitable problems of predicting future trends in market rates. The recommended share rate changed nine times from 1975 to 1978, compared with 52 changes in Minimum Lending Rate and 33 changes in clearing-bank base rates. Considerable variation occurs in the competitiveness of the societies' share rates relative to other institutions, which leads to substantial fluctuations in the societies' net intake of funds (Figure 6.3 in the Appendix). Although changes in net receipts are small in relation to total investment held by the societies, they are large in relation to the amount of new money they need to raise to provide mortgage funds adequate to maintain a stable housing market: for example, net receipts fell from £183 million during August 1976 to £23 million in November, then rose to £511 million in May 1977. In the 1973–4 slump net receipts fell from over £600 million in the second quarter of 1973 to minus £17 million in the first quarter of 1974 – a net loss of funds. Societies' competitive strength may also be affected by other factors. Insurance company 'income bonds' in 1973–4, index-linked retirement-issue National Savings Certificates in 1975, and attractive rates on National Savings Certificates in 1976–7, for example, gave societies strong competition. Changes in tax rates and management costs may also have an effect. But the major factor behind fluctuations in net receipts is the differential between societies' share rate and other interest rates.

Instability of funds

The societies' main sources of funds are net receipts of investment, mortgage repayments and mortgage interest (Figure 3.6 in the Appendix). Mortgage interest and regular monthly capital repayment are a relatively stable source of funds, being contractual payments to the societies. Premature redemption of loans, usually when a borrower is changing house, also generates a fairly stable flow and in any case usually generates equivalent demand for new loans. Mortgage interest and capital have grown steadily through the seventies and were little affected by the violent changes in the finance market in the period 1972 to 1975. However, the third main source of funds, net receipts, varies considerably, as we have seen, with the state of the finance market (Figure 6.3 in the Appendix), and is the main source of instability in the flow of funds available to the societies. The proportion of total funds contributed by net receipts has varied from 17 per cent in 1974 to 41 per cent in 1977. In the longer term, however, the contribution of net receipts to total funds has grown, so that the total flow of funds has become increasingly unstable.

Net receipts are the amount by which total intake of investment exceeds withdrawals. So although societies took in £15 889 million in 1978, withdrawals totalled £12 522 million, almost 79 per cent of total receipts, leaving net receipts of only £3367 million. As societies' receipts have grown over the years, so the rate of turnover of investment has increased. In 1945 withdrawals represented only 8 per cent of the total value of shares and deposits held at the start of the year; by 1978 this had risen to 39 per cent.[12] Net receipts have become increasingly unstable. The rate of withdrawal more than doubled from 1965 to 1978, while, more recently, the change in net receipts following a 1 per cent change in the societies' share rates relative to money market rates increased from £35 million a month in 1973 to £55–£60 million in 1976.[13]

Two main components contribute to fluctuation in net receipts. There is a certain amount of ebb and flow of existing funds, withdrawn when share rates are less competitive and returning when the societies' rates are more attractive. Thus the Chief Registrar reported in 1975:

> There is evidence to suggest that a substantial element of the net intake for the year resulted from the switching of larger investments from other savings and investment media. Almost certainly the amounts so received will have included the return of a substantial part of those investments withdrawn in pursuit of higher interest rates in 1973 and the early months of 1974. Building societies recognise that they are again possessed of these possibly volatile funds.[14]

But equally important is the diversion of money away from societies which they might otherwise have received had they been more competitive, or the increased inflow to societies when their rates are attractive of funds which might have gone to the banks or other institutions.

Fluctuations in net receipts can largely be explained by factors relating to the finance market, and the characteristics of investment holdings in the societies. The increasingly volatile nature of societies' receipts stems from changes in these two sets of factors; the first has in effect changed the rules of the game and the second has increased the pace of play and raised the stakes.

Market forces

As the societies have grown, they have become increasingly integrated with the general finance market and increasingly subject to its 'levelling influences' – investors' response to differences in interest rates. Up to the 1930s societies were relatively isolated from the general finance market, 'more or less shut off from the levelling influences of a market organisation'.[15] Competition from other institutions was limited and the level of savings attracted in by the societies was less crucially regulated by the level of interest rates than in more recent years, so that rates could be set with a greater degree of independence. Northern societies in particular faced less active competition from other institutions and were especially insulated from market influences – a factor contributing to their strength within the movement as a whole. In 1933, however, Bellman wrote that 'the movement, by the extent to which it – or rather the larger societies – has attracted the substantial investor is now definitely part of the organised capital market'.[16] As the societies grew and the finance market developed, so they became more subject to its forces. The 'Radcliffe Report' on the working of the monetary system in 1959 noted: 'In fixing interest rates the societies are keenly aware that they face severe competition . . . The sensitiveness of the societies to this competition and indeed the sensitiveness of the others to competition from the societies – illustrates the fundamental unity of the markets for loanable funds'.[17] At the same time as societies have become increasingly subject to market forces, the strength of these forces, and specifically changes in interest rates, has increased. This was emphasised following the change in monetary policy in 1971 heralded by the Bank of England in the article 'Competition and credit control'.[18]

Credit control has been a major element in government monetary policy aimed at maintaining the balance of payments and curbing inflation. Control of lending by financial institutions is one facet of monetary policy, the other main element being management of public expenditure and the national debt. Traditional forms of credit control comprised influencing interest rates, and hence borrowing, via the Bank rate and squeezing bank lending by squeezing banks' liquidity ratios. Banks had to maintain a proportion of assets in specified liquid assets of which treasury bills were a major part; by restricting the supply of treasury bills the Bank of England could, it was hoped, force banks to lend less in order to maintain the required liquidity ratio. By the early sixties, however, banks were finding ways round this type of control, and other institutions proliferated and expanded lending when banks were restricted; furthermore restricting treasury bills increasingly conflicted with the need to finance government spending and interest on the national debt. Therefore, in the sixties, the Bank turned to direct physical controls, first through Special Deposits called in from banks, which directly reduced their liquidity and encouraged them to lend less, and after 1965 through prescribed ceilings on total lending.

In 1971 the system of credit control was overhauled. The main objective was that credit be allocated among institutions and borrowers according to its cost – the rate of interest – which would be allowed to vary much more widely. Ceilings on bank lending were removed and the banks abandoned their cartel on interest rates. Direct credit restraint has been reintroduced since the mid-1970s (the banks' 'corset'). But targets for money supply and public-sector borrowing have become the key policy variable, which has made interest rates more volatile. For the building societies these changes have meant more aggressive competition from banks and other institutions on the basis of interest rates pushed up to higher levels and subject to more violent fluctuations. The authorities recognised that 'The greater freedom afforded to banks by the above proposals might lead them to compete for individuals' savings at present invested in public sector debt or in finance of housing',[19] and they reserved the right to give qualitative guidance on lending by banks and 'to consider the need to limit the impact on savings banks and building societies of competition by the banks for individuals' savings'. Measures were taken to restructure management of the national debt in order to accommodate wider fluctuations in interest rates; this right was invoked when bank deposit rates were restricted to $9\frac{1}{2}$ per cent from 1973 to 1975 (referred to earlier), but no more general strategy to protect the societies has emerged. These changes have induced much more frequent changes in societies' interest rates – for example, the recommended share rate, which changed only eight times in the sixties, changed 15 times from 1970 to 1978. As

Revell puts it, 'under the new system building societies can no longer afford to ride out periods of higher interest rates in the hope that they will quickly go away'.[20]

Invested funds

As the societies have grown, they have increasingly come to rely on funds which are by nature more volatile, more likely to switch between institutions following differences in interest rates. A substantial proportion of societies' funds are made up of relatively large investments – an estimated 42 per cent in amounts over £5000 by 1978 (Figure 4.6 in the Appendix) – and these have been much more volatile than small savings. Commenting on the slump in net receipts in 1973 (Figure 6.3 in the Appendix) the Registrar stated:

> It had become increasingly apparent in recent years that building societies were no longer the repository only for the savings of small investors. In many societies a substantial proportion of their funds had for several years been represented by comparatively large individual investments, very often up to the £10,000 limit (£20,000 for husband and wife) at which composite rate tax arrangements apply. In the circumstances of 1973 these larger investments proved, in the experience of many societies, to be more volatile than those of the more 'traditional investors' and it was considered to be their removal on a significant scale, for investment elsewhere at higher interest rates, which accounted for a very substantial part of the increases in withdrawals.[21]

Although there is evidence that large shareholdings were important to societies even between the wars – in 1932 a third of the Abbey Road Building Society's funds were in holdings of £5000 or more in 1974 terms[22] – large investments have become more important in recent years. A 1970 estimate based on Inland Revenue data, and giving very much a minimum figure, suggested at least 29 per cent of share balances (£2800 million) were in holdings of £5000 or more; by 1974 this had risen to 32 per cent and a BSA survey for the end of 1977 put the figure at 42 per cent.[23]

Although small savings represent a significant part of societies' funds, it is these larger amounts that account for most of the fluctuation in net receipts. About two-thirds of the month to month variation in net receipts associated with interest-rate changes in

1973–6 has been invested or withdrawn in amounts of £2000 or more, and most of the remaining variation has been in amounts of £500 to £2000. Receipts and withdrawals of amounts under £500 appear little affected by interest rates,[24] though they do vary for other reasons, particularly pre-Christmas or holiday demands for cash. The growing magnitude of fluctuations in net receipts suggests that large investors have become more sensitive to interest-rate differentials as well as accounting for an increasing proportion of societies' total funds.

'Small savers' have a limited range of investment opportunities, may lack knowledge of the savings market and have little to gain in absolute terms to justify switching funds around chasing small interest-rate differentials. Many small savers are anyway saving in a society to qualify for a mortgage. Investors with several thousand pounds to play with have a much wider range of alternatives open to them, much of these invested funds are professionally managed, and small differences in interest rates can generate large differences in absolute investment income. Furthermore, in the freer atmosphere since 'Competition and credit control', alternative investment media have proliferated and the scale of marketing and advertising has escalated. In particular, clearing and other banks often offer rates only just below money-market rates, considerably higher than the personal seven-day deposit-account rate. This was illustrated in 1973–4, when holding banks' deposit rate at $9\frac{1}{2}$ per cent did little to improve societies' net receipts, the diversion of funds to the banks continuing in response to the higher rates offered for large investments. For larger investments it is thus money-market rates which indicate the competition societies face rather than rates on small savings such as ordinary seven-day bank deposits.

Fluctuations in the level of mortgage-lending

Societies attempt to smooth out and insulate the flow of mortgage funds into the housing market from these sharp fluctuations in net receipts by changing their holdings of liquid assets. We can think of building societies as a reservoir *into* which flow mortgage interest and capital payments and net receipts, and *from* which flows the supply of mortgage funds. Mortgage interest and capital provide a relatively steady inflow and form the basis for a stable outflow of mortgage funds. But net receipts, as we have seen, vary considerably, flooding into the societies in some months and drying up in others. Societies absorb a certain amount of this fluctuation by varying their holdings of liquid assets, raising or lowering the level of funds stored in the reservoir. When receipts dry up, societies augment the level of lending by running down their liquid assets; when receipts are pouring in, they build up their liquidity again rather than flooding the housing market. For example, as receipts climbed steadily through 1977, mortgage-lending rose substantially, but part of the increase in receipts was absorbed by increasing liquid assets – the liquidity ratio rose from 18 per cent to 21 per cent during the year. Then when receipts fell off during 1978, the level of mortgage-lending was sustained by running down liquidity to 18 per cent by the end of the year (Figure 6.4 in the Appendix).

Varying liquidity is an integral part of societies' strategy in playing the finance market, supplementing the use of variable-rate mortgages. As Revell notes: 'Because societies must always operate on the basis of information relating to a past period and because the full effect of changes in interest rates is not felt for some time after the recommendation, liquidity ratios are likely to continue to rise or fall for a while'.[25]

The flexibility allowed by liquid funds is essential in allowing for this lag in response to changes in rates. As a more general means of stabilising mortgage-lending, changing liquidity has achieved some success. Major fluctuations in net receipts have certainly been ironed out, particularly since 1975. But strong variations in the level of mortgage-lending remain, reflecting the volatility of net receipts (Figure 6.4 in the Appendix), with serious repercussions in the housing market, to which we turn in Chapter 7.

7

Building societies and the housing market

Most people have to borrow to buy a house and most borrow from a building society. The volume of funds which societies channel from the finance market to the housing market, therefore, largely determines the effective level of demand for owner-occupied housing. This chapter looks at demand, supply and house-prices and the impact of house-prices on land-prices, the cost of housing relative to household incomes and, finally, the volume of funds absorbed by the private housing market.

Housing demand and supply

The level of demand for home-ownership is determined by the net rate at which new households are created, household incomes, the cost of house-purchase and the attractions of owner-occupation relative to other tenures. The relative attractiveness of owner-occupation is governed both by economic factors, including the level of subsidies to owner-occupiers, the effect of inflation on the real cost of borrowing, and capital gains from rising house-prices (in comparison with the yield on other investments), and by non-economic factors such as security of tenure and independence from (public or private) landlords. These are the underlying factors, but since few households can buy without building-society loans, it is above all the aggregate volume of lending by societies which determines *effective* demand in the housing market: 'given the dominant role of building societies as suppliers of house purchase finance, the amount of mortgage money advanced by building societies is the primary influence on how much of the underlying demand is made effective in the market'.[1] Since underlying demand for mortgages generally outstrips the volume of funds available, the volume of lending represents economic demand in the housing market. Note, however, that the relationship of household income to effective demand is mediated by how much societies will lend for a given income. Societies' lending criteria therefore influence the level of effective demand by determining the borrowing and hence the purchasing power of individual households. More generous lending criteria would tend to increase effective demand.

The supply of houses for sale on the market is a combination of additions to the total stock and that proportion of the existing stock which comes up for sale. The total stock is increased primarily by new house-building; net transfers from the public and private rented sectors and conversion from non-residential uses contribute to a lesser extent. The rate of new house-building is strongly influenced by the level of housing demand. A study commissioned by the Department of the Environment reported in 1975: 'An overriding impression created as a result of discussions with companies active in the industry was the extent to which their actions and opportunities are demand-determined . . . There was almost total agreement that the main expression of demand was the availability of mortgage finance from the building societies'.[2]

The rate of supply of new houses relative to demand, i.e. the rate of house-building, will *tend* to maintain prices at a level which covers building costs and builders' profit margins. The rate of building will tend to drop back when demand falls and rise when it increases, but time-lags and imperfections interfere with this process of adjustment. With excess demand, house prices will tend to rise faster than building costs; conversely, with excess supply relative to effective demand, costs will tend to catch up prices and squeeze builders' profit margins. Following the slump in mortgage-lending from early 1972 and through 1973 the rate of private house-building fell back sharply in 1973 and 1974 (Figure 7.1 in the Appendix) and since then has remained relatively low compared with rates of building over the previous decade – average annual housing starts for 1974–9 were about two-thirds the average for 1964–73.

'Many arguments have been put forward to explain the fall-off in housebuilding which make it appear to be essentially a supply problem. It is not. Indeed, as seen by builders . . . it is essentially a demand problem, linked above all to the availability of building society finance.'[3] An enquiry conducted by the House-Builders Federation in October 1978 found that 74 per cent of builders considered lack of readily available mortgage finance as the key factor limiting demand.

Fluctuations in the availability of mortgage finance are reflected in sharp changes in the house-building rate, which mirrors closely the pattern of lending over time (Figure 7.1 in the Appendix). Strong variation in mortgage availability and the level of effective demand for new housing seriously affect the viability and efficiency of the private house-building industry. Housing takes at least a year to construct and maybe three to four years to plan. So builders must attempt to gear the number of houses started now to the level of effective demand over a year ahead, while the time horizon for investment in land acquisition, purchasing materials and site preparation is considerably longer. This in effect means gearing investment to an estimate of building-society lending for house-purchase well in the future. In the past it has been almost impossible to predict the volume of funds which will be available over a year ahead to enable households to buy houses started now, with any degree of certainty. The Joint Advisory Committee guidelines may lead to some improvement in short-term predictability but are unlikely to improve builders' ability to plan land acquisition and site preparation efficiently.

Delays in selling completed houses, owing to lack of demand, can cause serious 'cash-flow' problems for house-builders, whereby revenue fails to cover regular costs, particularly given the extent to which the industry relies on borrowing as a source of working capital. Rising interest rates, which starve the building societies and may reduce demand for houses, also increase the rate at which builders clock up interest on their borrowed capital. Periodic changes in demand and hence in rates of house-building also reduce revenue available to cover companies' fixed costs and overheads. The financial problems produced by uncertainty and fluctuating demand contribute to the particularly high level of bankruptcy in the industry. The 1974 slump even brought down major companies, including Northern Developments, which built more houses in 1973 than any other company. Many other companies were supported by the state in 1974, when local authorities were encouraged to buy land and unsold houses, turning companies' unsaleable assets into ready cash:[4] for example, in April 1975 Newcastle District Council had bought or was negotiating to buy 1700 houses built for owner-occupation by a variety of firms, at a total cost to the authority of £13 million.

More generally, unstable demand for houses impairs the efficiency of the industry. Uncertainty as to levels of profits and share dividends of speculative house-building companies can make it difficult for such companies to raise share capital, leading to heavy reliance on borrowing as a source of capital. The structure of the industry as a whole tends to remain fragmented in relatively small, labour-intensive units with low fixed costs, relying heavily on subcontracting, which can respond more flexibly to changing demand patterns. Finally, fixed capital investment, labour-saving equipment and techniques are discouraged, as they lead to higher fixed costs and overheads, and financial inflexibility relative to the flow of revenue generated by changing rates of building and sales. Much of the instability in demand faced by builders is in effect absorbed by the labour force, which is laid off when demand is slack.

House prices

The price of owner-occupied housing is primarily determined by market mechanisms, that is by the interaction of supply and demand. Put simply, when demand rises relative to supply, house prices tend to go up; if demand falls, then prices tend to drop in real terms. With continuous price inflation established as a normal feature of the economy, market forces tend to be expressed in money terms in faster or slower rates of house-price inflation. We can recognise real changes in the price of housing by comparing house-price inflation with general retail-price inflation, and changes in the real cost of housing by relating house-price inflation to wage inflation. Prices in the owner-occupied sector are set by free-market forces in contrast to the private rented sector, where rents are restricted by legislation, and the local-authority sector, in which rents are set administratively, usually in relation to the nature of the individual houses.

Each time existing housing comes on to the market, its price is determined anew by the current state of the market and may bear little relation to what the house originally cost when new or to what any previous owner paid for it. So the price of existing housing is set by the interplay of supply and demand in exactly the same way as that of new housing. In fact, existing housing dominates the supply of housing for sale. New housing built in any one year represents no more than $1\frac{1}{2}$ per cent of the existing stock and less than a quarter of all houses which come on the market in a given time period. The dominance of existing housing in the supply of houses available for sale is crucial to an understanding of how the housing market hangs together, for it means that in the short term the supply of housing for sale is relatively fixed and in the long run it can expand only slowly. Furthermore, given the time-lags in planning, land assembly and actual construction, the house-building industry can only respond slowly to changes in demand. Therefore, although builders will *tend* to build more when demand expands and prices are pushed up and to cut back when demand falls, the industry's built-in time-lags mean that the supply of houses for sale cannot respond to short-term fluctuations in demand stemming from instability in mortgage-lending. Uncertainty about future mortgage availability reinforces this inertia by making builders' response, particularly to rising demand, more cautious. So although in the long run house prices relate to household incomes, in the short term they may be strongly influenced by the level of mortgage-lending. Short-term increases in the volume of funds flowing on to the market will tend to push prices up and a cutback will tend to reduce the rate of inflation.

This is graphically illustrated in Figure 7.1 in the Appendix, which relates price increases to mortgage-lending in the 1970s. Interest rates in general fell through 1970 and 1971, building societies' share rates became increasingly attractive and investment flooded in. Most of this intake of funds flowed straight through the societies to the housing market, and net lending doubled from £1088 million in 1970 to £2215 million in 1972. Relatively little of the inflow of funds was diverted into the societies' reservoirs of liquid assets; the aggregate liquidity ratio only rose from 17.8 per cent to 18.5 per cent over 1971 and actually had fallen back to 16 per cent by the end of 1972. The building industry responded to this sharp increase in effective demand, the quarterly rate of housing starts almost doubling from early 1970 to late 1971 (Figure 7.1 in the Appendix) but this increased supply fell far short of total demand. The result of the flood of mortgage funds was, therefore, the now infamous house-price boom of 1972–3.

House-prices, which had risen only 7 per cent in 1970 and 13 per cent in 1971, increased by 31 per cent in 1972 and 35 per cent in 1973 (Figure 7.2 in the Appendix).[5] The fastest increase was in the third quarter, July–September 1972, when the quarterly increase was 15 per cent, equivalent to an annual rate of over 60 per cent. Prices of existing houses led prices of new houses, rising earlier and faster. They increased 17 per cent in the third quarter of 1972 (an annual rate of 68 per cent) but the rate dropped to 7.5 per cent (30 per cent) over the first three months of 1973 when the increase in prices of new houses peaked at 14 per cent (over 55 per cent annually). This difference in timing of the price boom probably occurred because 'when the market is strong, the practice of builders offering houses for sale at the advertised prices slows down the rate of adjustment to the rise in demand; conversely when the market is weak, builders are more likely to try to hold to cost-determined prices rather than reduce them to try to make sales'.[6] The boom appears to have been led by demand rather than pushed by construction costs, since prices of secondhand houses rose rapidly relative to costs early on, followed later by prices of new housing. The building industry does not, in any case, seem to have suffered unduly from rising materials or labour costs until late 1973. The pattern of price inflation was repeated throughout the country, though increases were highest and came earlier in London and the South East of the country and lower and later towards the peripheral regions.

Towards the end of 1973, however, the general level of interest rates against which societies compete started to rise. Minimum lending rate rose from 7.5 per cent in June to 13 per cent by November, the societies' competitiveness was rapidly eroded and net receipts fell back sharply (see Figure 6.3 in the Appendix). Mortgage-lending in turn declined sharply, exacerbated by the recent rapid rise in house-prices, which eroded the volume of lending in terms of purchasing power over housing (Figure 3.1 in the Appendix) and the number of purchases which could be financed. Although the liquidity ratio fell from 18.5 per cent at the end of 1971 to under 15 per cent in early 1973, this did little to counteract the massive slump in lending. Builders cut back the number of houses started during the later months of 1973 and into 1974, and by the end of 1974 the number was little over a third the level two years previously. The estimated time-lag from start to completion of houses rose from about 12 months in 1971 and 1972 to over 19 months in 1975, and the number of dwellings virtually completed or completed but not sold rose from 13 000 in October 1972 to 56 000 in October 1975. The decline in effective demand rapidly lowered the rate of price inflation and prices rose only 11 per cent in 1974 and 8 per cent in 1975 (Figure 7.2 in the Appendix).

Societies' receipts and the volume of mortgage-lending recovered strongly from mid-1974, remained high over 1975, fell back over 1976, but rose strongly again in 1977, reflecting the changing competitiveness of societies' interest rates (Figures 6.3 and 6.4 in the

Appendix). Despite the substantial increase in lending over 1975 and early 1976, the number of houses started increased only slowly and remained low compared with previous upswings in the market. Although the growth in lending was spectacular in *money* terms, the purchasing power of this money in the housing market was little higher than that of mortgage-lending in 1971 and 1972, given the massive intervening increase in house-prices (Figure 7.1 in the Appendix). This same increase left house-prices historically high in relation to incomes and retail prices, moderating demand. However, the major factor was the relative increase in construction costs. Whereas in 1972 and 1973 house-prices increased much faster than builders' costs, from 1974 costs increased much more swiftly than house-prices (Figure 7.3 in the Appendix), squeezing builders' margins and hence depressing activity. During 1975 and 1976, for example, the *Building* housing-cost index rose 42 per cent, but prices of new houses only increased 17 per cent. Thus when mortgage-lending slumped in 1976, and interest rates for both builders and borrowers rose sharply, the rate of building quickly dropped back. House-prices rose relatively slowly from early 1974 through to mid-1977. But the increased volume of lending over the year was reflected in a faster rate of increase in house-prices, which easily outstripped the increase in building costs; thus in the 12 months to November 1978 the *Building* housing-cost index rose 10.4 per cent while prices of new houses increased by 24.8 per cent. The increase in house-prices relative to costs and improved profitability in house-building did not, however, produce a significant increase in building over 1978. Uncertainty as to future levels of lending and demand in the light of experience over the seventies has perhaps made builders more cautious. A House-Builders Federation survey in April 1978 indicated that 56 per cent of respondents still thought margins between costs and house-prices inadequate and in an October survey 74 per cent of respondents saw lack of mortgage finance as strongly limiting demand; on the supply side 84 per cent of respondents in October thought shortage of land at reasonable prices was the key factor limiting activity.

Looking back on the 1972–3 house-price boom, which has done much to shape fears and opinions about the housing market, it is unclear why house-builders failed to respond fully to the increased level of demand in 1971–2; somewhat similar booms in lending in 1962–4 and 1967–8, for example, were followed by a more commensurate rise in the building rate. But the building societies undoubtedly played a crucial role in setting off the boom, by making underlying demand effective in the market. Underlying demand was obviously high at the time, whether through the increase in the marriage rate or fears of the effects of the 1972 Housing Finance Act on public-sector rents; 'most of the additional demand to buy would have been ineffective, however, if building societies had not had the funds with which to meet the demand for loans'.[7] Furthermore, 'once the boom gets under way it is self sustaining for a time if credit is available; rising prices stimulate the demand to buy through generating fears of still further price rises to come'.[8] Rising prices also stimulate demand for housing as an investment, as households seek to borrow and buy as much as they can, conscious of rapidly escalating asset values. The cause of the boom is arguable but it could have undoubtedly been moderated if the lending by the societies had been kept down to a level commensurate with the supply of houses for sale. As *Housing Policy* concludes,

> The implication is that when the building societies' interest rates are especially competitive and the inflow of funds to them is large, there is no automatic mechanism that would ensure that they did not enable to become effective a greater demand for houses than could be met without undue increase in house prices. The further implication is that if the amount lent is to be matched in such circumstances to what the markets can take, it has to be done deliberately.[9]

Reflecting this view, the BSA/Government Joint Advisory Committee on mortgage finance reached agreement in 1975 on arrangements to stabilise mortgage-lending by assessing the amount of lending needed to maintain a healthy housing market and avoid undue price increases. Every six months the Technical Sub-Committee of the JAC estimates the appropriate level of lending and, after agreement from the JAC, the BSA takes steps to ensure this is not exceeded. Until early 1978 the agreed figures exceeded what the societies could achieve. In early 1978, however, house prices seemed to be rising threateningly. The quarterly rate of increase in prices of new houses (at mortgage approval), which averaged around 3.5 per cent over 1977, rose to 4.8 per cent in the first three months of 1978 and to 7.4 per cent over the third quarter of the year, equivalent to an annual rate of nearly 30 per cent. Prices of existing houses, in contrast to the 1972–3 boom, lagged behind but accelerated swiftly, rising 10 per cent over the third quarter (40 per cent annual equivalent). The societies agreed, though reluctantly, with the government to limit their normal lending for house-purchase by £70 million a month to £610 million net between 1 April and 30 June 1978; this amount was raised to £640 million in July and to £700 million for the first three months of 1979. Cutbacks were made in proportion to societies' assets. The societies' reluctance in accepting these 'guidelines' reflected partly some disagreement with the government that a price explosion was imminent and partly the opinion that prices were low relative to costs and some upwards adjustment was warranted to stimulate the building industry; but also, no doubt, the societies were wary of any form of creeping governmental control over their operations.

House prices and land prices

Different house-building companies operate different strategies regarding land purchase. Some, particularly the larger companies, buy land well before they want to build on it, and maintain substantial 'landbanks' – in June 1977 builders had land with planning permission sufficient for 353 000 dwellings, owned 14 000 hectares without planning permission and held options to buy a further 3600 hectares.[10] Land is often bought without detailed planning permission and some will not even be zoned in planning terms for residential uses. Other builders tend to buy land with planning permission as and when needed to maintain their desired output of houses. Despite these differences, however, land-prices are strongly influenced by the relationship of house-prices and building costs; the common belief that house-prices can be pushed up by rising land costs is thus generally untrue. Land-prices are in effect a residual value. Builders effectively estimate the price at which they can sell houses, subtract the cost of building and a normal profit margin from the selling price, and bid for land with the rest. So when house-prices are rising faster than building costs, as in 1972–3, land-prices will tend to be pushed upwards as builders bid away part of their increased margin; when, however, costs are catching up prices, squeezing builders' margins, as in 1974–5, builders will bid less for land in order to preserve their profit margins, and land prices fall back. So while the cost of housing land doubled from early 1972 to late 1973, it actually fell by 36 per cent from early 1974 to late 1975 (Figure 7.3 in the Appendix), and prices of land with outline residential planning permission were almost halved in many areas between 1974 and 1976. The price of land as a proportion of the selling price of the house rose from 17 per cent in 1971 to 25 per cent in 1973, then fell back to 14 per cent in 1976, when costs rose, squeezing profits.

Builders do tend to get a rather higher rate of profit when housing demand is buoyant and to suffer when it sinks back, but changes in demand are strongly expressed in changing land-prices. This was recognised in the report commissioned by the Department of the Environment on housing land availability, which recognised that:

> . . . prices of finished units (houses) are demand determined, through the availability of mortgage funds, whilst the price of land is determined on a competitive basis by housebuilders bidding . . . when a lot of house-buyers are chasing too few houses with too much building society money in their pockets, then housebuilders, having built on a speculative basis, will increase their prices to the market value. It was this situation which created the rapid rise in house prices during the three years 1970–1973, and which, on the down-turn, has forced house prices down in 1974. In this situation where house prices have risen more rapidly than increases in all other cost elements then the proportion of the final selling price which the builder can afford to devote to land will rise, without any reduction in the house-builder's normal profit margin. Moreover, the greater the proportion of the final selling price land becomes, the greater are the profits from holding land in a land bank.[11]

Much of the increase in effective demand in the early 1970s, based on building-society lending and reflected in higher house-prices, was thus passed on, via house-builders, to owners of land. Those builders with substantial landbanks, the largest 20 per cent or so, have themselves made considerable financial gains; for since house-prices and current land-prices had risen substantially, compared with the cost of land when it was originally bought, builders benefited from capital gains on land values. Thus the consultants' report for the DOE noted, 'Many housebuilders have made their profits (and hence have been able to keep in business) from the value of the land they hold',[12] while the *Investors Chronicle* suggested, more bluntly, that 'Despite appearances, housebuilding is only partially the business of putting up houses. The houses are the socially acceptable side of making profits out of land appreciation'.[13] Given these market mechanisms, building-society finance, which provides the effective demand to push up house-prices, which feed through to landowners, is then, despite appearances, only partially the business of financing owner-occupation. It is also the basis for the profits of landowners and dealers in land. The effects of house-price and, in turn, land-price inflation are not, however, confined to the market sector but rebound on to public housing, for 'there can be little room for doubt that the boom in prices for private house-building land in 1971–73 carried local authorities' land costs up with it'.[14] The policy implications of this analysis are that attention should be directed to demand factors, to the level of mortgage-lending in the first instance rather than to land availability.

> Fluctuations in the rate of housebuilding are seen by the industry to be essentially demand determined linked especially to the availability of building society finance. Attempts to influence house prices, building starts and completions by means of land availability per se are likely therefore to be very indirect, and of little relevance until the cyclical nature of demand, and the external financial influences upon it, can be ironed out.[15]

So despite the emphasis placed by respondents to the House-Builders Federation survey on land availability, and criticism of the level of mortgage availability, the government's attempt to control the level of lending appears justified.

House prices, retail prices and earnings

Between 1900 and 1970 house-prices increased $15\frac{1}{2}$ times, prices of consumer goods in general seven times and pre-tax incomes $10\frac{1}{2}$ times.[16] The price of houses has increased relative to other goods to the extent that, while rising incomes have increased households' purchasing power over goods in general, purchasing power over housing measured in terms of income has actually fallen. Though in the long run increases in the quality of housing account for part of the price increase in housing, 'there is no evidence that quality rose fast enough to account for the rise in house prices relative to the general price level since 1960. Thus there appears to be a long term tendency for house prices to rise relative to the general price level'.[17] Similarly building costs have risen in the long run no faster than prices in general and cannot account for the disparity.

House-prices consistently outpaced retail prices from 1959 to 1973, since when accelerating retail prices have closed the gap on slowly rising house-prices (see Figure 7.4 in the Appendix). The ratio of house-prices to incomes has fluctuated considerably since the late fifties, but in general house-prices have risen faster than earnings (Figure 7.4 in the Appendix). In the 1972–3 house-price boom the house-price to income ratio rose to over 4.8 by 1973, compared to a level of 3.5 typical of the previous few years, subsequently falling back as prices stabilised and earnings accelerated.[18]

Rising house-prices relative to incomes tend to increase the burden of mortgage payments, especially in the early years of purchase. Average initial payments as a percentage of earnings rose from about 22 per cent in the early sixties to a peak of 43 per cent in 1974, following the 1972–3 price boom, and only fell back to 28 per cent in 1978. Rising house-prices thus tend to put house-purchase increasingly out of reach of lower-income households. But although incomes tend to limit house-prices through limiting borrowing power, the societies' lending criteria have tended to become more liberal (detailed in Chapter 5), so that more can be borrowed on a given income. The effect of this increase in purchasing power has been to push up house-prices faster than earnings.

Increasing effective demand without ensuring a commensurate expansion in the supply of housing serves only to drive up prices, but this is inevitable where prices are set by market forces. So attempts to help first-time buyers by increasing their purchasing power may, in isolation, be frustrated, since the more efficient such policies are the faster will prices run away from first-time buyers. Increasing the volume of mortgage funds available to borrowers may, similarly, do little to help lower-income and first-time buyers unless the supply of housing for such purchasers is increased. As soon as the volume of funds expands enough for them to buy a decent house at current prices, market forces tend to push up prices out of reach. More generally, much of the benefit of tax relief on mortgage interest has probably gone to house-builders in higher house prices and, thereby, to those selling land (see Chapter 9).

The BSA has related house-prices to earnings in strict free-market terms, asserting that the market is 'an imperfect guide' but the 'best and fairest method we know of satisfying the "consumer"'.[19] The BSA claims, 'It is a contradiction in terms to say that house-prices are beyond the reach of most first-time buyers because house-prices are set by them', ignoring buyers who are existing owners; and not only is it 'incorrect to say that young couples are unable to afford owner-occupation, it is theoretically impossible for this to be the case'.[20] That this conclusion can be drawn from free-market economic theory merely demonstrates its bankruptcy. These theoretical conclusions simply prove that house-prices are not out of reach of those who can afford to buy. This 'theory' asserts that it is theoretically impossible that families in unfit housing, living with in-laws and at the tail end of council-house waiting lists, or who are refused building-society loans because their income is inadequate, cannot afford to buy a house, because it is only concerned with those who *can* buy.

House prices and mortgage funds

Finance for house-purchase is a strong and successful competitor in the finance market. Given that there are limits on the volume of finance within the economy available for competing uses, the efficiency and effects of finance within particular sectors is of considerable importance. In the private housing sector house-price inflation and the nature of the market in existing houses have particular implications for the use of funds. More specifically there are important contrasts with the structure of public-sector housing finance.

Loan finance for private house purchase must be raised to meet *current* market prices by each successive purchaser/borrower. For example, the average new house bought in 1965 cost about £2500 and a buyer obtaining an 80 per cent loan would borrow £2000. Kept in good condition, the same house sold in 1978 would cost about £14 000 and an 80 per cent loan would imply one of about £11 000. Thus mortgage-lending must expand on a massive scale in money terms simply to keep pace with house-price inflation. Thus from 1972 to 1975, for example, lending increased in money terms from £3649 million to £4965 million, but the number of houses bought with this money actually fell 3 per cent, and would have fallen 14 per cent had not the average advance fallen as a proportion of purchase-price from 72 per cent to 64 per cent. This happened because average prices more than doubled, from £5650 to £11 945. To the extent that house-prices have risen considerably faster than retail-prices, the volume of mortgage funds has to expand in real terms, i.e. faster than the general rate of price inflation, merely to maintain the same volume of transactions in the housing market, *ceteris paribus*. From 1972 to 1975 the volume of funds financing private house purchase increased by over a third in money terms but the number of houses bought with this money fell by 23 000.

The argument is rather more complicated than this, however, since the real issue turns on the proportion of expenditure on house-purchase funded by building societies that could in principle be diverted into other sectors, such as the production of alternative goods and services.[21] Loans to finance purchase of new houses do entail the consumption of real resources; 23 per cent of building-society lending (by value) in the seventies has funded purchase of new dwellings representing 57 per cent of all capital expenditure on new private houses and a quarter of all capital expenditure on housing over this period.

Sales of existing houses do not 'use up' funds in the same way because real resources are not utilised in the process. What is involved is a transfer of an existing asset: when a person borrows from a building society and buys a house, the person selling the house receives a cheque, a financial asset, so the money loaned by the society does not 'disappear'. Loans to finance the sale of existing houses do entail the consumption of real resources, however, if the proceeds are used to buy new housing, and their value should therefore be added to direct lending for purchase of new houses. As *Housing Policy* notes:

> The purchase and sale of second-hand houses are a transfer of ownership of existing assets, not a use of productive resources in the way that building a new house is. But to the extent that lending on second-hand houses is not matched by mortgage repayments then mortgage funds are being absorbed, net, in an exchange of ownership of existing assets.[22]

Repayments of existing loans fall far short of financing new lending because of the large number of existing houses sold other than by existing owners moving house. Building-society lending on existing housing totalled £7205 million in 1978, but mortgage capital repayments on *all* housing, new and existing, only came to £3638 million.[23] According to an estimate in *Housing Policy*, the number of secondhand houses coming on to the market that were not owned subject to a mortgage was probably at least 300 000 in 1971—mainly houses sold after outright owners had died, but also landlords selling up.[24] Since over 90 per cent of first-time buyers and 75 per cent of existing owners buy with a mortgage, a high proportion of these houses formerly owned outright must obviously be bought with a mortgage. 'The amounts advanced for the purchase of second-hand houses from sellers who are not owner occupiers moving, and so cannot use the money to help pay for the purchase of a fresh house, are thus extremely large, and a substantial call on mortgage funds.'[25]

With the growing number of elderly people in the population the volume of funds involved is likely to increase significantly. Much of this money is probably paid out to heirs and legatees, passing on wealth accumulated in the form of housing, including benefit from increasing market values. Significantly, the proportion of houses owned outright rather than with a mortgage does not therefore rise through time as borrowers pay off their loans, reducing the total volume of funds tied up in house purchase, because of the number of houses subsequently purchased with a mortgage. The proportion of all owner-occupied houses owned outright actually fell, from 50 per cent to 44 per cent between 1966 and 1978.

The volume of funds absorbed is further increased to the extent that existing home-owners borrow more than they need to meet the difference between the price of the house they are buying and the amount of the existing loan they have to repay. Additional mortgage funds are thus called for to fund the encashment by the buyer of part of the value of his previous house. There is thus considerable 'leakage' of cash out of the private housing market, both in the purchase of existing houses from sellers who are not owner-occupiers moving and in encashment by existing owners moving. This absorbs a substantial volume of mortgage funds, and raises the volume of lending needed to support a given level of transactions. The implications of this leakage out of the housing market, funded in part by the societies, for the use of real resources depends on how this money is spent.

Rising house-prices thus generate an expanding demand for mortgage funds, which are absorbed in the sale of both new and existing houses. This contrasts with the public sector. Local authorities, like private owners, borrow to purchase new housing. However, unlike in the private sector, once purchased the housing does not return to the market to be revalued everytime the occupier moves. So although initially loan payments may be high, the burden in real terms is rapidly reduced by inflation, as in the case of owner-occupiers. And whereas when an owner-occupier moves, the house is sold at its current market price and the buyer must borrow enough to cover this, the local authority has only the historic cost to meet. The local authority does not need to borrow to cover the previous occupant's capital gain, for there are no private capital gains in the public rented sector. Local authorities operate on what is known as the 'pooled historic cost' principle. Rents on most local-authority housing over about 20 years old are greater than the current cost to the authority of loan repayments, maintenance and management because inflation has reduced the real cost of loan charges in respect of these houses. This surplus is normally used to reduce the rents charged on newer housing bought at prices nearer to the current level, so tenants of newer housing do not bear the full burden of the current cost. The local authority has only the historic costs of its dwellings to meet, and new finance to purchase housing at current market prices need only be raised when dwellings are *added* to the stock, not every time an occupant moves. This contributes to the considerable difference in average capital debt between the sectors — £4000 per mortgaged house and £2500–£3000 for each public-sector house at the end of 1976. The expansion of the owner-occupied sector relative to public housing may thus have major implications for the utilisation of financial and real resources within the economy, in addition to the crucial issues of housing policy considered in Chapters 8 and 9.

8
Policies for home-ownership

Support for the continued expansion of home-ownership is now a central element of housing policy. According to the *Housing Policy* Green Paper prepared under the last Labour government, 'The Government welcome this trend towards home ownership, which gives many people the kind of home they want . . . [and] . . . reduces the demands made on the public sector. . . . The Government will therefore promote measures to widen still further the opportunities for home ownership'.[1] The building societies are seen as crucial to this aim. 'Their dominant role in financing home ownership is probably unique among countries where home ownership is the largest tenure, and places their operations at the centre of housing policy.'[2] They 'occupy a pivotal position in the growth of home ownership', and 'The Government hope and expect that the building societies will be ready to shoulder still greater responsibility and to extend their voluntary co-operation with central and local government in the expansion of home ownership within the framework of the national housing policy.'[3] The Conservative government returned to office in 1979 can be expected to carry forward these aims with redoubled enthusiasm.

While positive support for the expansion of owner-occupation places much greater emphasis on the private market sector, the Green Paper argued: 'Greater emphasis on home ownership does not mean less social emphasis in housing policy. On the contrary, the widening of entry into home ownership for people with modest incomes will help solve housing problems which used to be faced by the public sector, as well as satisfying deep-seated social aspirations'.[4] The Green Paper outlined a series of measures to widen access to home-ownership, which, it was estimated, might increase from 55 per cent of the housing stock to around 59 per cent by 1986 in

England and Wales.[5] In response to the measures introduced by the Labour administration to widen access, the Green Paper suggested, 'it is reasonable to expect that the number of first-time buyers might run into tens of thousands a year, over and above those who were helped to buy sooner than they could otherwise have done'.[6] The emphasis in housing policy on expanding home-ownership – which the change of government in 1979 will only intensify – raises the question of mortgage supply and of the terms on which loans are made available, particularly to lower-income first-time buyers. Given that many lower-income households can only afford older, cheaper housing, this in turn focuses attention on mortgage-lending in the inner city and, in the context of policies to revitalise the inner city, on the impact of lending policies on urban decay and the improvement programme. This chapter considers the supply of mortgage funds in general, the terms on which loans are made available to individual borrowers, and the impact of mortgage-lending in the inner city, in the context of the emphasis in housing policy on the expansion of home-ownership and specific measures to achieve this aim.

Funds for house purchase

At the most general level the continued growth of home-ownership is conditional upon the supply of mortgage funds. Two related issues are involved: first, the short-term stability of the flow of funds, which affects first-time buyers, existing owners wanting to move, and the house-building industry; and second, the long-term adequacy of the supply of funds to meet demand for loans.[7]

Stabilisation

There are two basic approaches to stabilising the flow of mortgage-lending, which may in practice be combined. First, societies can try and reduce fluctuations in investment receipts. The increasing use of term shares to tie down volatile money is likely to continue, though their higher interest rates threaten societies' operating margins. Their expansion could be accommodated by the growing practice of charging differential mortgage rates, raising the rate progressively with the amount borrowed. This might be carried a stage further by issuing long-term 'mortgage bonds' (discussed below). More frequent changes in societies' share rates in line with competing interest rates could help stabilise receipts; but the flexibility of mortgage rate is limited by the notice required for changes, the desire to avoid frequent changes which disrupt borrowers' budgets, and to some extent the administrative cost. Share rates could, however, be varied more than mortgage rates. This would mean that societies would tend to make lower than normal surpluses when competing rates were high and higher than normal surpluses when competing rates were low, but over time the two would even each other out.

The second approach is to attempt to insulate the flow of mortgage-lending from fluctuations in investment receipts by societies operating a 'stabilisation fund' or drawing on fresh sources of extra money when they are short of funds. Societies have in the past used their liquid assets to some extent as a stabilisation mechanism. Liquidity is built up when societies are competitive, and released to supplement lending when receipts drop back. In spring 1976 liquidity was built up to 22 per cent of total assets as against the customary minimum working liquidity of 15–16 per cent. This provided about £1500 to £1750 million extra mortgage funds, sufficient to offset a 2 per cent increase in interest rates for about 12 months.[8] These funds were adequate to cope with the $2-2\frac{1}{2}$ per cent increase in rates in March–May 1976, but not with the further 4 per cent increase in the autumn, which would have required a much larger stabilisation fund. One obstacle to accumulating a more substantial stabilisation fund is that societies may be paying investors more than they can get by investing liquid assets in the money market, and thereby incurring a loss. According to *Housing Policy*, the government might in future carry this loss by accepting part of societies' funds for investment in the National Loans Fund at an interest rate which would not involve any loss to the societies, subject to agreement through the Joint Advisory Committee on the level of mortgage-lending and stabilisation funds.[9] Societies might also supplement lending when receipts from conventional sources are low by raising short-term loans on the money market when general interest rates are temporarily high; though money-market interest rates were high, the borrowing would be short term and limited in volume, and the total cost much less than raising the additional funds by increasing the rates paid on *all* shares. An example in *Housing Policy* indicates that the cost of responding to a 4 per cent increase in general interest rates by borrowing on the money market would push up the mortgage rate 0.7 per cent, as against $4\frac{1}{4}-4\frac{1}{2}$ per cent if share rates were increased across the board.[10] Societies might raise short-term money by issuing securities like banks' certificates of deposit, or possibly through an intermediate public or private body. The Labour government also indicated it would, in exceptional circumstances, consider short-term loans from public funds, as in 1974. While the details of Conservative policy have yet to emerge, financial support for the societies would be at least as likely as under the last Labour government.

A major objective in stabilising mortgage-lending is to provide a steadier level of effective demand for private housing, allowing private house-builders to plan production and hence encourage the supply of new houses. This could be facilitated by extending arrangements whereby builders are allocated advance quotas of mortgage funds for buyers of their housing who meet the societies' status requirements, thus removing some of the uncertainty. Quotas assure builders that potential purchasers will not be frustrated by inability to raise a mortgage, so 'the size of such quotas and how far ahead they reach are very important to builders in deciding how many houses to start'.[11] It has sometimes been suggested that societies should expand their lending to house-builders to finance land-purchase and construction, and that short-term loans to finance production be converted into long-term loans to house-buyers, through the quota system. But since there is little evidence that lack of development finance from their customary sources, primarily the banks, has been a major problem for builders,[12] extending the mortgage quota system would probably have a much greater impact.

Housing Policy expressed the belief that stability could be increased by developing the voluntary arrangements with societies through the Joint Advisory Committee. It recommended that societies should build up liquidity as 'stabilisation funds' to higher levels, keep their share rates more in line with competing rates, adopting a more flexible relationship between mortgage and share rates, and be prepared to raise short-term loans on the money market. Further development of quotas for builders was also suggested.

Adequacy of funds

Forecasts indicate that the funds societies have to raise to meet demand for mortgages will need to increase substantially in real terms – from £4340 million in 1976 to £6300–£6500 million by 1986

(1976 prices) – as owner-occupation continues to expand and measures to widen access to home-ownership take effect.[13] Societies' receipts of 'small savings', amounts under £500, are likely to rise in line with incomes but, with demand for mortgage funds rising distinctly faster than incomes, a rapid increase in receipts of 'large' money will be required. Net receipts might grow fast enough to meet demand. If not, one possibility would be for societies to offer higher interest rates in general (therefore raising the mortgage rate), though competition might simply cause their rivals to increase their rates also. *Housing Policy* has suggested that it is 'possible that the building societies will only be able to meet demands placed upon them for advances if they supplement their traditional sources of finance by raising funds from other financial institutions'.[14] The larger building societies might be able to deal direct with the institutions, but a special financial intermediary is suggested. This might raise short-term loans for stabilisation as well as long-term mortgage funds. Possible sources of long-term funds would be life assurance and pension funds, large private investors, or banks (for one-year money renewed by rolling over). Though interest rates on this money would be higher than for traditional sources, it would represent only a small part of societies' total funds. Such an agency might be private, owned and controlled by the societies, or a public body with greater government involvement.

One possibility for tapping new funds and attracting institutional investment would be for societies to issue mortgage bonds, modelling themselves more on the European mortgage banks. The latter issue long-term, fixed-interest bonds, which can be bought and sold at their prevailing market price. Societies would, however, meet strong competition from central and local government and company bonds if they developed in this direction. Significantly, mortgage bonds have drawn institutional investors into financing house-purchase in other European countries on a far greater scale than in Britain, where direct mortgage finance by institutions such as banks and insurance companies has been very limited and indirect investment by institutions through intermediaries such as the building societies virtually non-existent. In Sweden, for example, housing bonds are taken up by commercial banks, savings banks, insurance companies, and particularly the National Insurance Pension Fund, which holds employers' contributions to the National Pension Scheme and had over half its assets in housing bonds at the end of 1970.[15] Corporate bodies lacking the expertise or desire for direct mortgage-lending can thus participate indirectly in housing finance by taking up bonds issued by the mortgage banking institutions.

Institutional investment in finance for house-purchase might be achieved by counting investment in mortgage bonds or other investment in building societies as part of legally required reserves or liquid funds. In Italy, for example, part of the commercial banks' reserves can be held in housing bonds, and Swedish housing bonds count towards the liquid assets commercial and savings banks must maintain. Control has been carried further in Sweden in the form of 'investment guidelines', whereby insurance companies and the National Insurance Pension Fund must place a proportion of their increase in funds in specified 'priority assets', which include direct mortgage-lending and mortgage bonds as well as government-supported projects and government bonds. Additionally, in 1973 the banks and Pension Fund agreed to increase their net holding of housing bonds above the previously arranged level to meet the rapidly developing shortage of mortgage finance for buying newly completed housing. The commercial banks, which provide much of the short-term finance for new building in the form of 'building credits', also agreed to convert part of their holding of short-term building loans into long-term house-purchase loans. These measures served to minimise the impact of the short-term famine in finance for house-purchase, which in Britain at this time led to a wave of bankruptcies in the building industry, massive unemployment, and stagnation in investment in new house-building. In Sweden the combination of control and co-operation has ensured a steady flow of mortgage funds, contributing both to short-term stability and long-run adequacy in the volume of lending. If in the future building societies need to draw on institutional funds to supplement traditional sources, reserve and liquidity regulations or investment guidelines might therefore be considered.

Financial barriers to home-ownership

Assuming that a stable and adequate flow of mortgage funds can be achieved, a second obstacle to the continued expansion of home-ownership is the financial burden of the deposit and mortgage payments first-time buyers face. This is particularly heavy in the early years, given the phenomenon of 'front loading' (Chapter 5 and Figure 5.5 in the Appendix). *Housing Policy* therefore concentrated attention on schemes to ease the financial burdens in the early years of house-purchase to aid low-income first-time buyers and widen access to home-ownership, advocating low-start loans, higher percentage loans, increased lending on older property in inner-urban areas, and introducing a savings bonus and loan scheme.

Low-start loans

Payments on a normal repayment mortgage are fixed in money terms for the life of the loan unless mortgage rates change, whereas borrowers' incomes generally rise in money terms in line with inflation, and for many people also in real terms with pay increases on top of this general rise. The proportion of a borrower's income represented by mortgage payments is thus high initially but falls progressively through time. Payments on low-start loans are initially lower, but higher subsequently than on a normal repayment mortgage; they flatten out the decline in the real cost of mortgage payments, offsetting to some extent the high initial burden. A great variety of schemes is possible.[16] Two national schemes have been devised, while some local authorities and building societies operate their own alternatives. The National Economic Development Office in 1972 developed a scheme that is used by a number of authorities and the Greater London Council. Payments are interest only in the first year but rise constantly by a fixed percentage over the mortgage term. With high interest rates, deferring capital repayment makes little difference, however, since early payments on a normal mortgage are mainly interest anyway – with an 11 per cent mortgage rate the scheme reduces the first year's payments on a typical loan by only 7 per cent net of tax relief. A scheme devised by the DOE and BSA in 1975 also defers part of the interest payments in the early years, and reduces typical net payments by 20 per cent in the first year; the reduction diminishes progressively, and repayment of the extra debt starts in year 11. In practice, however, the scheme proved over-complicated.

Building societies have granted few low-start loans so far, compared with over 10 per cent of local-authority loans in 1975. Successful schemes are operated in a number of other European countries: in Norway a flexible repayment scheme is linked to trends in income and a Swedish scheme links repayments to the building cost index. Low-start loans carry greater risk than normal mortgages. They require adequate safety margins to ensure that rising incomes keep well ahead of rates of increase in scheduled repayments, and to avoid the (increasing) outstanding debt getting ahead of house-prices, which would leave the loan partly unsecured. Delayed capital repayment also reduces the return flow of funds available for relending by societies, so that the volume of funds needed to support a given number of loans is increased. A limited increase in the use of low-start loans might, however, provide significant assistance to a substantial minority of low-income house-buyers, particularly in conjunction with the option-mortgage scheme, which, although benefiting non-taxpayers, increases borrowers' initial payments in comparison with those of a borrower benefiting from a tax-relief mortgage.

A different form of low-start payments scheme is provided by the 'half and half' scheme, whereby a household buys a long lease on one half of the house for half its market value, and pays half the rent which would be due if the house were rented normally. Mortgage payments thus relate to only half the market value of the house, but the occupier can buy the rented part of the house at any time. Initial outgoings in a local-authority scheme might be 30 per cent less than on a full mortgage. 'Half and half' schemes were first operated by Birmingham Council in 1975 and other authorities have followed suit.[17] The government has encouraged their development both as a permanent form of tenure and as a stepping-stone to full home-ownership.

Higher percentage loans

Recognising that the need to raise a substantial deposit to cover the gap between the price of a house and what a building society will lend can be a major obstacle for potential first-time buyers, the government has urged societies to offer higher percentage loans. The average advance to first-time buyers by building societies in 1975 was 76 per cent of average purchase-price, compared with 90 per cent for local authorities, which may suggest societies could be more liberal. Although societies commonly lend above their 'normal' percentage provided the 'excess' is covered by some form of guarantee or additional security, they have been reluctant to grant 100 per cent loans (see Chapter 5). Local authorities are empowered to guarantee loan repayments to societies under the 1958 Housing (Financial Provisions) Act, but societies have argued that the cover provided and administrative speed is not comparable with the commercial scheme agreed with the insurance companies. The BSA recently arranged for commercial guarantees to cover loans up to 100 per cent, which may allow an increase in higher percentage loans. Many lower-income borrowers could, however, already obtain 100 per cent loans, in theory, under the Option Mortgage Guarantee Scheme. The government has suggested that in the context of local co-operation, local authorities could offer guarantees on dwellings in particular areas to assure societies of their lasting future. It has further been suggested that local authorities offer 'topping-up' loans – second loans to supplement a loan from, say, a building society – similar to the insurance company second mortgages offered higher up the market. This might, however, lead societies to refuse or reduce the first loan, but could be useful if societies were limiting the size of loans because they were short of funds. As the Labour government indicated, legislation may be necessary to clarify and strengthen local authorities' powers to give guarantees and grant topping-up loans to support building-society lending to low-income, first-time buyers.

The government homeloan scheme

The Labour government demonstrated its commitment to expanding home-ownership with the introduction of a savings bonus and loan scheme for first-time buyers under the 1978 Home Purchase Assistance and Housing Corporation Guarantee Act. There are two parts to the scheme. First-time buyers who have saved for at least two years with a recognised savings institution, have kept at least £300 in their account throughout the 12 months before asking for a loan, and have saved at least £600 in total at that time, qualify for a £600 additional loan from the lending institution. No interest or capital repayments are made on the loan for the first five years – worth about £6.30 a month before tax relief on a 25-year loan with an 11.75 per cent mortgage rate. The lending institution initially receives this £600 from the government; after five years it repays the government, replaces the £600 from its own funds, and the borrower repays the loan with interest along with the rest of the mortgage. The borrowers' payments therefore rise after five years. The main qualifying lending institutions are most building societies, local authorities, trustee savings banks, the major banks, and insurance companies; these are also qualifying savings institutions, along with the National Savings Bank and Girobank – the savings and lending institution need not be the same, though, and building societies will continue to encourage prospective borrowers to save with them. Purchasers who qualify for a loan will also receive a tax-free savings bonus of at least £40; and every additional £100 in their account over the 12-month period brings an extra £10 bonus up to a maximum of £110 for savings of £1000 or more. Two final conditions are that the property price must not exceed a regional house-price limit, initially set so that about two-thirds of first-time buyers in each region would qualify, and that the total loan must be at least £1600 and 25 per cent of the purchase-price of the property.

The scheme encourages saving and, through the bonus and loan, adds to buyers' initial financial resources. The £600 loan can either increase the total loan obtained or, if this would push the total over the value of the property, reduce payments for the first five years. The scheme does not, however, guarantee or give priority in actually obtaining a loan. It has been estimated the scheme will cost about £100 million in its first full year but after five years, when loans start to be repaid, the net annual cost will drop to around £15 million per annum. The size of benefits, house-price limit and conditions can be altered under the Act. As currently structured, the level of assistance is relatively low, and a case could be made for concentrating the resources devoted to the scheme more strongly on lower-income purchasers by setting a lower house-price limit if the government wished to aid those on the margins of home-ownership, and excluding buyers paying higher than basic income tax rates from the scheme. The effect of the scheme in practice cannot, however, be observed until the two-year qualifying period elapses and the first loans are granted. The Conservative government has expressed its strong commitment to such a scheme and, indeed, has suggested the need to increase the level of aid introduced by Labour.

Mortgage-lending and the inner city

Housing Policy specifically advocated that societies should 'extend further their lending on older property, especially in inner urban areas'.[18] Many householders can only afford older, cheaper, inner-city type housing. The Department of the Environment's study of 'starter homes' gives the example of a one-bed starter home in Oldham costing £6950 extendable to two or three bedrooms for £1000, whereas a two-up, two-down terrace house in the same areas would sell for £2000–£3000 unmodernised and £3500–£5500 modernised.[19] Older homes may also offer more space and better access to work, shops and entertainments than new suburban housing; but the major disadvantage is likely to be higher expenditure on repairs and maintenance (see Chapter 9). Many lower-income households will be unable to buy a house unless they can obtain loans to purchase older houses, and may remain trapped in inferior accommodation in the private rented sector or face long waits for scarce council housing. Indeed, for many, buying a cheap inner-city house may be the only chance to acquire something approaching a decent house, owing to shortages in other sectors.

Building societies do lend a considerable (and increasing) proportion of their funds to those buying older housing. But there remains a substantial proportion of the older housing stock, particularly cheaper, inner-city type houses, conversions, and unmodernised houses, which they are reluctant to accept as loan security, given that their funds are limited and safer alternatives are available elsewhere; they have also suggested that householders should not be encouraged to buy such houses, which may prove financially burdensome and poor investments (see Chapter 5). There is a certain amount of justification in the societies' arguments, particularly perhaps those related to uncertainty about local authorities' housing programmes in the context of the switch in emphasis nationally from rebuilding to improvement. As they are private-sector financial institutions, there is little reason to expect them actively to expand into more risky mortgage business unless in response to governmental or social pressure or the unlikely event of a surplus of funds to lend out. Societies tend to see older inner-city housing areas, with some justification perhaps, as the territory and problem of local authorities.

Societies could undoubtedly expand lending on older, cheaper property to some extent with little real increase in risk. Their total mortgage losses in 1977 were only £311 000, 0.0009 per cent of their total assets of £34 200 million. The investors themselves lost nothing, since societies make provision for losses out of the surplus they earn – this amounted to just over £1 million in 1977. Losses of individual societies are insignificant: in 1978, for example, the Bristol and West lost only £1881 and the Leicester £2000, on total mortgage assets of £458 million and £1014 million respectively.

There might, however, be some increase in arrears if societies were lending to borrowers of more marginal financial status. *Housing Policy* suggests that, 'since mortgage losses have been so low for all societies, it is hard to see that societies that have taken less restrictive attitudes have been running any significant risk',[20] and argues that societies should 'give due weight to social factors when deciding what priority to give to applications for mortgages . . . (but) . . . this does not mean that building societies should allow sound judgement to supersede commercial judgement'.[21] *Housing Policy* also says that, 'while the building societies must certainly satisfy themselves about the security of the funds invested with them, the government consider that they could without risk go further in supporting the objectives of the national housing policy and that they should do so'.[22]

An effective mortgage-guarantee system could in theory allow societies to expand lending on older, inner-city property without risk to investors, though administrative costs of arrears could increase. Both the Building Society Indemnity and the Option Mortgage Guarantee Schemes insure only the top slice of the loan, the 'excess'. A clarified and strengthened local-authority guarantee scheme applying to the entire amount loaned, and fully underwriting any risk to the societies along the lines suggested in Labour's proposed 1979 Housing Bill, might largely have met societies' objections to down-market lending. Insurance could cover borrowers below a certain income level; the purchase of property below a given value or over a certain age; the purchase of all property within certain areas defined by local authorities, in consultation with the building societies, so as to include inner-city areas and specifically General Improvement Areas, Housing Action Areas and other priority areas, thus orientating building-society lending specifically towards local housing policy; or purchase of other awkward categories of housing such as converted flats. Such a scheme might enable and encourage but not ensure more liberal building-society lending policies. A more positive move would be to expand direct lending by local authorities.

Local authorities have in the past lent proportionately more of their funds to lower-income households and first-time buyers, lent on more liberal terms, and lent more on older, inner-city property than the building societies (Chapter 5). However, the succession of public-expenditure cuts since 1975 has severely reduced the volume of local-authority lending, and while the building-societies' support lending has replaced local-authority lending to some extent, there has nevertheless been little specific liberalisation of societies' lending policies. Local authorities operate under different constraints and with different objectives to building societies. They are housing authorities with a general responsibility to meet housing need in their area, and their financial status as public bodies is backed by their ability to borrow and levy rates. Different patterns of mortgage allocation from the societies are therefore possible, and perhaps appropriate and necessary for authorities to fulfil their responsibilities and role in the housing system. Thus an increase in direct local-authority lending may therefore be more appropriate than attempts to persuade societies to abandon 'conservative' lending policies and 'red lining', or to operate a more liberal support-lending scheme.

The expansion of local-authority lending is, however, constrained by the desire to control public expenditure on the grounds of monetary policy. In the short term, mortgage-lending by local authorities does increase public-sector borrowing. However, in the long term, loans are repaid with interest and costs covered. So lending increases the public-sector debt but does not increase expenditure as such. Frank Allaun has described the cuts in local-authorities' mortgage-lending as 'wholly illogical': 'If a person takes a mortgage out at the town hall, that is public expenditure. If he crosses the High Street and gets one at a building society, that is not'.[23] The effect on the economy as a whole is little different if a local authority borrows and on-lends to house-buyers or if a building society takes in investment and increases mortgage-lending. A way round these controls could probably be found if a strong case was put to the Treasury. Funds were, for example, recently raised for housing associations via the merchant banks, avoiding public-expenditure constraints.

It is sometimes suggested that local authorities be permitted to set up building societies under the appropriate Act; but authorities' lack of expertise and the small fragmented scale of such societies would make them inefficient and possibly risky. Alternatively a National Building Society might be set up to channel mortgages via local authorities to priority borrowers. A much simpler proposal, strongly supported within the Labour Party and the subject of two private members' bills introduced by Frank Allaun, is for bulk lending by building societies to local authorities for on-lending to individual borrowers. This would allow local authorities to allocate a much larger volume of total mortgage funds in accordance with social priorities and local housing strategies. It would obviate the need for liaison between societies and authorities over each individual application, as under the support-lending scheme or an improved local-authority guarantee scheme. Most significantly it would assure both interest payments and the security of this portion of societies' funds, as interest could be paid by local authorities to societies at the normal share rate and authorities would bear any extra cost generated by increased arrears. A scheme on these lines is already operated in Northern Ireland through the Housing Executive. Since such a scheme would in effect guarantee the riskiest portion of societies' lending with minimal administrative effort and absolve them from responsibility and criticism of their policies relating to the lower end of the market, it could attract some support. Fear of government interference and control, if not 'creeping nationalis-ation', has, however, generated strong opposition in some quarters of the building-society movement. A figure of 10 per cent of building-society funds to be allocated in this way has been suggested. It could be distributed to local authorities through the same administrative system as used for lending based on direct public expenditure. Again, however, if funds were actually loaned to local authorities, they would count towards public expenditure and the relevant regu-lations would need modification. A block-lending scheme would, however, appear to be the simplest and most effective measure to expand lending to lower-income households buying older, cheaper houses in the inner city. At the same time, local authorities should be encouraged to develop positive mortgage policies in the context of their Housing Strategies and Investment Programmes.

Housing Policy sees the local authorities' role, however, as that of 'co-operating' with and providing a framework for building-society activity, building on the 'working partnerships' established under the support-lending scheme. Under the system of Housing Investment Programmes introduced in 1978–9, designed to enable local autho-rities to present co-ordinated analyses of housing conditions in their area and to formulate coherent policies and programmes of capital spending, authorities are expected to relate their own proposals 'more explicitly to the housing contribution likely to be made by the private sector and other agencies'.[24] The Green Paper advocates that authorities should complement the work of building societies especially in areas of older housing by providing topping-up loans, guarantees, and improvement and repair grants 'to improve the security of building society loans', and should keep societies informed of their local housing strategies and plans for specific areas:

> Such co-operation should help ensure increased lending on houses which are old or in a poor state of repair. It should also help to reduce 'red-lining' – the withdrawal by societies of mortgage lending from declining areas. . . . Building societies and local

authorities, by working together at the local level, can assist in revitalising older urban areas including inner city areas.[25]

Those buying inner-city housing who *cannot* raise a building-society or local-authority loan often turn to banks and finance houses. Interest rates are high and repayment terms short, so that mortgage payments are much higher than on conventional loans, and there are often onerous conditions attached to the contracts (see Chapter 5). In the inner city, therefore, the costs and risks of house-buying to those least able to afford it tend to increase. According to Karn, 'The bigger the gap left by the building societies and local authorities in minimising their *own* risk, the greater the role played by these institutions and the greater the ultimate risk to the buyers'.[26]

Inner-city decay and the improvement programme

Mortgage-lending and the expansion of home-ownership in older inner-city areas tend to encourage increased investment in house repairs, maintenance and improvement, including, specifically, grant-aided improvement. In 1976 owner-occupied houses were better maintained age for age than pre-1914 private rented housing, and inter-war and post-war local-authority housing; and half the houses brought up to full amenity standard between 1967 and 1971 were in the owner-occupied sector, which accounted for only a third of all houses lacking amenities in 1967.[27] *Housing Policy* suggests specifically that the sharp rise in improvement activity after 1969 was due in part to the sharp increase in local-authority lending, mainly on older housing, and that 'The number of transactions in the stock of old dwellings is important because improvement often follows a change of residents'.[28] Increased owner-occupation tends to generate a more stable social structure by maintaining family occupancy and a more 'balanced' community, retaining or attracting back younger people and skilled workers, in contrast to the transient structure of the older inner areas. Mortgage-lending by building societies and local authorities in particular, and the expansion of inner-city home-ownership, are therefore important factors affecting the rate of urban decay and the success of grant-aided and area-improvement policies. The significance of this relationship between lending and improvement has been emphasised in the context of two major trends: first, the decline of the private rented sector, since transfer of ownership from renting to owner-occupation has clearly encouraged maintenance and improvement; second, the shift of emphasis in housing policy away from wholesale clearance and redevelopment towards preservation and improvement, particularly since 1974, which has focused attention on the housing market and mortgage supply in these older areas.

From the mid-sixties at least local-authority lending has been linked to improvement policies. The priority lending categories established in 1965 included specifically those buying older, smaller property, and after the 1969 Housing Act this became 'more particularly persons who want to acquire a house with a view to subsequently improving it for their own occupation with the help of the provisions of the Housing Act 1969' (see Chapter 5). The building societies' role was recognised by the government, which approached the BSA following the introduction of General Improvement Areas in 1969 seeking the societies' co-operation, and contacted local authorities, suggesting they should inform building societies locally about their plans for improvement. In many cities, however, local-authority General Improvement Areas and, particularly, Housing Action Areas are in localities which attract very few building-society loans, in contrast to local-authority loans, which tend to be concentrated in improvement areas.[29] However, as the Birmingham example quoted in Chapter 5 suggests, local authorities themselves are often unable through lack of funds, or unwilling to, expand general lending in the inner city.

In the specific case of grant-aided improvement there remain problems of co-ordinating building-society loans and local-authority grant procedure (see Chapter 5). If societies *are* to increase lending on property to be improved with grants, then authorities must be prepared to commit themselves to grants before (though conditional on) actual purchase, and to waive their right to reclaim loans if the property, where it is bought with a building-society loan, is sold within five years. Prior commitment to grants could prevent buyers having to raise expensive bridging finance while improvements are carried out, with no definite assurance of a building-society loan when they are completed. The building societies' practice of withholding part of a loan until specified repairs or improvement are completed obviously further discourages purchase of older housing, particularly by lower-income households; an effective local-authority guarantee scheme might encourage a more liberal attitude.

Lack of mortgage-lending on inner-urban areas tends, therefore, to impede improvement policies and to accelerate urban decay. This is part of a more general dynamic process of urban development, whereby existing inner-city housing is written off at an accelerated rate in favour of new, primarily suburban housing, for which demand is stimulated. Harvey in particular has linked this process to the expansion of the automotive-based, suburban, consumer life-style, functioning to maintain aggregate demand in the economy in general and to support, specifically, the profitability of the private speculative house-building industry. Building societies' mortgage quotas reserved for those nominated by private house-builders stand in direct contrast to societies' reluctance to lend on older inner-city housing. Meanwhile commercial city-centre redevelopment schemes move outwards. It is worth stressing, however, that the large-scale abandonment of inner-city housing seen in many American cities has not developed in Britain, for, despite the lack of building-society and also local-authority lending in these areas, the private market continues to provide a basis for profitable trading in older property by drawing on bank, finance house and other sources of finance.[30]

Building-society and local-authority lending policies thus contribute to the general structuring of urban space by financial and governmental institutions. Harvey, writing of the USA, characterised inner-city decay and suburban growth as a basic process of capitalist urban development, and there is evidence in the case of the USA for the specific transfer of funds away from the inner city.[31] In part this occurs through institutions withdrawing from inner areas, refusing new loans and 'transferring' funds by financing sales in the suburbs. But information revealed through the American Mortgage Disclosure Act also indicates that the proportion of funds received from investors in the inner city which is returned there in the form of loans for house purchase can be very low. Savings banks in Boston were reinvesting 70 per cent of their intake from upper-income areas, but as little as 12–20 per cent of deposits received from investors in older neighbourhoods were reinvested in those areas.[32] The success of the British building societies in attracting money from small savers and low-income investors (20 per cent of investors earn too little to pay income tax), in contrast with the societies' lending policies towards low-income households in the inner city, suggests that a similar transfer of funds out of inner areas to finance suburban development is likely to be taking place. And there is also some evidence of building societies withdrawing from the inner city, refusing new loans in areas where previously they would lend. In Saltley, Birmingham, for example, until 1950 it was easy to get a

building-society loan, but as property deteriorated and leases
declined to under 40 years, societies became reluctant to lend on this
property – from 1950 to 1959 they supplied nearly 70 per cent of all
loans, but this fell to only 8 per cent by 1972–4.[33] Mortgage-lending
by building societies and from other sources is thus part of a general
process of investment and disinvestment in the urban system by
financial and government agencies, which structures both the
housing market and the pattern of urban development.

9
Home-ownership and housing policy

With housing policy now firmly wedded to the expansion of home-ownership, the role of owner-occupation in housing policy and the housing system as a whole is of major importance. This final chapter considers two key issues. First it broadens the context of the discussion by examining housing taxation and subsidy and the financial support granted to house-buyers and home-owners relative to local-authority tenants. Then it considers the expansion of home-ownership as an element of housing policy looking in particular at the extent to which this represents an appropriate strategy to meet the housing need of lower-income households and at its implications for the housing system as a whole.

Housing taxation and subsidy

The question of housing taxation and subsidy bears directly on the distribution of housing costs and of income and wealth both within the owner-occupied sector and between owners and renters. There has been considerable debate focusing not only on alternative subsidy and taxation policies but also on the basic question of what actually constitutes a subsidy. In relation to owner-occupation there are three main issues at stake: tax relief on mortgage interest, exemption from tax on imputed rental income, and exemption from tax on capital gains.

Tax relief on mortgage interest

Under the original system of income tax introduced in 1803 borrowers paid interest and other annual payments to the lender net of tax. This applied to all loans, not only those for house-purchase.

From 1925–6, under a special arrangement, borrowers from building societies paid interest in full but could claim interest payments against their income-tax liability. This was legally formalised in 1951, and, since the introduction of the unified system of tax rates in 1973, relief has been given through borrowers' PAYE codes. Full tax relief has always been available at whatever rate the borrower is liable to pay. Since 1969 tax relief on interest paid by individuals has been restricted to loans for the purchase or improvement of property except in the period 1972–74 when universal tax relief on loan interest was largely restored. Since 1974 tax relief has also been restricted to loans relating to property to be commercially let and to loans up to £25 000 on the sole or main residence of the borrower, a divorced or separated wife (*sic*), or a dependent relative, thus ruling out second houses, for example. Thus, although tax relief is a long-established part of the tax system, not originally designed to assist owner-occupiers, it is now confined to mortgaged house-buyers and is widely accepted to be a specific form of subsidy. The option-mortgage subsidy gives aid roughly equivalent to tax relief at the basic rate to non-taxpayers. The government thus included tax relief and option mortgage subsidy in its definition of 'general assistance' adopted in *Housing Policy*.

The total cost of tax relief and option-mortgage subsidy was estimated to be £1240 million in 1976–7. It has been increasing rapidly and in real terms doubled between 1971–2 and 1976–7 (Figure 9.1 in the Appendix). This large increase is mainly explained by the rise in house-prices at a faster rate than general prices, and by substantial increases in tax and interest rates. The reduction in mortgage and tax rates in 1977–8 reduced tax relief slightly in real terms to around £1115 million (1976 prices), but higher mortgage rates and accelerating house prices pushed the total up in 1978–9. Between 1971 and 1975 tax changes accounted for 35 per cent, higher mortgage rates for 20 per cent and increased mortgage debt for 45 per cent of the £635 million increase. The contribution of increased mortgage debt is particularly significant, since mortgage debt inevitably rises with rising house-prices. According to *Housing Policy*, 'the trend is for the total mortgage debt *per mortgagor* to rise – and with it the gross interest payments made and the tax relief and option mortgage subsidy claimed'.[1]

Tax relief currently gives greatest help to those least in need. The higher the borrowers' tax bracket and the larger the loan they can afford to take out, the more subsidy they receive. Tax relief at the basic rate reduces a mortgage rate of 11.75 per cent to 7.87 per cent for a basic (33 per cent) taxpayer, to 5.88 per cent for a 50 per cent taxpayer and only 4.7 per cent for a 60 per cent taxpayer.

Tax relief per individual thus tends to rise with income, in contrast to subsidies in the public sector (central government and rates subsidies), which are roughly constant over the income ranges (see Figure 9.2 in the Appendix). The average subsidy to mortgaged owners (£140) and to council tenants (£139) was roughly equal in 1974–5.[2] But whereas the ratio of subsidy to income fell rapidly the higher the income group in the public sector, in the private sector the ratio fell only slowly. The average subsidy to those with incomes under £2500 was £132 for tenants and £91 for owners. Tenants earning over £5000 received £154 but owners got £273. Rent rebates raise the average subsidy per tenant to £160 but concentrate aid even more strongly on lower-income groups. Tax relief thus follows the biblical logic of 'to them that hath shall be given'.

Criticism has also been levelled at the efficiency of tax relief as a form of subsidy. Tax relief subsidises the consumption of housing, increasing demand but affecting supply only indirectly through the price mechanism. On the one hand, it is suggested that consumption subsidies encourage households to occupy more housing space than they need by buying bigger and bigger houses – this is reinforced by the prospect of capital gains and the high performance of housing as an investment. Thus part of the housing stock becomes under-occupied while severe housing need exists elsewhere in the housing system. On the other hand, it is argued that the benefits of tax relief are, in part at least, illusory, since they are capitalised in land-prices and house-prices. Stafford has argued: 'Although the tax paying owner occupier may receive the immediate benefit, the demand and supply conditions in the market will determine who ultimately gains. Given the relative price inelasticity of the supply of housing, much of the gain has probably gone to the supplier of the house, and through him to the seller of the land'.[3]

There have been many varied proposals to reform this highly inequitable subsidy structure. The Labour Party has proposed abolishing tax relief at higher than basic rates, replacing mortgage tax relief with a universal mortgage subsidy equivalent to tax relief at the basic rate, and reducing the £25 000 ceiling on eligible loans to something approaching average house-prices, varied on a regional basis. Limiting relief to the basic rate would have saved the Exchequer £110 million in 1976–7,[4] which might have been directed to help lower-income households. A universal subsidy could be paid direct to lending institutions, which would then charge a lower mortgage rate (as currently for option mortgages). This would also eliminate the complication of tax-relief assessment and allowance by the Inland Revenue. Assistance might also be concentrated in the early years of house-purchase. Currently, owners moving benefit from tax relief on the full first year's interest on a new and normally larger loan. On the 'single annuity' principle proposed by the Housing Centre Trust relief would only be allowed on the amount of interest which would have been paid on a 25 year loan taken out at the date the original mortgage commenced.[5] For example, an owner moving from a house mortgaged for £10 000 after seven years and taking out a new loan for, say, £15 000 would receive tax relief only on the interest due on the second mortgage as if it had been taken out seven years before, and relief would end after 25 years. A further limit would confine relief to interest calculated on the amount of the first mortgage − £10 000 in the example. The organisation Shelter has proposed limiting relief to the first ten years of a mortgage, while the London Boroughs Association suggested replacing tax relief with annual cash grants for first-time buyers.[6] Cash grants could help bridge the deposit gap, reduce house-buyers' need to borrow, and facilitate an effective low-start loan scheme.

Substantial reform is obviously called for. But according to *Housing Policy* the Labour government was 'firmly committed to the continuance of tax relief on mortgage interest and option mortgage subsidy. This is essential if the steady growth of home ownership is to be maintained'.[7] The commitment was also for continuance in its present form, for it is argued in *Housing Policy* that change would disrupt family budgets, and house prices at the top end of the market, hit financially those with middle as well as higher incomes (the beleaguered 'middle-management'), and finally that concentrating aid on first-time buyers would reduce housing and job mobility. Again, the Conservative government is likely to back up those proposals and, indeed, may yield to the arguments of the BSA that the current £25 000 limit on loans qualifying for tax relief should be raised. The crucial point remains that to help low-income households and those in greatest housing need, subsidy to the top end of the market should be cut and diverted to the lower reaches. Prices at the top end of the market could usefully fall, any changes could be phased in, while the financial resources of existing owners who have been buying over several years are usually such that limiting subsidy on the single annuity principle or to a fixed term would have little effect on mobility.

Exemption from tax on imputed rental income

Owner-occupiers receive benefits in the form of the use of their house which have an imputed cash value equal to the rent they would have to pay to obtain similar housing. In other words, they receive an imputed rental income. The owner-occupier of a house worth an annual rent of, say, £1000 clearly has £1000 more income at their disposal than someone with the same income who must pay out £1000 in rent for equivalent housing. Logically the owner-occupier should pay tax on £1000 more than the renter. If the owner had invested their capital elsewhere rather than buying a house, they would generally be taxed on the income from that investment.

Until 1963 owner-occupiers were taxed under Schedule 'A' income tax as part of a general system of taxing both actual (landlords') and imputed (owner-occupiers') income from property. The tax was levied on valuations based on market rents, in a similar manner to rates, with an element to cover the cost of repairs deducted from the income before the tax was levied. There had been no general revaluation of property since 1935 and values on which the tax was levied were left far behind by rising market rents. The situation came to a head in 1963 with the transfer of rating valuation to the Inland Revenue and the imminence of a fresh valuation which would have greatly increased the tax payable by owners. Although the Royal Commission on the Taxation of Profits and Incomes had recommended in 1955 that Schedule 'A' be retained in order to maintain equity between owners and (public and private) tenants, the government decided in 1963 to abolish the tax, largely for political reasons. Since 1963 landlords have been taxed directly on rental income rather than on assessed values. When abolished, Schedule 'A' was only netting about £50 million, though up to date valuations would have increased this maybe fourfold. It has been estimated that currently the yield would be well over £1000 million per year; owner-occupiers' total imputed rental income in 1975 was £3283 million.[8]

Under taxation conventions the costs of acquiring and maintaining an asset are deductable from the income derived from that asset before tax is levied. Thus mortgage interest and the cost of repairs and maintenance qualify for relief against tax on imputed rental income. One cannot therefore argue that *both* tax relief on mortgage interest *and* exemption from tax on imputed rental income are subsidies to the owner-occupier. But it can, however, be argued that the real subsidy according to consistent principles of taxation is exemption from tax on imputed rent, not tax relief on mortgage interest. Without the tax there is, logically, no justification for the tax relief. It is therefore clearly wrong to argue that outright owners with no interest payments and no tax relief are unsubsidised, since they are the most heavily subsidised by exemption from tax on imputed rent. According to *Housing Policy*, 'Where the home owner is buying his house on mortgage and therefore paying mortgage interest the argument is that, as these interest charges are allowable for tax, a charge on imputed rent is needed to preserve equity with the tenant whose rent is not allowable for tax'.[9]

The argument turns on whether owner-occupied houses are investment goods producing a taxable income or are consumption goods, different in degree but not kind from consumer durables like cars and washing machines on which the benefits derived are not taxed. Tax relief on mortgage interest implies that owner-occupied housing is an asset. If it is argued that it is a consumer durable, then tax relief should be withdrawn. But in fact one can argue strongly that the difference in degree of benefit, life and disposable value turns owner-occupied housing into an asset rather than a consumer durable. Housing is, for example, taken to be an asset by building societies and other institutions which grant loans secured against it, and also when it is owned by landlords and companies.

Introducing a tax on imputed rental income would increase equity both within the owner-occupied sector and between owners and renters; it would encourage repairs and maintenance, since these would be tax-deductible; and would yield tax revenue in excess of £1000 million. Allowing tax relief on mortgage interest would avoid adverse effects on first-time buyers, while outright owners and those with low interest payments on which to claim relief would bear the heaviest burden. The Royal Commission on the Distribution of Income and Wealth concluded: 'In view of the relative size of the benefit which can accrue to an owner occupier we believe there is a strong case for having alternative distributions of income, one including and one excluding imputed rents'.[10] *Housing Policy*, however, does not include exemption from tax on imputed rent as an element of 'general assistance'; it discusses such a tax only briefly and fails to estimate and make explicit the cost and effects of exemption.

Exemption from capital gains tax

As house prices rise above the price an owner originally paid, the owner makes a capital gain. The gain equals the current market price of the house minus its original purchase price, less the amount of any loan still to be repaid. There is currently no tax on capital gains realised in cash terms on a sole or main residence. Since this exemption is uniquely available to home-owners, and tenants receive no equivalent benefit, it can be argued that its value should be counted as an element of assistance to owner-occupiers which is not available to tenants. When framed in 1965, however, capital gains tax specifically exempted owner-occupiers' gains from tax.

It is often suggested that owners' capital gains are unreal, since they cannot be realised in money terms while the owner occupies the house, and that when one house is sold, the next must be bought at similarly inflated prices unless the owner is trading down the market. There are several arguments against this.[11] First, when moving, part of the capital gain is commonly turned into cash by owners borrowing more than they need to cover the difference between the price of the new house and the proceeds from selling the old one. The Department of the Environment Movers Survey indicated that in 1973 over 60 per cent of movers realised net cash proceeds over £500 and 16 per cent realised over £3000, despite the building societies' policy of taking movers' cash proceeds into account in deciding how much they will lend to existing owners. Total proceeds in the UK were almost £400 million.[12] This form of capital gain derives from borrowing, specifically borrowing at rates of interest which do not compensate investors for the falling value of money due to inflation. House-buyers generally have been able, therefore, to borrow at negative interest rates.

Second, the wealth of owners (both borrowers and outright owners) increases whether they choose to realise it in the form of money or of housing. An owner who bought 20 years ago could sell up and start renting from a local authority or private landlord, but with the capital gain from selling the house at current prices in their pocket. The current market value can also be used as mortgage security to raise loans; various commercial schemes have also been developed specifically to generate income for retired persons by capitalising part of the value of their property.

Third, since house-price inflation has consistently outpaced general inflation, owners have made substantial gains over renters –

it has been impossible for renters to obtain returns on investment comparable to those from house-price increases. So even if owners had to plough back all their capital gains when moving house, their gains enable them to keep up with prices, whereas non-owners are increasingly left behind. As Saunders has pointed out, such gains made from uneven inflation are achieved at the expense of new buyers.

Finally it must be remembered that capital gains are ultimately passed on to the owner's heirs or legatees either as cash or a house: 35 per cent (£1770 million) of building-society lending in 1976 went to purchasers of existing housing not being sold by owner-occupiers moving – mainly sales of deceased owners' homes, indicating the scale of the wealth passed on in this way.[13]

Exemption from capital gains tax increases demand for owner-occupied housing as an investment particularly when prices are rising fast. This extra demand drives prices up even faster. Capital invested in housing maintains its value in real terms, whereas most other forms of investment lose against inflation in the long run, even taking interest into account. By facilitating the accumulation of wealth in the form of housing, exemption from tax on owners' capital gains tends to create a gap between owners and renters in terms of housing conditions and costs, and wealth. It has been estimated that capital gains tax at 30 per cent would yield currently about £500 million a year.[14] Again, *Housing Policy* discusses exemption from capital gains tax only briefly and fails to acknowledge it as part of 'general assistance' to owners.

Assistance to owners and council tenants

The relative level of subsidy to owner-occupiers and council tenants has become a major issue in the discussion of housing policy. *Housing Policy* devotes an entire chapter to the subject but concludes: 'There is *no* incontrovertible way of making the comparison between home owners and local authority tenants to show the extent of the advantage of one group over the other – or even to show which group "does better".'[15] The different ways the comparison can be made and the various assumptions and estimates needed produce radically different results, and analyses have more often served to support prejudice over the desirability of one or other form of tenure than form a basis for rational discussion.

Housing Policy defined 'general assistance' as tax relief and option-mortgage subsidy to owners, and exchequer subsidies and rate-fund contributions to local-authority housing costs. In 1977–8 subsidy to house-buyers amounted to £1347 million and to local-authority tenants £1440 million. Dividing these totals by the number of households in each tenure reveals that the average subsidy in 1975–6 was £217 per mortgaged owner-occupier and £215 per local-authority tenant (see Figure 9.3 in the Appendix).[16] Dividing tax relief and option-mortgage subsidy by all owners rather than those with a mortgage produces an average subsidy per household of £121. But since only those paying mortgage interest receive this subsidy, outright owners should not be counted in when calculating the average. If assistance *is* to be averaged over *all* owners, the appropriate subsidy is, logically, exemption from tax on imputed rent rather than tax relief. Rent rebates to local-authority tenants added a further £387 million to the total public-sector assistance and raised the average per tenant to £280 in 1975–6. However, rebates are an element of income support designed to alleviate poverty and should therefore not be counted as a housing subsidy. Since rebates are specifically related to tenants' income, they are excluded from the Green Paper's definition of 'general assistance'.

The cost of subsidies on local-authority rented housing and tax relief on owner-occupied housing can also be compared by estimating subsidy and tax relief generated by a new house in each tenure over the whole of its useful life rather than averaging totals over number of households. *Housing Policy* suggests on this basis that the subsidy on owner-occupied houses might vary from £3305 to £6495, and on local-authority housing from £5630 to £13 805. However, these calculations both ignore any grants towards costs of maintenance or improvement of owner-occupied housing, and assume the council house to be worth nothing after 60 years of useful life while assuming that owner-occupied house-prices rise either at or 2 per cent below the rate of interest. A more realistic range of subsidy on owner-occupied housing may therefore be worked out to be £7129 to £17 217.[17] Purely numerical comparisons are, however, misleading. Local authorities bear the extra costs of high-density building to meet housing needs in inner-urban areas where land is short, and in slum-clearance areas. They bear the extra cost of providing housing for special social needs – sheltered housing, for example, and housing for the disabled. On top of this, local authorities purchasing new housing to add to their stock of housing to let pay higher interest rates than house-buyers – in 1976–7 10.5 per cent (estimated pool rate of interest) as opposed to 7–8 per cent (mortgage rate after basic-rate tax relief). Since both local authorities' building and finance costs are higher per dwelling than in the owner-occupied sector, subsidies per dwelling must obviously be higher as well. Two final qualifications must be made. First, assistance to house-buyers is help towards the cost of acquiring a personal capital asset subsidising future exchange value as well as housing costs or use value. Second, the efficiency of assistance in social and economic terms is related to the recipient's need: £100 is worth more to a family earning £2500 than one earning £5000. Since, despite considerable overlap, local-authority tenants in general earn less than owners, assistance is more efficient pound for pound in the public than private housing sector, particularly remembering the relative distribution of subsidy over the different income groups in each sector.

Home-ownership and housing need

Housing policy is now firmly wedded to the continued expansion of home-ownership within the context of a system of subsidy and taxation which gives substantial support to owner-occupiers. The Labour government fostered co-operation with the building societies and introduced legislation to widen access to home-ownership particularly to lower-income households, which the incoming Conservative administration is likely to support and extend. A strategy to encourage building society lending to lower-income households buying inner city housing was evolved on the basis of increasing guarantees and subsidies to underwrite any increased risk to the societies. Proposals included local-authority topping-up loans and improved guarantees, environmental improvements and improvement and repair grants provided on terms which encouraged building-society lending by increasing the security of loans on older property. Yet even the Labour government was strongly criticised by its own left wing and by other 'radicals' for not going far enough. Greater assistance to first-time buyers and block loans to local authorities or even nationalisation of the societies[18] in pursuit of more liberal lending policies were proposed. Campaigns against 'red lining' and conservative lending policies and in favour of increased state control spurred on the development of policies which increasingly guarantee and subsidise mortgage-lending and support the expansion of owner-occupation. In fact, of course, these proposals and campaigns, radical as they may have seemed, moved *further* in the direction of support for expanding private home-ownership and a housing system based on market forces. Consequently, the vigorous campaigns of a left-wing Labour Member of Parliament like Frank Allaun[19] were loudly re-echoed by such established property interests as the British Property Federation, which both believes that 'building societies could, without losing money, take a considerably greater element of risk over the status of the persons to whom, and the quality of property on which they lend' and 'deplores the cessation of local authority lending to housebuyers',[20] and the Royal Institute of Chartered Surveyors, which recommended that 'as soon as practicable, local authorities should recommence their home loans service'.[21] Those who operate and profit from the private market obviously have an interest in maintaining and expanding the flow of mortgage funds, on which demand, sales and market values depend.

This leaves us with the basic question of the extent to which the expansion of home-ownership represents an effective and appropriate solution to the housing need of lower-income households, and the implications of an expanding owner-occupied sector for the housing system as a whole. It is now fairly widely accepted that there will always be a significant proportion of the population for whom home-ownership is not possible because of their income or employment, because it would be inappropriate or is unwanted. And the Labour government, at least, denied that it intended 'to devise schemes which would lead into home ownership those who cannot realistically be expected to maintain mortgage repayments even with some additional initial assistance'.[22] Yet there is important evidence that already the expansion of owner-occupation among lower-income households, particularly in older housing areas – a specific aim of Labour policy – is causing serious problems.

Poor home-owners

In the first half of 1977 a fifth of all homeless families outside London came directly from owner-occupation, and a further large but unknown proportion came originally from owner-occupation via a stay with relatives or friends.[23] The insignificant level of building-society mortgage arrears and possessions are frequently used as evidence that societies could liberalise lending (see Chapter 8). Yet local authorities, usually lending more generously on older, cheaper housing than the societies, appear to have experienced considerable problems with arrears, suggesting the general problems which could arise with a down-market expansion of owner-occupation. One study in 1976 suggested local-authority arrears were seven times those of building society arrears, although the difference in respect of possessions was smaller; there was considerable variation between authorities, which may in part have reflected different practice in managing arrears cases.[24]

A more detailed analysis by Karn indicates the scale and nature of the arrears problem which may be generated by increased lending on inner-city areas.[25] She studied arrears and possessions in a sample of 400 mortgages granted by Birmingham City Council between 1964 and 1971, up to October 1975; during this period the Council was applying fairly standard income criteria, similar to those operated by building societies, but was more willing to lend on slightly older and cheaper housing, though still not reaching the poorest buyers or oldest, most deteriorated owner-occupied housing. It was found that 21 per cent of mortgages repaid by October 1975 had 'failed' through repossession, or through sale under threat of repossession or with arrears problems on the main or a second mortgage. Of mortgages still outstanding, 16 per cent were 'at risk', mainly through being over six months in arrears. There was an extremely high incidence of second mortgages from finance houses in cases of failure and severe arrears. Karn suggests that, though moves to control second mortgages by finance houses are welcome, these institutions are responding to a need created by the problems of low incomes in relation to house-purchase and maintenance costs; they exacerbate but do not create the debt problem. Exactly the same argument applies where banks and finance houses supply the main loan for house-purchase, again commonly in older inner areas, where they respond to a need which is unmet by more conventional lenders. Karn argues that a safety net must be provided, preferably through enabling local authorities to buy the property and rent it back to households who get into mortgage difficulties. Councils can already do this with the agreement of people in arrears; but a repossessed house must be sold on the open market. Labour's proposed 1979 Housing Bill aimed to relax this stipulation. The provision of a general safety net is appropriate, because mortgage difficulties because of illness, unemployment, marital break-up or expensive repairs etc., which can cause crises for low-income borrowers on tight budgets, are difficult to spot in advance. However, as Karn points out, this would 'make no difference to the fundamental problem of the relationship between incomes and the cost of owner occupation and therefore to the likelihood that the owner will default'.[26]

This study indicates that attention must be focused on the total costs incurred by owner-occupiers, including repayments on second loans to cover deposits, and repair and maintenance costs, as well as payments on the main mortgage. Costs of repairs, maintenance and improvement in particular are crucial in relation to policies aiming to expand inner-city owner-occupation of older, cheaper housing. Older housing means greater repair and maintenance costs; the 1976 house-condition survey indicated that 67 per cent of pre-1914 owner-occupied houses needed repairs costing at least £250, compared with 38 per cent of inter-war and 3 per cent of post-war houses.[27] Owners with heavy mortgage commitments, including second loans perhaps, and maybe also faced with the cost of buying the freehold of their property, cannot easily afford the costs of maintenance or improvement of old, rapidly deteriorating property. Again the problem is the fundamental conflict between incomes and housing costs. Inner-city owner-occupied housing tends therefore to deteriorate, despite government improvement programmes,[28] and though prices of such housing have risen, they have fallen behind the general rate of house-price inflation. Owners find increasing difficulty in selling and in maintaining capital appreciation to enable them to trade up and out of the inner city. In the longer term they face the prospect of being trapped in deteriorating, increasingly obsolete housing of declining capital value.[29] In more general terms policies which see increasing owner-occupation as encouraging improvement and stemming the tide of inner-city decay are likely to be frustrated. To the extent that such policies *do* succeed, real improvements in the stock take place and the cost is borne by the owner-occupiers, it is likely that low-income families will be displaced, and their housing problems shifted elsewhere in the city, by middle-class 'gentrification' and purchasers able to bear the costs of maintenance and improvement.

Proposals to restructure subsidies in the owner-occupied sector to give greater help to lower-income house-buyers by, for example, changes in tax relief might have some impact on the relationship between income and housing costs, and would therefore be welcome. But their effect would be limited: the supply of houses in the lowest price ranges is unlikely to expand much in direct response to this increased demand, since there is limited scope for further contraction of the private rented stock and building costs largely rule out an increase in new housing in the lowest ranges. Nor does evidence suggest that new building higher up the price scale would cause an increased supply of better housing to filter down to the lower ranges of the market.[30] Much of the apparent benefit from increased subsidy to lower-income house-buyers would thus be lost as prices at the bottom of the market were simply pushed up, benefiting existing but not prospective owners. More generally, reforms which liberalise mortgage-lending and widen access to home-ownership must be welcome if in the short term they increase the availability of decent housing to lower-income households for whom the public or private rented sectors provide no alternative. But as a long-term aim of housing policy the continued expansion of home-ownership and particularly the more radical proposals to liberalise and underwrite mortgage-lending are obviously questionable.

Despite the popular ideology of home-ownership, and the property-owning democracy, that 'everybody gains', it is not only those who cannot obtain their own home that lose. It can also be the poor home-owners at the bottom of the scale who lose out in the face of rising maintenance costs, declining asset values and vulnerability to mortgage failure. Thus the division between tenants and owners on which much of the debate over housing policy and levels of subsidy has turned can be misleading. 'The real divide is between those who gain from the working of the new housing market – wealthy owner occupiers and exchange professionals in particular – and those who lose, generally tenants and working class owner occupiers'.[31] Behind the specific problem of housing provision is the basic conflict between low wages in relation to housing costs and the inherent conflict between private investment and social need.

The role of public housing

Public housing has significantly weakened the link between low incomes and poor housing in Britain, and contributed to raising the standard of the housing stock. In the owner-occupied sector, however, housing is allocated by the logic of economic demand, by prices set in the market. Allocation is based on the ability of households to buy rather than in relation to their need for housing. Owners acquire not only the right to occupy housing but also the right to dispose of it on the market for whatever price it will fetch, retaining the proceeds of the sale. They acquire not only the use value of the dwelling but also the exchange value. Council housing is, on the other hand, allocated according to some logic of need, by administrative procedures. Households pay to occupy but cannot dispose of dwellings. They acquire the use value but not the exchange value of the dwelling. The cost of housing to the tenant is based on the historic cost of providing it rather than its current market price, incorporating through the pooled rent system an element of cross subsidisation from tenants of older housing, who pay more than the historic cost of their dwellings, to those of newer housing, who pay less. Within this framework, rent levels are set according to the quantity and quality of accommodation each dwelling unit offers. So the owner-occupied sector is organised by the logic of exchange value and economic demand, the public sector by the logic of use value and social need.

Market mechanisms are such that lower-income families can obtain only the poorest owner-occupied housing. This is inevitable, given great inequality of income and a housing stock which varies greatly in type and quality. This implies that increased emphasis on the provision of public-sector housing is the best solution to the housing problems of low-income households, calling for a halt to council-house sales and building for sale, and an expansion of council building for rent.[32]

The continued expansion of owner-occupation increasingly relegates public housing to a residual, welfare role, socially stigmatised as accommodation for 'second-class citizens'. The growth of home-ownership at the direct expense of the public sector through council-house sales – a policy vigorously pursued by the Conservative government elected in 1979 – accelerates and exacerbates these effects; for it is generally the best of the public housing stock which is sold off and the better-off tenants who buy, with at best a minimal financial gain to local authorities.[33] So long as council housing is conceived of as housing for only those with special needs, provided for those who cannot afford home-ownership, and mainly for working-class families with children, the contrasts with the private sector will be divisive. To prevent this, and to provide real choice in the housing system, the public sector would have to be broadened to provide for general housing needs available to all, completely reversing the policies of the present government.

A significant shift in the balance of taxation and subsidy from better-off home-owners, who currently make substantial financial gains from the housing system, and towards the public sector would facilitate greater balance between the tenures, in terms of access and benefits. But the problems of council housing must be clearly recognised and faced up to. First, the quality of public-sector construction has varied greatly in the past, and certain periods have produced particularly low quality, unpopular housing – the cost-cutting of the 1950s when quality was sacrificed for quantity, and the systems building of the 1960s, which produced the tower blocks in particular. The emphasis in the future must be on good quality design and construction. Second, the quality of management needs funda-mental changes to give tenants greater freedom and, where appro-priate, participation in management. Tenants currently suffer from considerable bureaucratic paternalism, restrictions on the use and modification of their homes, and lack of security of tenure. Recognition of these severe problems does not, however, imply rejecting the public sector as a general form of housing provision. As Murie puts it, 'Restriction on tenants' degree of freedom and independence, paternalism and patronising landlordism are not features of public provision which are made essential by con-sideration of need'.[34] Tenancy agreements giving security of tenure and legal entitlement to repairs and other services in return for rent paid should be introduced, and authorities required to recognise and to negotiate agreements with democratically elected tenants' asso-ciations. Tenants should also have the right to decorate, modify and improve their homes, and be given financial recognition of their investment through rent allowances or payments when they leave the house. Tenant participation and, in particular, the evolution of co-operative housing out of the public sector should be encouraged, possibly on the pattern of Scandinavian countries.[35] In Norway, for example, council housing has been converted to co-operative ownership on an experimental basis in the context of the develop-ment of a charter for tenants' rights and participation in management.

Reform of public housing, coupled with more equitable distri-bution of subsidy within the owner-occupied sector, more socially oriented building-society lending policies, and a shift in housing subsidy towards the public sector, could go far towards achieving real choice and equitable treatment within the housing system as a whole, and breaking the link between low income and bad housing. Inequalities in housing provision reflect and arise from inequalities due to the wider socio-economic structure; but the purpose of social policy in relation to housing should be to break this link. It may be, however, that the existing rights of owner-occupiers over the sale of dwellings, and increased property values, remain inconsistent with the provision of housing as an equitable social service.[36] This implies that the right to sell dwellings at a price determined by market mechanisms cannot be reconciled with a housing system designed to allocate housing according to social need. Thus some form of control over sale, prices and allocation in the private sector may be necessary if households in different tenures are to receive equivalent treatment.

Such a system might involve dwellings being sold to democratically constituted public agencies or co-operatives at a price determined by the purchasing agent, subject to appeal, in relation not to the forces of supply and demand but in relation to the replacement cost of the dwelling. The purchasing agencies would be responsible for allocating dwellings according to social priorities related to need. The design of an efficient and equitable administrative allocative mechanism is a problem to which no satisfactory solution has emerged from debates on the allocation of the existing council stock. But while there is probably no one 'equitable' system possible, it must be borne in mind that attempts to design methods of allocating the existing public stock have been conducted in a context of existing shortage in relation to need and catering for particular groups rather than general housing needs. Such a system of housing agencies would allow for considerable flexibility in forms of tenure, payment, and division of responsibility for management between household and agency. Within the general framework of price control there would be great freedom of choice. In conjunction with the reforms of the present public sector discussed earlier such a scheme would in effect merge the two main forms of housing tenure, eliminating the polarisation of the housing system into owner-occupation versus council housing.

The role of the building societies

Building societies are manifestly efficient financial institutions competing strongly for personal savings and channelling loan finance into the housing market. In the housing system their current role is almost exclusively one of funding individual house purchase. They have a strong vested interest in the maintenance and expansion of home-ownership, since this constitutes the market for their funds and influences their own ability for continued expansion in their present form; this is reinforced by a political and ideological commitment to private housing formed partly in the context of their relations with other agents in the private sector in the fields of house-building, estate agency, finance and insurance. Their character is essentially that of private-sector financial institutions. The need for an adequate and stable flow of mortgage funds and for more equitable lending policies has already been considered (Chapter 8). It has also been argued that housing problems which have been blamed on the societies stem to a large extent from the basic conflict between low wages relative to housing costs and the lack of adequate social housing provision. In the context of the more fundamental changes in the nature of housing provision discussed above, building societies might evolve into general-housing finance agencies. They could, for example, fund the growth of a significant co-operative housing sector, if housing policy developed in this direction. The societies' role is obviously, then, dependent on the evolution of housing policy, and arguments for change in their role must be based in housing policy rather than isolated political or ideological commitment. Control over a proportion of building-society funds or national-isation of major building societies *might* be welcome, but not as an end in itself. The question then raised would be how their funds were to be deployed. The crucial issue would remain, as now, one of housing policy.

Abbreviations

The following abbreviations appear in the sources to the figures, the notes
and references section and the bibliography.

BSA   Building Societies Association.

CRR   *Chief Registrar of Friendly Societies Annual Report: Building
Societies* (HMSO).

HPGP *Housing Policy: a consultative document*, Cmnd. 6851 (HMSO,
1977).

HPTV *Technical Volume* to *Housing Policy: a consultative document*,
parts I, II and III (HMSO, 1977).

RC2   *Royal Commission on Friendly and Benefit Building Societies*, 2nd
Report, Parliamentary Papers, vol. XXVI (HMSO, 1872).

Appendix
The figures

FIGURE 2.1   The growth of financial institutions, 1913–63 (£m)

	1913	1923	1938	1948	1964	1963/1913	1963/1948
Building societies	66	125	759	1 038	4 331	65	4.2
PO savings bank	187	273	524	1 970	1 793	10	0.9
Trustee savings banks	69	103	243	764	1 591	23	2.1
Friendly societies	53	80	152	206	260	5	1.3
Industrial and provident societies	78	188	361	666	1 179	15	1.8
Industrial assurance companies	56	123	359	640	1 297	23	2.0
Other life assurance	380	–	1 322	1 478	4 240	13	3.3
Bank deposit and current accounts	–	1 674	2 277	5 912	7 971	–	1.3
National savings certificates	–	445	519	2 104	2 685	–	1.3

SOURCE: E. J. Cleary, *The Building Society Movement* (Elek, 1965).

FIGURE 2.2 Building society progress, 1900–78

Year end	Number of societies	Share accounts (000s)	Borrowers (000s)	Loans in year (£m)	Total assets (£m)	Total assets at constant prices (£m)*
1900	2 286	585	–	–	60	1 000
1910	1 723	626	–	9	76	1 267
1920	1 271	748	–	25	87	458
1930	1 026	1 449	720	89	371	3 092
1940	952	2 088	1 503	21	756	5 400
1950	819	2 256	1 508	270	1 256	3 221
1960	726	3 910	2 349	560	3 166	5 863
1970	481	10 265	3 655	1 954	*10 819*	*10 819*
1971	467	11 568	3 896	2 705	12 919	10 677
1972	456	12 874	4 126	3 630	15 246	8 565
1973	447	14 385	4 204	3 513	17 545	8 601
1974	416	15 856	4 250	2 945	20 094	9 523
1975	382	17 916	4 397	4 908	24 204	10 170
1976	364	19 991	4 609	6 183	28 202	10 847
1977	339	22 536	4 836	6 745	34 288	12 290
1978	316	24 999	5 108	8 808	39 538	11 466

* Total assets in terms of purchasing power over housing at 1970 prices. House-price index from *British Economy Key Statistics 1900–1970* (London and Cambridge Economic Service, n.d.) and *Occasional Bulletin* (Nationwide Building Society).

SOURCE: *BSA Bulletin* (BSA, 1979), except final column, which are author's calculations.

FIGURE 2.3   Housing completions in England and Wales since 1920

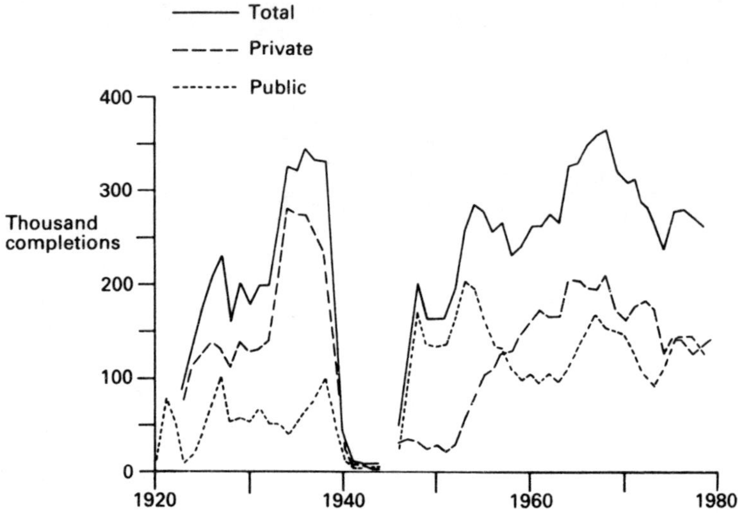

SOURCE: Up to 1965, B. R. Mitchell and H. G. Jones, *Second Abstract of British Historical Statistics*, University of Cambridge Applied Economics Department, Monog. 18 (Cambridge, 1971); 1965 onwards, *Housing Statistics Great Britain* and *Housing and Construction Statistics* (HMSO).

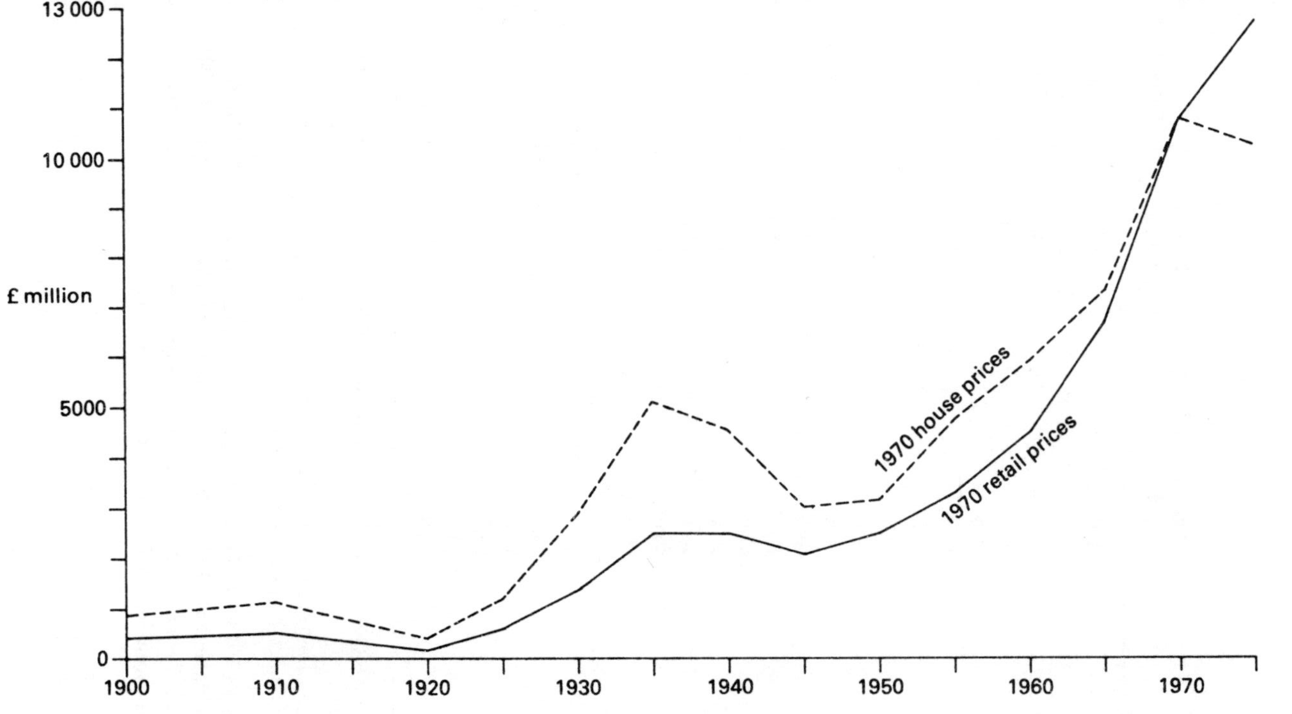

SOURCE: Real value of building societies' total assets expressed in terms of purchasing power over retail-prices and house-prices at 1970 level. Assets from *Building Societies Yearbook* (Franey). House prices index derived from *British Economy Key Statistics 1900–1970* (London and Cambridge Economic Service) and *Occasional Bulletin* (Nationwide Building Society). Retail-prices index derived from *BEKS* 'average value of consumer expenditure' and *Economic Trends* (HMSO) 'all items index'.

FIGURE 2.5   Housing tenure in Britain, 1914–78*

| Year | Percentage of all households | | | |
	Owner-occupied	Public rented†	Private rented	Other‡
1914	10.0	1.0	80.0	9.0
1938	25.0	10.0	56.0	9.0
1945	26.0	12.0	54.0	8.0
1951	29.0	18.0	45.0	8.0
1956	34.0	23.0	36.0	7.0
1960	42.0	27.0	26.0	6.0
1961	43.0	27.0	25.0	6.0
1962	44.0	27.0	24.0	5.0
1963	44.6	28.0	22.0	5.4
1964	45.6	28.1	20.9	5.4
1965	46.5	28.2	19.9	5.4
1966	47.1	28.7	18.8	5.4
1967	47.9	29.2	17.7	5.3
1968	48.8	29.5	16.6	5.3
1969	49.4	30.0	15.8	5.2
1970	50.0	30.4	14.9	5.1
1971	50.5	30.6	18.8	
1972	51.5	30.5	18.0	
1973	52.3	30.5	17.2	
1974	52.7	30.8	16.5	
1975	53.0	31.3	15.7	
1976	53.3	31.7	15.0	
1977	53.6	31.9	14.5	
1978	53.9	32.3	13.8	

* Discrepancies in additions in this table and in others are due to rounding.

† Local authorities and new towns, and other public bodies.

‡ Includes housing associations.

SOURCE: 1914–56, D. Butler and A. Sloman, *British Political Facts 1900–1975* (Macmillan, 1975). 1960–77, *Annual Abstract of Statistics* (HMSO); *Housing Trends*, first quarter 1979 (Nationwide Building Society); 1978 figures estimated by Nationwide Building Society.

FIGURE 2.6   The regional pattern of housing tenure in 1977

	Total number (000s)	Percentage of total number		
		Owner-occupied	Public rented*	Private rented†
Northern	1 171	45.1	40.8	14.1
Yorks and Humberside	1 834	53.6	32.9	13.5
North West	2 416	57.8	30.5	11.7
East Midlands	1 413	55.8	29.5	14.7
West Midlands	1 864	54.8	34.2	11.0
East Anglia	701	56.2	27.1	16.7
Greater London	2 709	47.5	30.6	21.9
Rest of South East	3 657	61.1	24.6	14.3
South West	1 626	62.1	22.3	15.6
England	17 391	55.5	29.6	14.9
Wales	1 042	58.8	29.0	12.2
Scotland	1 942	34.1	54.4	11.5
Great Britain	20 375	53.6	31.9	14.5

* Local authorities and new towns.
† Includes housing associations and other tenures.

SOURCE: *Housing and Construction Statistics*, No. 25 (HMSO, 1978).

FIGURE 2.7   Socio-economic group and income of households in different tenures in 1977, Great Britain (%)

	Owners		Tenants		
	Outright owners	Mortgaged owners	Local authority	Unfurnished private	Furnished private
Socio-economic group					
Professional and managerial	27	34	6	16	20
Intermediate and junior non-manual	22	23	14	21	36
Skilled manual etc.	33	33	48	35	22
Semi-skilled manual etc.	14	8	23	22	18
Unskilled	4	1	9	6	5
Income					
Up to £1500	7	1	5	10	16
£1500–£2999	32	16	43	41	45
£3000–3999	29	32	35	28	27
£4000 or over	33	51	17	21	13

SOURCE: Derived from *Social Trends*, No. 9 (HMSO, 1979).

FIGURE 3.1   Assets of institutions holding mainly personal savings, 1966–78 (£ million)

Year end	Building societies	National savings	Trustee savings banks	Unit trusts*	Personal bank deposits	Insurance companies†	Private superannuation funds	Building societies' share of total (%)
1966	6 350	8 335	2 151	553	7 466	10 596	3 365	16
1967	7 523	8 472	2 272	788	8 250	11 802	3 719	18
1968	8 357	8 547	3 265	1 349	8 932	13 164	4 280	18
1969	9 336	8 452	2 411	1 344	9 240	14 201	4 468	19
1970	10 940	8 589	2 542	1 316	10 062	15 452	4 673	20
1971	13 067	9 220	2 797	1 953	11 015	17 100	6 175	21
1972	15 386	10 103	3 155	2 553	12 910	19 101	7 028	22
1973	17 709	10 438	3 366	2 097	16 317	22 918	6 199	22
1974	20 289	10 599	3 535	1 407	19 290	24 357	5 108	24
1975	24 364	11 320	3 849	2 555	19 373	27 819	7 706	25
1976	28 131	12 350	4 217	2 622	20 736	30 695	9 156	26
1977	34 680	14 640	4 534	3 432	21 266	35 377	12 760	28
1978	39 692	16 424	4 999	3 873	24 490	40 034	14 431	28

* Market values.
† Book values. Includes the holdings of Commonwealth companies' life funds, 1967–75.

SOURCE: *Factual Background* (Bristol and West Building Society).

FIGURE 3.2   Personal savings institutions: net investment from personal sector, 1966–78 (£ million)

Year	Building society shares and deposits	Local authority securities	Bank deposits	Unit trusts	Life assurance and superannu- ation funds	All national savings	Trustee savings banks	Building societies' share of total (%)
1966	724	246	250	105	1 241	−35	121	27
1967	1 099	129	740	84	1 372	125	121	30
1968	767	191	682	258	1 508	77	93	22
1969	895	226	308	186	1 507	−113	46	29
1970	1 490	−45	822	89	1 735	107	131	34
1971	2 034	−232	953	46	1 930	612	255	36
1972	2 193	−82	1 767	203	2 935	813	358	28
1973	2 162	358	3 381	162	3 354	268	211	22
1974	1 993	725	2 973	31	3 493	45	169	21
1975	4 172	749	989	100	4 426	632	314	37
1976	3 405	1 799	1 320	78	5 398	791	368	26
1977	6 099	502	561	26	6 121	1 916	317	39
1978	4 879	202	3 239	116	7 976	2 130	468	26

SOURCE: *Financial Statistics* (HMSO).

FIGURE 3.3 Annual net amount loaned for house purchase (total loaned − amount repaid) by building societies, insurance companies, local authorities and banks, 1959–78, UK

Year	Building societies		Insurance companies		Local authorities†		Banks		Total*
	£m	%	£m	%	£m	%	£m	%	£m
1959	231	64	35	10	26	7	70	19	362
1960	240	63	68	18	42	11	30	8	380
1961	221	55	81	20	67	17	30	8	399
1962	276	67	61	15	47	11	30	7	414
1963	422	74	34	6	59	10	55	10	570
1964	546	72	53	7	121	16	35	5	755
1965	459	65	91	13	168	24	−15	−2	703
1966	667	88	61	8	53	7	−25	−3	756
1967	823	85	34	4	68	7	40	4	965
1968	860	89	71	7	9	1	25	3	965
1969	782	93	83	10	−18	−2	−5	−1	842
1970	1 088	88	36	3	72	6	40	3	1 236
1971	1 600	92	13	1	107	6	90	5	1 736
1972	2 215	80	2	–	198	7	345	12	2 761
1973	1 999	72	121	4	355	13	310	11	2 785
1974	1 490	68	120	5	559	23	90	4	2 202
1975	2 768	81	67	2	620	16	60	2	3 428
1976	3 618	97	13	–	67	1	70	2	3 737
1977	4 100	96	22	1	5	−1	120	4	3 921
1978	5 096	95	47	1	−57	−1	270	5	5 356

* Excludes advances by new towns and the Housing Corporation, which totalled: 1971, £12 million; 1972, £22 million; 1973, £46 million; 1974, £113 million; 1975, £135 million; 1976, £105 million; 1977, £28 million; 1978, £ −34 million.
† Includes loans for improvement etc., housing associations, and sale of council houses.

SOURCE: *Housing and Construction Statistics* (HMSO).

FIGURE 3.4   Sources of finance for house purchase and average price paid in England and Wales, 1973

	First-time purchasers		Existing owners	
	% of buyers	Average price (£)	% of buyers	Average price (£)
Building society	71	7 680	63	11 630
Local authority	12	5 945	2	6 935
Insurance company	4	8 280	5	14 490
Bank	3	7 840	5	13 265
Private loan	3	5 680	2	11 905
Ready money*	6	6 095	24	10 515

* Proceeds of previous sale or money available.

SOURCE: *HPTV*, II, Table VII.1.

FIGURE 3.5   Building societies' aggregate balance sheet, 1978

Liabilities	£m	% of total	*Assets*	£m	% of total
Shares and deposits	37 334	98.4	Mortgage assets	31 598	79.9
Taxation and other	622	1.6	Investment	6 064	15.3
			Cash	1 351	3.4
			Office premises	458	1.1
			Other	67	0.2
Total	**38 062**	**100.0**	**Total**	**39 538**	**99.9**
Reserves (assets minus liabilities)				**1 476**	**3.7**

SOURCE: *CRR* (1978).

FIGURE 3.6   Flow of building society funds, 1978

Sources of funds	£m	%
Net increase in shares and deposits*	3 535	33
Mortgage capital repayments	3 615	34
Mortgage interest payments	2 770	26
Interest and net profits from cash and investments	733	7
Insurance commission	65	1
Miscellaneous (net)	9	–
Total	**10 726**	**101**

Figure 3.6 (*continued*)

Use of funds	£m	%
Mortgage loans	8 808	82
Added to holdings of cash and investments	5	–
Interest paid out on shares and deposits†	660	6
Taxation	817	8
Management expenses (excluding depreciation)	341	3
Office premises and other fixed assets	95	1
Total	**10 726**	**100**

* £16 355 million receipts minus £12 820 million withdrawals.

† As opposed to credited to investors' accounts, thus increasing shares and deposits. Total interest due on shares and deposits in 1978 was £1 735 million, of which £1 173 million was credited to accounts.

SOURCE: *CRR* (1978).

Figure 3.7   Building societies' income and expenditure, 1978

Income	£m	%
Mortgage interest (including option mortgages)	2 770	79
Investment and bank interest	661	19
Commission	8	–
Rents from letting office premises	10	–
Total	**3 506**	**99**
Expenditure		
Management expenses	363	11
Share, deposit and loan interest	2 244	67
Income tax on share and deposit interest	667	20
Corporation tax	90	3
Total	**3 364**	**101**
Income minus expenditure	142	
Exceptional or non-recurrent items (net)	70	
Added to general reserves	**212**	

SOURCE: *CRR* (1978).

FIGURE 3.8   Size distribution of the societies, 1977

Size	Number	Assets (£m)	% of number	% of assets
Largest five societies*	5	18 391	1.5	53.6
Others over £100 million assets	27	12 045	8.0	35.1
Assets £25–100 million	49	2 675	14.5	7.8
Assets £2–25 million	132	1 105	38.9	3.2
Assets below £2 million	126	72	37.2	0.2
All societies	339	34 288	100.0	100.0

  * Halifax, Abbey National, Nationwide, Leeds Permanent, Woolwich Equitable.

SOURCE: *CRR* (1977).

FIGURE 3.9   Societies, branches and mergers, 1966–78

Year end	Societies*	Branches	Societies merging in the year
1966	576	1 213	14
1967	554	1 542	21
1968	525	1 662	27
1969	504	1 807	24
1970	481	2 016	22
1971	467	2 216	16
1972	456	2 522	13
1973	447	2 808	10
1974	416	3 099	30
1975	382	3 375	32
1976	364	3 696	13
1977	339	4 130	18
1978	316	4 411	22

  * The change in numbers of societies from year to year reflects societies removed from the register for reasons other than mergers (e.g. dissolution), and also new societies registered. Mergers include 'engagements transferred' and 'unions'.

SOURCE: *CRR* (1978).

FIGURE 3.10   Concentration of building society assets, 1930–78

Year end*	Largest five societies (%)	Largest 20 societies (%)	Total assets (£m)
1930	39.1	65.0	371
1940	38.0	60.7	756
1950	37.3	62.5	1 256
1960	45.3	68.6	3 166
1970	50.1	77.4	10 819
1975	52.9	82.3	24 204
1976	53.7	82.8	28 202
1977	53.6	83.3	34 288
1978	54.4	84.0	39 713

* Balance sheet dates differ between societies such that there is small error in the figures but a realistic trend.

SOURCE: *BSA Bulletin*, No. 16 (BSA, October 1978).

FIGURE 3.11   Other directorships held by directors of the Halifax Building Society in 1978

G. N. Hunter (vice-chairman)
Hillards Ltd (chmn)
Hunter and Smallpage Ltd (chmn)
John Foster and Son Ltd
Robert Glew and Co Ltd
Wormalds, Walker and Atkinson Ltd (chmn)

T. J. Burrows
Curry and Co Ltd

J. L. Hanson
Parkland Textiles (Holdings) Ltd
Park Land Hotel Ltd

D. I. Hunter
of Henry Cooke, Lumsden & Co, stockbrokers
Arkwright Nominees Ltd
CS Nominees Ltd
English National Investment Co Ltd

Henry Cooke, Plan Investment Ltd (chmn)
Lindow Investment Co Ltd
Hallstead Securities Ltd
OCH Nominees Ltd
Pownall Investment Co Ltd
Ridgefield Nominees Ltd
St Ann's Trust

A. S. Monckton
Penk (Holdings) Ltd (chmn and man.)
Penk Ltd (chmn and man. dir.)
Penk Products Ltd (chmn)

Sir James H. I. Whittaker (vice-chairman)
Auchanfree Estate Co
Auchanfree Shareholding Co Ltd
Babworth Home Farm Ltd
Economic Forestry Group Ltd

FIGURE 3.11 (*continued*)

Economic Forestry Holdings Ltd
Forest Farms (Babworth) Ltd
Hesley Estates Co
Moorside Investment Trust Ltd
National Carbonising Co Ltd
Tiln Bulbs Ltd
Tiln Farms Ltd
Updown Investment Trust Ltd
United World College of the Atlantic

J. H. Denham
Bradford Pty Trust Ltd (man.) and subsidiaries
Cliffe Hill Second Investments Ltd

R. P. Hornby
J. Walter Thompson Co Ltd

A. N. Stockdale
Associated Dairies Ltd (chmn and dir.) and four subsidiaries

Adel Investment Trust Ltd
Asda Stores Ltd and two subsidiaries
Austragrades Chemists Ltd
Bramhams Foods Ltd
15 dairy and creamery companies
Farm Stores Ltd
G. E. M. Super Centres Ltd
Greens of Mexborough Ltd
Grimshawe Holdings Ltd
Independent Garages Ltd
J. Bradbury and Sons Ltd
Leeds Cricket, Football and Athletic Co Ltd
Manor Garage (Wakefield) Ltd
Moorlea Garages Ltd
Moorlea Garages Factors Ltd
P. R. Grimshawe and Co Ltd
Robert Hardman Ltd
Steeton Investments Ltd
Valu Petroleum Co Ltd

Also directors of the Halifax but without other recorded directorships were Sir Raymond Potter (chairman), T. I. Kerr, D. S. W. Lee, M. Macaskill (general manager), M. Mackintosh, J. O. Spalding (general manager), F. G. Sykes (general manager), and A. J. Thayre (chief general manager), the last four having the position of executive directors.

SOURCE: *Building Societies Yearbook* (Franey, 1978); *Directory of Directors* (Thomas Skinner Directories, 1978).

FIGURE 3.12 Building society connections in Tyne and Wear county

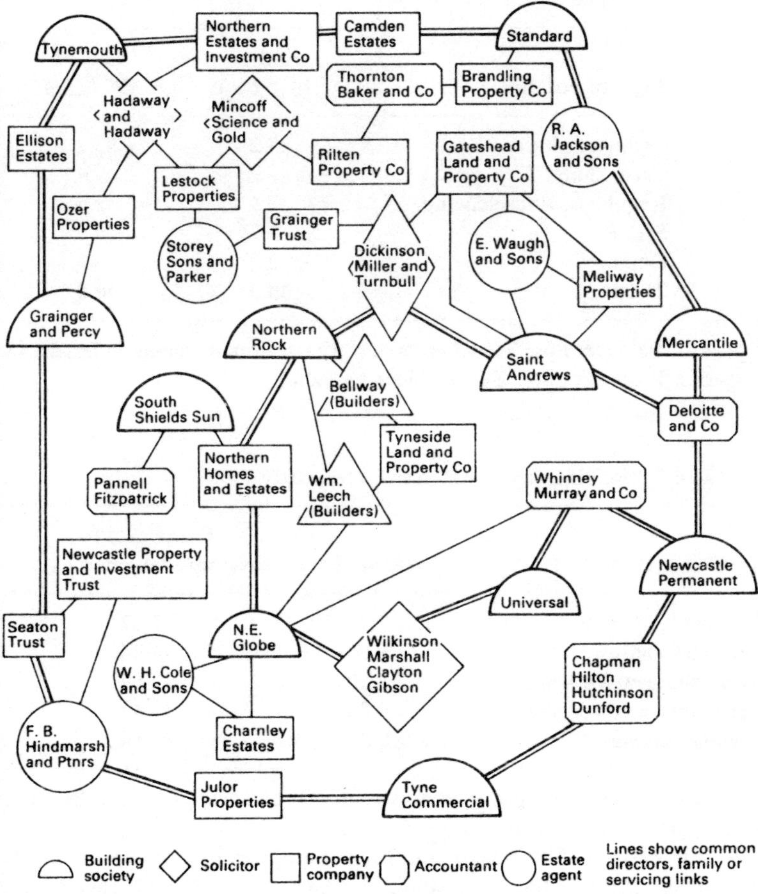

SOURCE: *Profits Against Houses* (Community Development Project Information and Intelligence Unit, 1976).

FIGURE 4.1   Proportion of total investment in building societies in different types of account

Type of account	End of 1975 (%)	End of 1977 (%)
Ordinary shares	85.2	83.2
Term shares	7.2	9.4
Regular savings schemes	2.4	2.5
SAYE	1.2	0.9
Deposit	3.5	3.9
Total	**100.0**	**100.0**

SOURCE: BSA (see note 7 to Chapter 4, p. 193). Estimate based on largest 18 societies. Properties are of investment by value.

FIGURE 4.2   Building-society interest rates, early 1979

Type of account†	Net rate (%)	Gross rate to basic-rate taxpayer (%)*
Deposit	7.75	11.57
Ordinary shares	8.00	11.94
Term shares (two years)	8.50	12.69
Term shares (three years)	9.00	13.43
Regular savings	9.25	13.80

* Gross rate assuming income tax at 33 per cent. Gross rate = net rate × (100/100 − tax rate).

† Subject to a £15 000 maximum. Term shares usually require a minimum investment (£100–£1000, depending on the society). Regular savings are usually limited to a maximum per month (typically £50).

These rates were typical of large societies in early 1979. Many smaller societies were offering slightly more, usually up to 0.25 % extra. These figures indicate the general structure of rates for the different types of account. Current actual levels are given in the *Building Societies Gazette*.

FIGURE 4.3 Market penetration of different forms of saving and investment

Type of account	Percentage of UK adults	
	1970/1	1975/6
Clearing bank current accounts	30	38
Clearing bank deposit/savings accounts	16	18
Other bank deposits	n.a.	9
Building society accounts	20	34
National Savings Bank accounts	25	25
Trustee Savings Bank accounts	n.a.	13
Endowment assurance	42	44
Unit trusts	6	9
Stocks and shares	6	7

SOURCE: BSA (see note 7 to Chapter 4, p. 193) from *The London Clearing Banks* (evidence by the Committee of London Clearing Banks to the Committee to Review the Functioning of Financial Institutions, 1978), derived from Target Group Index.

FIGURE 4.4 Percentage of households' financial assets held by different investment institutions, 1966 and 1976

	1966	1976
Building societies	8.3	17.8
Banks	10.4	13.6
National savings	11.5	7.9
Central and local government securities	7.5	6.2
Company securities	26.9	16.5
Unit trusts	0.7	1.2
Equity in life assurance and pension funds	20.8	25.3

SOURCE: BSA (see note 7 to Chapter 4, p. 193), calculated from 'Personal Sector Balance Sheets', *Economic Trends* (January 1978).

FIGURE 4.5   Social class of investors

| Type of investment | Percentage of social class investing | | Ratio of A–B to D–E |
	A–B	D–E	
Current bank account	67.2	14.3	4.7
Bank deposit account	29.5	13.2	2.2
Building society	40.8	12.1	3.4
Life assurance	31.3	21.1	1.5
National Savings Bank	17.1	10.8	1.6
Stocks and shares	15.4	0.5	30.8
Trustee Savings Bank	7.5	10.5	0.7

SOURCE: Economists Advisory Group (see note 8 to Chapter 4, p. 193). According to the Registrar-General's classification, A and B represent higher and intermediate managerial, administrative, and professional occupations, and D and E semi-skilled and unskilled manual occupations and state pensioners.

FIGURE 4.6   Analysis of size of building-society accounts

Size category	Number of accounts (000s)	Percentage of total	Balances held (£m)	Percentage of total
Up to £100	7 418	31.1	191	0.6
Over £100 up to £500	5 417	22.7	1 422	4.5
Over £500 up to £1000	3 239	13.6	2 404	7.6
Over £1000 up to £2000	3 089	13.0	4 459	14.1
Over £2000 up to £5000	3 046	12.8	9 862	31.2
Over £5000 up to £10 000	1 343	5.7	9 474	29.9
£10 000 and over	266	1.1	3 830	12.1
Total	**23 818**	**100.0**	**31 642**	**100.0**

SOURCE: BSA (see note 7 to Chapter 4, p. 193). The figures are based on returns provided by 11 societies, representing 71.0 per cent of total investment balances. SAYE balances are excluded.

FIGURE 5.1   Structure of annual payments on a capital repayment mortgage

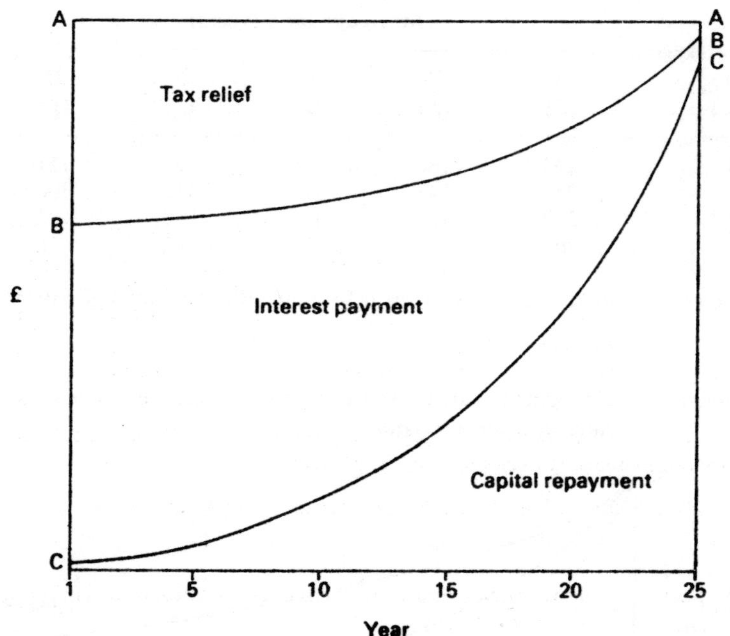

Shows capital repayment, interest payment and tax relief at the basic, 33 per cent, rate over the life of a 25-year repayment mortgage in constant money terms and constant interest rate.

A   = gross payment before tax relief, capital and interest.
B   = net payment after tax relief at 33 per cent.
C   = capital repayment.
AB = 33 per cent AC.
AC = gross interest before tax relief.

FIGURE 5.2   Monthly mortgage repayments, mortgage term and interest rates

Mortgage rate (%)	Mortgage term (years)				
	5 (£)	10 (£)	15 (£)	20 (£)	25 (£)
14	243	160	136	126	121
12	231	148	122	112	106
10	220	136	110	98	92
8	209	124	97	85	78

Shows monthly mortgage payments before tax relief on a loan of £10 000.

FIGURE 5.3   Mortgage payments as a proportion of income given various rates of income inflation

Shows average mortgage payments for a typical loan repaid over 25 years with the mortgage rate at 11 per cent, as a percentage of average income in the mid-1970s.

FIGURE 5.4   Mortgage repayments and earnings, 1963 and 1970–8

Purchased April of	Average new house price (£)	Average initial mortgage repayment (£ p.a.)	Average earnings (£ p.a.)	Average initial repayments as a percentage of average earnings*	Average actual repayments in April 1976 (£ p.a.)	Average actual repayments as a percentage of average earnings in April 1976
1963	3 156	198	933	21	277	7
1970	5 082	398	1 543	26	475	13
1971	5 630	440	1 725	26	528	14
1972	6 947	521	1 922	27	656	18
1973	10 023	850	2 179	39	951	26
1974	11 160	1 061	2 446	43	1 061	29
1975	12 273	1 166	3 162	37	1 166	31
1976	13 309	1 219	3 734	33	1 264	34
1977	14 274	1 381	4 087	34	n.a.	n.a.
1978	16 843	1 318	4 702	28	n.a.	n.a.

* Initial repayments based on an 80 per cent loan at recommended mortgage rate on house of average price, and *before* tax relief. Earnings are the average for fully employed males over 21 years.

SOURCE: *BSA Bulletin*, No. 7 (1976), and No. 15 (1978) (BSA).

Figure 5.5   'Front loading' of mortgage payments as a proportion of income

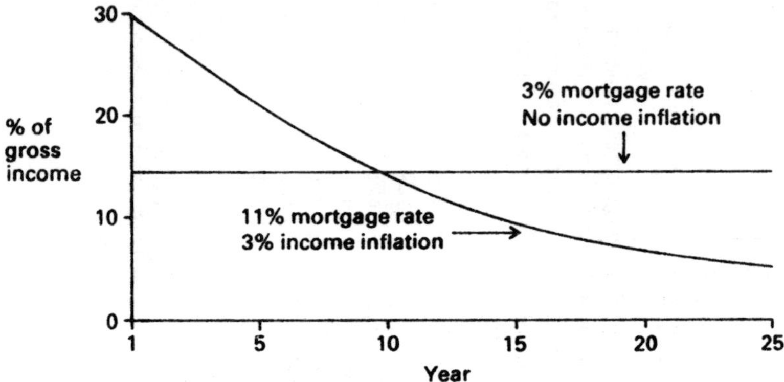

Source: *HPTV*, I, Table IV. 23.

Figure 5.6   Typical building-society lending criteria

Class of property

A. Properties built since 1930 of conventional construction, structurally sound, well maintained, with garage or space and in an appropriate residential location.

   Properties built pre-1930 of conventional construction which are structurally sound, have been modernised, rewired as appropriate, have been well maintained, with garage or garage space and are in an appropriate location.

   Purpose-built flats with a minimum unexpired term of not less than 80 years.

B. Properties built since 1930 which, through lack of one or more of the requirements defined for Class A properties, do not qualify for that classification.

   Properties built during period 1918 to 1930 which are structurally sound but which fall short of a Class A grading.

   Flats or maisonettes which fall short of top grading.

C. Pre-1918 housing, particularly terraced houses, lacking garage space and in a secondary location but otherwise structurally sound and modernised.

D. Properties which for particular reasons are only of a minimal acceptable standard. Unmodernised properties could go into this category with proper assurances for modernisation being given.

Figure 5.6 (*continued*)

Class	Maximum term (years)	Maximum loan as % of valuation	
		Without insurance	With insurance
A	25	80	95
B	25	75	95
C	20	70	90
D	15	60	80

Maximum loan as a multiple of income (9.7 per cent mortgage rate)
    30-year term 3 times gross annual salary
    25-year term $2\frac{3}{4}$ times gross annual salary
    20-year term $2\frac{1}{2}$ times gross annual salary
    15-year term $2\frac{1}{4}$ times gross annual salary
    10-year term 2 times gross annual salary

1. This is a *typical* example. Individual societies vary and do not apply rigid criteria to individual applications.
2. Loans may be subject to retentions or undertakings to complete repairs.
3. Gross salary normally discounts bonus, overtime etc; but where these form a regular and recognised element of income, 50 per cent may be taken into account. The multiple factor will usually be applied to the higher income in the case of husband and wife and the maximum loan increased by an amount equivalent to one year's income of the other partner.

SOURCE: H. R. Walden, 'Building Society Lending Policies', in *Co-operation Between Building Societies and Local Authorities* (BSA, 1978).

FIGURE 5.7   Characteristics of UK building-society borrowers, 1978

	Percentage of number of loans granted		
	All buyers	First-time buyers	Former owner-occupiers
Income p.a.			
Under £4000	22	27	18
£4000–£4999	22	24	21
£5000–£6999	33	33	33
£7000 and over	23	16	29
Age			
Under 25	18	33	6
25–29	25	29	23
30–34	22	17	27
35–44	21	13	28
45–54	10	6	12
55 and over	3	2	4
Amount borrowed			
Under £7000	21	21	20
£7000–£9999	29	34	24
£10 000–£12 999	28	30	26
£13 000 and over	23	15	29
Summary			
Proportion of all loans	100	47	53
Houses costing under £9000	15	26	9
Borrowers earning under £5000	44	51	39
Borrowers under 25	18	33	6
Loans over 94 per cent of purchase price	10	18	3
Deposit under £1000	21	39	5

SOURCE: *BSA Bulletin*, No. 18 (BSA, 1979).

FIGURE 5.8 Characteristics of dwellings mortgaged to building societies in UK, 1978

House-price	Percentage of number of loans granted		
	All buyers	First-time buyers	Former owner-occupiers
Under £9000	15	26	6
£9000–£10 999	15	21	9
£11 000–£12 999	16	20	12
£13 000–£14 999	13	14	13
£15 000–£19 999	21	14	27
£20 000 and over	20	6	32

Age and type of house	Percentage of number of loans granted					
	Pre-1919	1919–39	1940–60	Post-1960	New	All ages
Bungalow	–	2	1	5	2	10
Detached house	3	3	1	8	7	22
Semi-detached house	4	9	3	12	5	3
Terraced house	13	4	1	5	3	7
Flat	3	1	–	2	1	8
All dwellings	24	19	7	32	18	100

House-price, income and loan size, 1970–8

	Average (£)			Ratios		
	House-price	Loan	Income	Loan/price	Price/income	Loan/income
1970	4 975	3 591	1 928	72.2	2.58	1.86
1971	5 632	4 104	2 187	72.9	2.58	1.88
1972	7 374	5 195	2 474	70.5	2.98	2.10
1973	9 942	6 181	2 923	62.2	3.40	2.11
1974	10 990	6 568	3 411	59.8	3.22	1.93
1975	11 787	7 347	4 036	62.3	2.92	1.82
1976	12 704	8 288	4 644	65.2	2.74	1.78
1977	13 650	8 819	5 193	64.6	2.63	1.70
1978	15 594	10 144	5 746	65.1	2.71	1.76

SOURCE: *BSA Bulletin*, No. 19 (BSA, 1979); and *Housing and Construction Statistics* (HMSO).

FIGURE 5.9   Red-line areas and areas of minimal building society lending

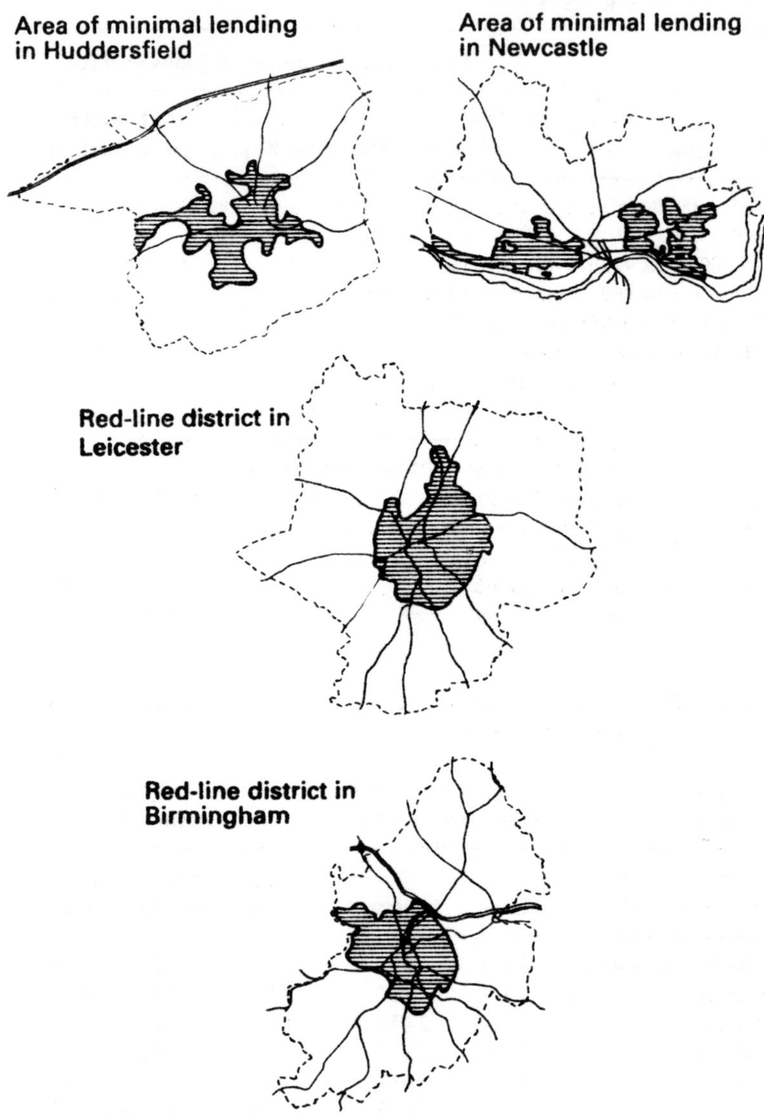

SOURCE: *Roof* (July 1976).

FIGURE 5.10   Local-authority mortgage-lending constraints

Financial year(s)	Constraint	Circular(s)
1965–8	Annual lending in any authority not to exceed average for three years prior to April 1965 (£130 million)	62/65, 65/65, 7/67, 68/67
1968–9	80 per cent of previous year (£104 million)	41/68
1969–70	£30 million first six months, £25 million second six months (£55 million)	8/69, 75/69
1970–1	£155 million	29/70
1971–5	No limit on lending in priority categories	22/71, 39/72
1975–6	£250 million (at 1974 survey prices) and 50 per cent of 1974–5 lending in each authority	64/75
1976–7	£220 million (at 1975 survey prices). Expenditure up to 85 per cent of allocation authorised	80/76

FIGURE 5.11   Loans on older property by building societies and local authorities, 1975

Age of property	% of building-society loans	% of local-authority loans
Pre-1919		
Under £4000	4	23
£4000–£5999	18	25
£6000 and above	77	51
All prices	19	62
Inter-war	19	20
Post-war	43	12
New	19	6
(Total loans)	(651 000)	(102 000)

SOURCE: Derived from *HPTV*, II, Table VII. 7.

FIGURE 5.12   Building-society and local-authority mortgages, 1975

	Building societies	Local authorities
Total loans granted	601 000	102 000
Average purchase price (£)	9 549*	7 130*
Average loan size (£)	7 292*	6 420*
Average ratio of loan to price (%)	76*	90*
Average ratio of loan to income (%)	1.94*	1.99*
First-time buyers (%)	47	88
Borrowers under 25 (%)	33*	46
Borrowers earning under £2500 p.a. (%)	41	16
Borrowers earning over £5000 p.a. (%)	7	21
Pre-1919 houses (%)	19	62
Houses costing under £6000 (%)	57	7
Houses costing over £12 000 (%)	6	36
Option mortgages (%)	20*	53
Low-start loans (%)	–	11
Loans over 95 per cent of purchase price (%)	1*	33*

* Refers to first-time buyers only; since local authorities lend predominantly to this category, this provides a more meaningful comparison.

NOTE: Percentages indicate the proportion of loans from each source individually in each category, not the proportion of all loans from both sources.

SOURCE: Building Societies Mortgage Survey and Local Authority Mortgage Survey, Reproduced in *HPTV*, II, Ch. 7, and *Fact and Figures*, No. 9 (BSA, 1977).

FIGURE 6.1   Investment yields on personal savings, January 1979 (£%)

	Stated yield*	Equivalent gross yield at tax of 33%*
Building societies, £15 000 maximum per society		
Deposits	7.75	11.57
Shares	8.00	11.94
Three-year term shares: £100–£1000 min.	9.00	13.43
Regular savings	9.25	13.81
Four-year insurance-linked	11.87	17.72
Savings certificates, 18th issue, 5 years	8.45	12.61
National Savings Bank investment dept	12.00	12.00
Finance house deposits, three-month	12.88	12.88
Bank deposits, average	10.00	10.00
SAYE, 2nd issue, seven years	8.62	12.87
Local authorities, varies, three-month	12.44	12.44
Trustee Savings Bank, special deposits	8.00	8.00

* Stated yields represent the return to a non-taxpayer. Equivalent gross yield represents the return to a basic (33 per cent) taxpayer.

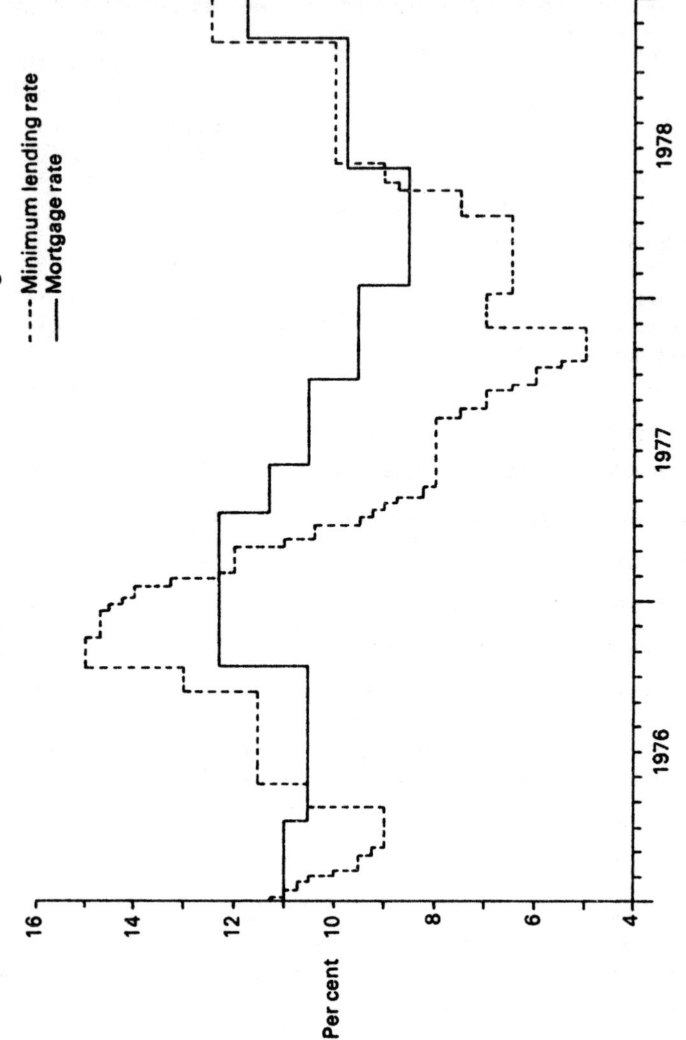

FIGURE 6.2   Building societies' mortgage rate and bank minimum lending rate

SOURCE: *Financial Statistics* (HMSO).

FIGURE 6.3   Building-society competitiveness and net receipts, 1973–8

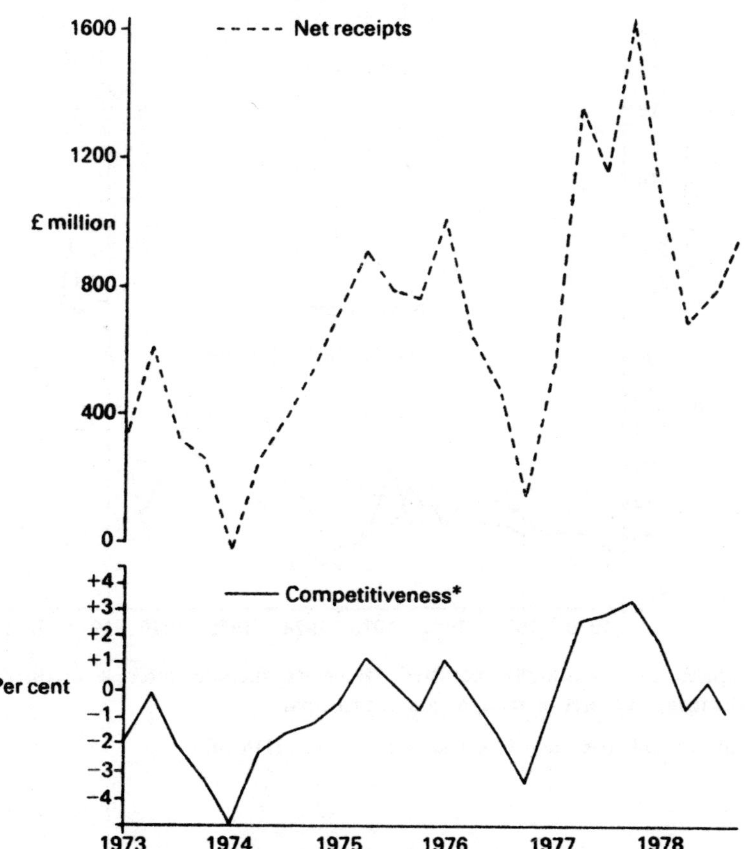

* Competitiveness measured as recommended building-society share rate grossed-up at the basic (standard) rate of income tax, minus the local-authority three-month deposit rate. The latter has been shown to be the best proxy for the general level of interest rates against which societies compete.

SOURCE: *Evidence submitted by the BSA to the Committee to Review the Functioning of Financial Institutions* (BSA, 1978) p. 29.

FIGURE 6.4   Receipts, liquidity and mortgage lending, 1970–8

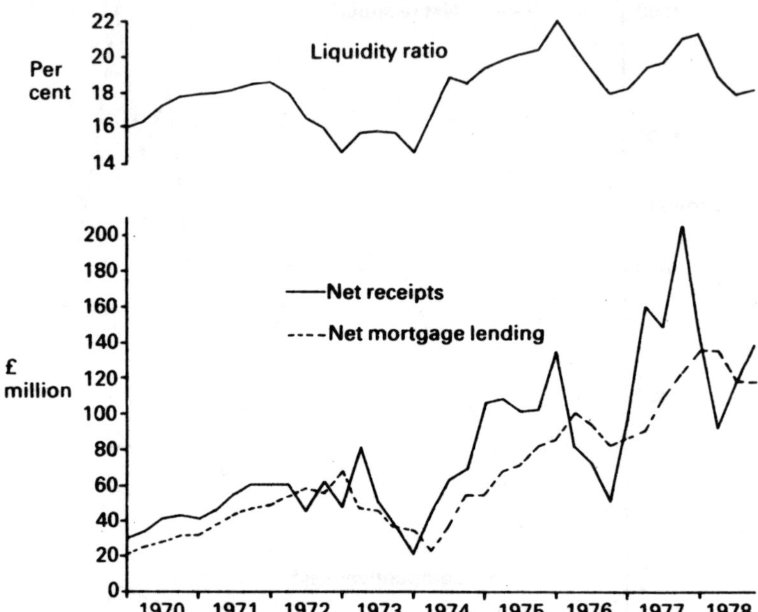

Figures are seasonally adjusted. Receipts include interest credited. Mortgages are net of repayments of principal.

SOURCE: *Housing and Construction Statistics* (HMSO).

FIGURE 7.1 Mortgage-lending, house-building and house-prices, 1970–8

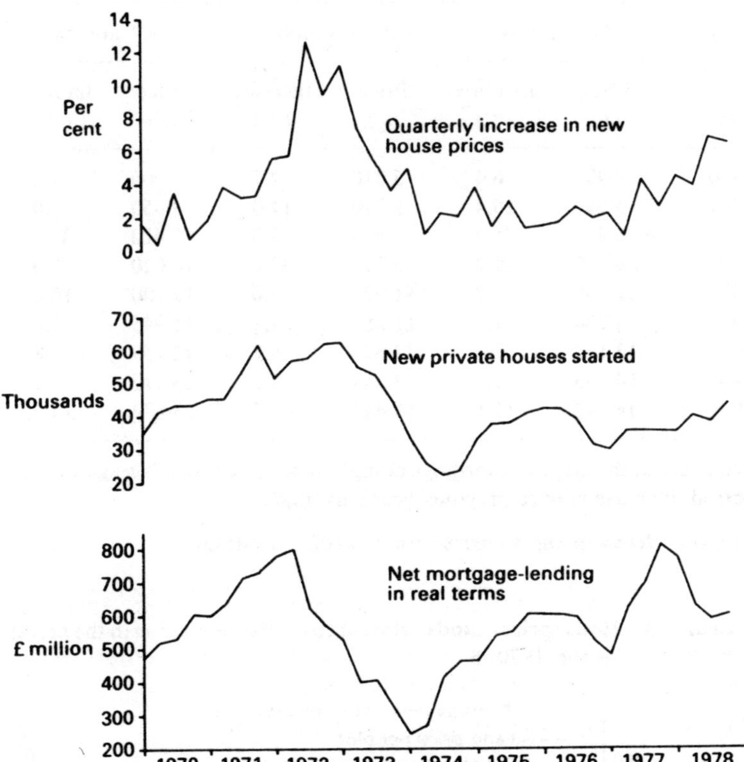

Mortgage-lending and house-building seasonally adjusted. Average prices at mortgage-completion stage. Mortgage-lending expressed in terms of purchasing power over new houses at average 1970 prices.

SOURCE: *Economic Trends* (HMSO).

FIGURE 7.2   Average house prices, 1970–8

Year	New houses		Existing houses		All houses	
	Price (£)	Increase (%)	Price (£)	Increase (%)	Price (£)	Increase (%)
1970	4 990	6.4	5 010	7.7	5 000	7.3
1971	5 510	10.4	5 710	14.0	5 650	13.0
1972	6 920	25.6	7 610	33.3	7 420	31.3
1973	9 630	39.2	10 710	33.6	10 020	35.0
1974	11 140	15.7	11 090	9.0	11 100	10.8
1975	12 234	9.8	11 880	7.1	11 945	7.6
1976	13 132	7.3	12 679	6.7	12 759	6.8
1977	14 343	9.2	13 589	7.2	13 712	7.5
1978	16 792	17.1	15 447	13.7	15 674	14.3

Prices are at the stage of mortgage completion. Price is the average over the period; increase is over previous year's average.

SOURCE: *Housing and Construction Statistics* (HMSO).

FIGURE 7.3   House prices, land costs and costs of construction in the private sector, 1970–8

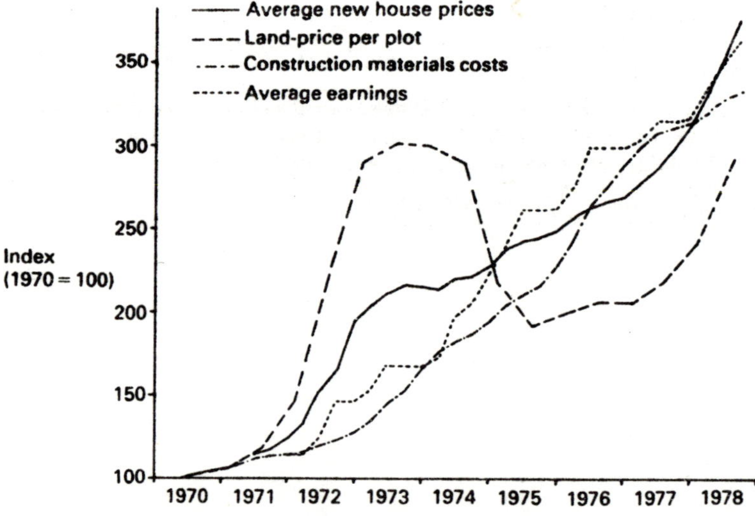

SOURCE: *Housing and Construction Statistics* (HMSO).

FIGURE 7.4   House-prices, retail-prices and earnings, 1956–77

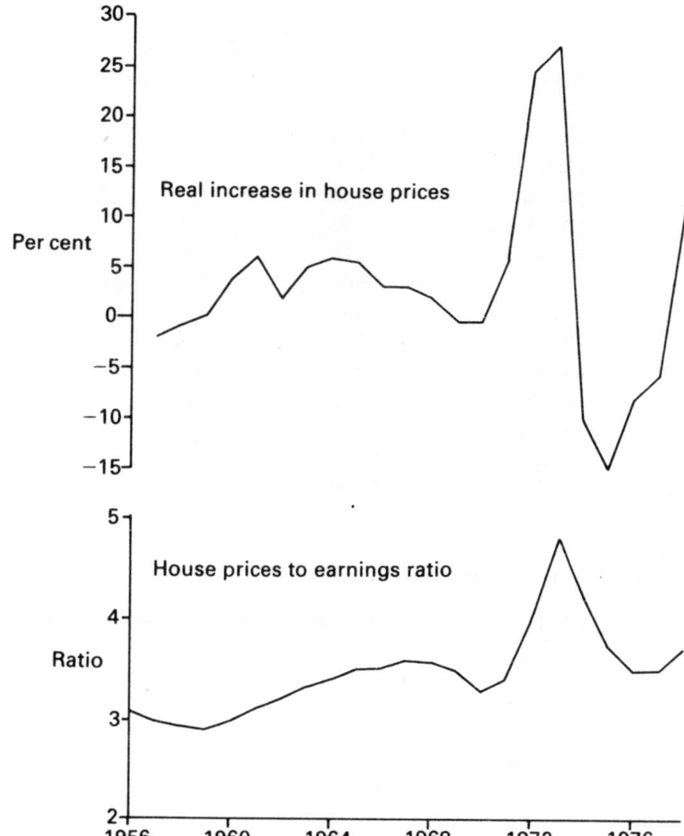

Average new house prices are at mortgage approval; average earnings relate
to employed males 21 or over; retail prices are derived from the 'all items'
index in *Economic Trends*. Increases are calculated over the previous year.
The real increase in house-prices is house-price increases minus retail-price
increase. House-prices to earnings ratio is house-prices divided by earnings.

SOURCE: *BSA Bulletin*, No. 15 (BSA, 1978).

FIGURE 9.1   Tax relief on mortgage interest and option-mortgage subsidy (£m)

Year	Current prices	Constant (1976) prices
1965/6	135	355
1966/7	155	395
1967/8	180	445
1968/9	200	470
1969/70	245	540
1970/1	300	620
1971/2	330	635
1972/3	395	710
1973/4	560	925
1974/5	770	1 075
1975/6	970	1 095
1976/7*	1 240	1 240
1977/8†	1 260	1 115

* *HPTV* estimate.

† *BSA Bulletin* estimate.

SOURCE: *HPTV*, II, Table VI.26; and *Facts and Figures*, No. 13 (BSA, 1978).

FIGURE 9.2 Subsidy to owners and public-sector tenants in different income ranges, 1974–5

Income of head of household and wife (£)	Average tax relief or option-mortgage subsidy (£)	Average general subsidy per tenant (£)	Average general subsidy and rent rebate per tenant (£)†
Under 1000	59	120	166
1000–1499	73	132	180
1500–1999	91	157	180
2000–2499	104	137	144
2500–2999	101	147	147
3000–3499	129	154	154
3500–3999	129	148	148
4000–4999	148	164	164
5000 and over	273*	154	154
All ranges	141	139	161

* Average tax relief in range £5000–£5999 was £179 and in the range £6000 and over £369.

† Rebate averaged over all tenants in income range, not only those receiving rebate.

SOURCE: *HPTV*, I, Tables IV.34 and IV.35.

FIGURE 9.3   Subsidy level to owner-occupiers and local-authority tenants, UK 1967/8–1977/8, current prices

Tax year	Tax relief and option-mortgage subsidy (£ m)	Subsidy to local-authority tenants (£m)	Average assistance per owner-occupier (£ p.a.)	Average assistance per owner-occupier with a mortgage (£ p.a.)	Average assistance to local-authority tenants (£ p.a.)
1967/8	180	200	22	40	39
1968/9	202	231	24	43	44
1969/70	244	280	28	49	51
1970/1	297	311	33	58	55
1971/2	327	328	36	61	57
1972/3	391	324	42	71	56
1973/4	556	432	58	98	73
1974/5	760	827	78	131	137
1975/6	957	1 066	96	162	173
1976/7	1 320	1 296	138	218	198
1977/8	1 347	1 440	121	217	215

SOURCE: 1967/8–1975/6, *HPTV*, II, Table V.1, except 'Average assistance per owner-occupier with a mortgage' which is calculated by means of figures for mortgaged owner-occupiers from *Housing Trends: Fourth Quarter 1978*, (Nationwide Building Society); 1976/7–1977/8, subsidy figures from *Social Trends* (HMSO) and average subsidies calculated from *Housing Trends, Fourth Quarter 1978*.

Notes and references

A list of abbreviations appears on p. 148.

Introduction

  1. *HPGP.*

Chapter 1

  1. *RC2*, p. 8.
  2. S. J. Price, *Building Societies: their Origin and History* (Franey, 1958).
  3. E. J. Cleary, *The Building Society Movement* (Elek, 1965) p. 46.
  4. *RC2*, p. 15.
  5. Ibid.
  6. *RC2*, p. 16.
  7. *RC2*, pp. 16–17.
  8. *RC2*, p. 7.
  9. *RC2*, p. 21.
10. *CRR*, 1974, p. 5.

Chapter 2

  1. See A. A. Nevitt, *Housing Taxation and Subsidies* (Thomas Nelson, 1966).
  2. See H. Bellman, *Bricks and Mortals* (Hutchinson, 1949); and H. Bellman, *Capital, Confidence and the Community* (Heffer, 1938). Also H. W. Richardson and D. Aldcroft, *Building in the British Economy between the Wars* (University of Glasgow, 1969); and H. W. Richardson, *Economic Recovery in Britain 1932–39* (Weidenfeld and Nicolson, 1967).
  3. E. J. Cleary, *The Building Society Movement* (Elek, 1965) p. 205.

4. See *Economist*, 18 February 1939, quoted in Cleary, *The Building Society Movement*, p. 197.

5. *Building Societies Gazette*, December 1933, p. 900, quoted in Cleary, *The Building Society Movement*, p. 205.

6. Bellman, *Bricks and Mortals*, p. 130.

7. Cleary, *The Building Society Movement*, pp. 187–8.

8. E. S. Watkins, 'Building Societies' in G. D. H. Cole (ed.), *Studies in Capital and Investment* (Gollancz, 1935).

9. Nevitt, *Housing Taxation and Subsidies*, p. 107.

10. D. Coates, *The Labour Party and the Struggle for Socialism* (Cambridge University Press, 1975) pp. 68–9.

11. M. Pinto-Dushinsky in V. Bogdanor and R. Skidelsky (eds), *The Age of Affluence 1851–64* (Macmillan, 1970) pp. 61–2.

12. S. Clarke and N. Ginsburg, 'The Political Economy of Housing', in *Political Economy and the Housing Question* (CSE Housing Workshop, 1975).

13. R. Crossman, *The Diaries of a Cabinet Minister* (Hamish Hamilton and Jonathan Cape, 1975) vol. 1, p. 383, referring to the 1964 election.

14. Ibid, p. 325.

15. Ibid, p. 377, referring to the 1966 election.

16. Ibid, p. 568, to the Chancellor of the Exchequer in a meeting on public expenditure cuts.

17. *Fair Deal for Housing*, Cmnd. 4728 (HMSO, 1971).

18. *Widening the Choice: the next steps in housing*, Cmnd 5280 (HMSO, 1973).

19. *HPGP*, p. 50.

20. *HPGP*, p. 50.

21. *HPGP*, p. 68.

22. H. Bellman, *The Silent Revolution* (Methuen, 1928) p. 31.

23. Ibid, p. 31.

24. H. Bellman, *The Building Society Movement* (Methuen, 1927) p. 54.

25. Quoted in the introduction to Bellman, *The Silent Revolution*.

26. 'British Homes: the building society movement', reprinted from the Building Society number of *The Times*, 31 May 1938, p. 40.

27. N. Branson and M. Heinemann, *Britain in the Nineteen-Thirties* (Panther, 1973) p. 205.

28. Report of an address to the Northumberland and Durham BSA by N. Griggs, Secretary-General of the National BSA, *Building Societies Gazette*, May 1976.

29. L. Sklair, 'The Struggle against the Housing Finance Act', in R. Miliband and J. Saville, *The Socialist Register* (Merlin Press, 1975).

30. But see Community Development Project, *Profits Against Houses* (CDP Information and Intelligence Unit, 1976), and M. Ball, 'British housing policy and the house-building industry', *Capital and Class*, 4, 1978, pp.

78–9, which indicate the real base for conflict between home-owners and those who supply finance and deal in housing.

31. *The Times*, 'British Homes', p. 3.
32. G. Lee, *The Services of a Building Society* (Hodder and Stoughton, 1964) pp. 11 and 13.
33. *Building Society Affairs*, No. 83 (BSA, 1975).
34. *HPGP*, p. 50.
35. Quoted in Bellman, *The Silent Revolution*, p. 29.
36. See the argument of F. Engels, *The Housing Question* (Progress, 1872, 1970) and, more recently, M. Castells, *The Urban Question* (Edward Arnold, 1977) pp. 145–69. This and other perspectives are discussed in P. Saunders, 'Domestic property and social class', *International Journal of Urban and Regional Research*, 2.1, 1978, pp. 233–51.
37. J. Rex and R. Moore, *Race, Community and Conflict* (Oxford University Press, 1967).
38. Branson and Heinemann, *Britain in the Nineteen-Thirties*, p. 206.
39. The slogan of the Community Development Project pamphlet *Profits Against Housing*.
40. D. Harvey, 'Labour, capital and class struggle around the built environment in advanced capitalist societies', in K. Cox (ed.), *Urbanization and Conflict in Market Societies* (Methuen, 1978).
41. Following, but extending, the argument of R. Haddon, 'A minority in a welfare state society', *New Atlantis*, 2, 1970, pp. 80–133.
42. G. Carchedi, 'On the economic identification of the new middle class', *Economy and Society*, 4, 1975, pp. 1–86.
43. See P. Hirst, 'Economic classes and politics', in A. Hunt (ed.), *Class and Class Structure* (Lawrence and Wishart, 1977).

Chapter 3

1. Revell estimates the societies' share of small-unit retail deposits held by persons to have increased from 29 per cent in 1957 to 51 per cent by 1970. J. Revell, 'UK Building Societies', Report 3, Annex 1 of OECD, *Housing Finance: Present Problems* (1974) p. 71.
2. *Housing and Construction Statistics* (HMSO, 1978).
3. Financial information in this section is derived from the Registrar's Report, *CRR*, 1978.
4. Information in this section is derived from *BSA Bulletin*, *CRR*, and *Building Societies Yearbook* (Franey).
5. *CRR*, 1973, p. 11.
6. See *CRR*, 1973, pp. 11–12.
7. J. Revell, *The British Financial System* (Macmillan, 1973) p. 384.
8. *CRR*, 1969.

9. Quoted in M. Harloe, *et al*, *The Organisation of Housing* (Heinemann, 1974) p. 82.

10. P. Williams, 'The role of financial institutions and estate agents in the private housing market', Working Paper No. 39 (Centre for Urban and Regional Studies, Birmingham University, 1976) p. 30.

11. *Building Society Management*, Building Society Administration Booklet No. 1, 5th ed (Building Societies Institute, 1973) p. 9.

12. Revell, *The British Financial System*, p. 367.

13. Temperance Permanent Building Society, *Into the Future* (1973) p. 19.

14. Information derived from *Building Societies Yearbook*, *Building Societies' Who's Who* (Franey), and *The Directory of Directors* (IPC Business Press).

15. D. S. Byrne, 'The property world in and around North Shields', North Tyneside Community Development Project, 1975; *Profits Against Houses* (CDP Information and Intelligence Unit, 1976).

16. See 'European Developments' in *Evidence Submitted by the Building Societies Association to the Committee to Review the Functioning of Financial Institutions* (BSA, 1978).

17. For a detailed account of the BSA and its relation with the government and other bodies see M. Boléat, *The Building Societies Association* (BSA, 1979).

18. *HPTV*, II, p. 106.

Chapter 4

1. *CRR*, 1974, p. 15.

2. A. Mason, 'Societies' investment portfolio must aim at longer-term, more stable money', *Building Societies Gazette*, January 1979, pp. 60–4.

3. See 'Taxation of building society interest', *BSA Bulletin*, 17, 1979.

4. The example is based on the share rate (8 per cent) and basic rate of income tax (33 per cent) current at the time of writing. The example may be recalculated to take account of subsequent changes in share interest or tax rates as follows:

$$\text{Gross equivalent for basic rate taxpayer} = \text{net share rate} \times \left(100/100 - \text{basic tax rate} \right)$$

Thus currently:

$$8\% \times (100/100 - 33\%) = 11.94\%$$

The gross equivalent for higher-than-basic-rate taxpayers can be calculated as follows:

$$\begin{array}{c} \text{Gross equivalent} \\ \text{for higher-rate} \\ \text{taxpayer} \end{array} = \begin{array}{c} \text{gross equivalent} \\ \text{for basic rate} \\ \text{taxpayer} \end{array} - \left[\begin{array}{c} \text{gross equivalent} \\ \text{for basic rate} \\ \text{taxpayer} \end{array} \times \begin{array}{c} \text{investor's} \\ \text{marginal} \\ \text{tax rate} \end{array} \div 100 \right]$$

Thus currently for a 55 per cent taxpayer:

$$11.94\,\% - (11.94\,\% \times 55\,\% \div 100) = 5.37\,\%$$

5. *Guide to Building Society Finance* (BSA, 1974) para. 5.51, p. 58.

6. J. Revell, 'UK Building Societies', Report 3, Annex 1 of OECD, *Housing Finance: Present Problems* (1974) p. 73.

7. Figures quoted in *Evidence Submitted by the Building Societies Association to the Committee to Review the Functioning of Financial Institutions* (BSA, 1978).

8. Figures in this section for 1974 are from a report produced by E. V. Morgan of the Economists Advisory Group, *Personal Savings and Wealth in Britain* (*Financial Times*, 1974).

9. *Economic Trends* (HMSO, January 1978), reproduced in BSA, *Evidence Submitted by the Building Societies.*

10. BSA, *Evidence Submitted by the Building Societies*, p. 15.

11. *Financial Statistics* (HMSO).

Chapter 5

1. *HPTV*, II, p. 142.

2. *CRR*, 1977.

3. *HPTV*, I, Table IV.32.

4. *Co-operation Between Building Societies and Local Authorities* (BSA, 1978) p. 19.

5. J. Tunnard, 'Marital Breakdown and the Loss of the Owner Occupied Home' and 'Housing Advice Notes' (on owner-occupiers with mortgage difficulties), both in *Roof*, Shelter, March 1976; see also J. Tunnard and C. Whately, *Rights Guide for Home Owners* (Child Poverty Action Group, 1977).

6. C. Lambert, 'Building Societies, Surveyors and the Older Areas of Birmingham', Working Paper No. 38 (Centre for Urban and Regional Studies, University of Birmingham) p. 37.

7. Figures in this section are from *BSA Bulletin* (*Facts and Figures* before October 1978), and *Housing and Construction Statistics* (HMSO), unless otherwise noted.

8. *BSA Bulletin*, and *Social Trends* (HMSO).

9. *The Mortgage Department*, 8th ed. (Building Societies Institute, 1972) p. 17.

10. R. H. Barbolet, 'Housing-classes and the socio-ecological system', Working Paper No. 4 (Centre for Environmental Studies, 1969) p. 37.

See also M. Harloe *et al*, *The Organisation of Housing* (Heinemann, 1974) p. 89.

11. Centre for Urban and Regional Studies Housing Monitoring Team, 'The structure and financing of building societies', Research Memorandum No. 64 (CURS, 1978) p. 28.
12. M. J. Boddy, unpublished PhD research.
13. *HPTV*, II, pp. 78–9.
14. Boddy, unpublished PhD. research.
15. *Planned Savings* publishes an annual building-societies' survey, detailing lending policies regarding different property types. That for 1977 appeared in September 1977, and for 1978 in August 1978.
16. *BSA Bulletin*, No. 16, 1978, and *Housing and Construction Statistics*, No. 25 (HMSO, 1978).
17. *HPTV*, II, p. 88, and I, 63.
18. *Building Society Management*, Building Society Administration Booklet No. 1, 5th ed. (Building Societies Institute, 1973) p. 23. See also P. Williams, 'Building societies and the inner city', *Transactions, Institute of British Geographers*, n.s., 3.1.1978, for a detailed review and analysis of this subject; and E. Low, 'The red (and green) lining of America', *Roof*, Shelter, November 1977.
19. *Mortgage Lending Procedure: a Model*, 5th ed. (Building Societies Institute, 1975) p. 23.
20. *Building Societies Gazette*, April 1977, p. 314.
21. Evidence on red lining in various cities was drawn together in S. Weir, 'Red line districts', *Roof*, Shelter, July 1976. This drew on the work of several researchers and organisations, including P. Herrington, research officer, Leicester Shelter Group; Lambert, 'Building Societies, Surveyors etc.' (Birmingham); North Hyde Park Residents' Association and South Headingly Community Association (Leeds), *Memorandum*, March 1976; M. J. Boddy, 'The structure of mortgage finance: building societies and the British social formation', *Transactions, Institute of British Geographers*, n.s., vol. 1, No. 1, 1976 (Newcastle); S. S. Duncan, 'Self-help: the allocation of mortgages and the formation of housing sub-markets', *Area*, vol. 8, No. 4, 1976 (Huddersfield); P. Williams, 'The role of institutions in the inner London housing market: the case of Islington', *Transactions, Institute of British Geographers*, n.s., vol. 1, No. 1, 1976; V. A. Karn, 'Priorities for local authority mortgage lending: a case study of Birmingham', Research Memorandum No. 52 (Centre for Urban and Regional Studies, University of Birmingham, May 1976) p. 12.
22. Lambert, 'Building Societies, Surveyors etc.', p. 33.
23. *Yorkshire Evening Post*, 16 December 1975; and *Building Societies Gazette*, May 1977, p. 426, respectively.
24. *Building Societies Gazette*, May 1976, p. 432.

25. See 'The provision of building finance', annexe to *Evidence submitted by the Building Societies Association to the Committee to Review the Functioning of Financial Institutions* (BSA, 1978), and *HPTV*, II, pp. 152–3.
26. Annual Returns to the Chief Registrar of Friendly Societies.
27. Department of the Environment, *Circular* 24/66.
28. DOE *Circular*, 38/78. Relevant *Circulars* include 22/71, 39/72 and 67/74.
29. *HPTV*, II, p. 154, note 13.
30. DOE *Circular* 29/70.
31. Cmnd. 6393 (HMSO, 1976) p. 71.
32. *HPTV*, II, p. 109.
33. *HPTV*, II, p. 79.
34. *HPTV*, II, p. 109. See J. O. Spalding, 'The building society support scheme for local authorities', and M. Boléat, 'Co-operation between building societies and local authorities–origins, methods and effects', both in *Co-operation Between Building Societies and Local Authorities* (BSA, 1978); M. L. Harrison, 'The local authorities/building societies support scheme in Leeds', *Housing Research Working Paper*, No. 2 (Dept of Social Policy and Administration, Leeds University, 1977); *Roof*, May 1977, p. 70; and N. McIntosh, 'Mortgage support scheme holds the lending lines', *Roof*, March 1978.
35. Spalding, p. 15.
36. Boléat, 'Co-operation between building societies and local authorities', p. 31.
37. Karn, 'Priorities for local authority mortgage building', Birmingham Community Development Project, 'Local authority mortgages in Saltley?', 1975; G. Green, 'Property exchange in Saltley', (Birmingham CDP, 1975); 'Private Housing and the Working Class', Final Report Series, No. 3 (Benwell Community Project, 1978).
38. See, for example, *Building Societies Gazette*, January 1979, pp. 60–4.

Chapter 6

1. See J. Revell, 'UK Building Societies', Report 3, Annex 1 of OECD, *Housing Finance: Present Problems* (1974).
2. *Financial Statistics* (HMSO).
3. For example, see S. T. Graham, 'Money supply controls are ineffective unless societies' funds are included', *Building Societies Gazette*, January 1979; and 'Mr. Stow replies to bank critics of societies' competition', *Building Societies Gazette*, May 1978.
4. See D. T. Llewellyn, 'Do building societies take deposits away from banks?', *Lloyds Bank Review*, January 1979; and *Evidence Submitted by the BSA to the Committee to Review the Functioning of Financial Institutions* (BSA, 1978) pp. 19–26.

5. Reported in BSA, *Evidence Submitted*, p. 7.
6. *Banking and Finance* (Labour Party, 1976) p. 5.
7. National Economic Development Office, *Finance for Investment* (1975) p. 134.
8. *Financial Statistics* (HMSO).
9. BSA, *Evidence Submitted*, p. 33.
10. See the discussion in *HPTV*, II, Chapter 7.
11. *HPTV*, II, p. 136.
12. Graham, 'Money supply controls are ineffective', p. 61; and *BSA Bulletin*, No. 18, 1979.
13. *HPTV*, II, p. 133.
14. *CRR*, 1977, p. 2.
15. H. Bellman, 'Building societies: some economic aspects', *Economic Journal*, vol. 33, March 1933, p. 20.
16. Ibid, p. 20.
17. *Report of the Committee on the Working of the Monetary System*, Cmnd. 827 (HMSO, 1959).
18. 'Competition and credit control', *Bank of England Quarterly Bulletin*, June 1971.
19. Ibid, p. 192.
20. OECD, *Housing Finance*, p. 74.
21. *CRR*, 1973, p. 2.
22. Bellman, 'Building societies: some economic aspects'.
23. *HPTV*, II, pp. 129–31, and *BSA Bulletin*, No. 16, 1978.
24. *HPTV*, II, p. 132.
25. OECD, *Housing Finance*, p. 48.

Chapter 7

1. *HPTV*, II, p. 50. Several studies have, in contrast, argued the importance of the real cost of housing, including incomes, the rate of household formation, the price (mortgage rate), and availability of credit, in particular, as determining demand and house-prices. See C. Whitehead, 'House prices: what determines them and how can they be controlled?', *Centre for Environmental Studies Review*, No. 3, 1978.
2. Department of the Environment, *Housing Land Availability in the South East* (HMSO, 1975) p. 38. A consultant's study.
3. Ibid, p. 6.
4. See Department of the Environment, *Circular* 70/74, 1974.
5. House-price statistics are from *Housing and Construction Statistics* (HMSO), and relate to 'mortgage completion', when houses are actually purchased rather than 'mortgage approval' (two–three months earlier) unless noted otherwise, since the former are more comprehensive in the early seventies.

6. *HPTV*, I, p. 171.
7. Ibid, p. 173
8. Ibid, p. 72.
9. *HPTV*, II, p. 51.
10. Department of the Environment, *Private Enterprise Housing Enquiry*, July 1977.
11. Department of the Environment, *Housing Land Availability in the South East*, p. 48.
12. Ibid, p. 8.
13. *Investors Chronicle*, 8 January 1974.
14. *HPTV*, I, p. 172.
15. Department of the Environment, *Housing Land Availability in the South East*, p. 2.
16. London and Cambridge Economic Service, *The British Economy: Key Statistics 1900–1970* (Times Newspapers, n.d.).
17. *HPTV*, II, p. 50.
18. *BSA Bulletin*, 15, 1978, presents statistics and analysis relating house-prices and earnings.
19. BSA Chairman, *Building Society Affairs*, 76 (BSA, 1973).
20. *Evidence Submitted by the Building Societies Association to the Housing Finance Review* (BSA, 1976) p. 15, and repeated in *BSA Bulletin*, 7, 1976, p. 14; and by M. Boléat, *Building Societies Gazette*, June 1976.
21. See *Evidence Submitted by the Building Societies Association to the Committee to Review the Functioning of Financial Institutions* (BSA, 1978) pp. 19–24.
22. *HPTV*, II, p. 112.
23. Ibid, pp. 112 and 117, expands on this argument.
24. Ibid, p. 113.
25. Ibid, p. 113.

Chapter 8

1. *HPGP*, p. 45.
2. Ibid, p. 50.
3. Ibid, p. 68.
4. Ibid, p. 68.
5. *HPTV*, I, p. 153, based on 'A forecast of housing prospects in the medium term', Chapter 3 of *HPTV*, I.
6. *HPGP*, p. 63.
7. See the discussion in *HPTV*, II, pp. 127–42.
8. *HPTV*, II, p. 136.
9. *HPGP*, p. 66.
10. *HPTV*, II, p. 139.
11. Ibid, p. 153.

12. *Evidence Submitted by the Building Societies Association to the Committee to Review the Functioning of Financial Institutions* (BSA, 1978) pp. 38–9.
13. *HPTV*, II, pp. 109–27 and 139–42.
14. *HPGP*, p. 66
15. J. Revell, *Flexibility in Housing Finance* (OECD, 1975) pp. 71–2; 'Sweden: key characteristics of institutions and instruments of housing finance', paper prepared within the Sveriges Riksbank, Stockholm, September 1974; D. L. Cohen and D. R. Lessard, 'Mortgage innovation to facilitate investment in housing: the case of Sweden', mimeo, 1974.
16. Revell, *Flexibility in Housing Finance*. See also J. W. Christian, 'Escalating payment mortgages for low and moderate income families in developing countries', International Union of Building Societies and Savings Associations *Newsletter*, No. 61, April 1976, pp. 4–6; and Dr B. von Hoffman, 'Systems of housing finance – Europe', IUBSSA *Newsletter*, No. 64, March 1977, p. 7.
17. See D. Hughes, 'Half-and-half mortgages: what they're about', and S. Weir and B. Kilroy, 'Equity sharing in Cheshunt', *Roof*, November 1976.
18. *HPGP*, p. 52. For a detailed discussion of this subject as a whole see P. Williams, 'Building societies and the inner city', *Transactions, Institute of British Geographers*, n. s., vol. 3, No. 1, 1978.
19. *HPTV*, II, p. 150.
20. *HPTV*, II, p. 98.
21. *HPGP*, p. 63.
22. Ibid, p. 50.
23. *Hansard*, col. 465, 21 April 1977.
24. Department of the Environment, 'Housing Strategies and Investment Programmes: arrangements for 1978/79', DOE *Circular* 63/77 (HMSO, June 1977).
25. *HPGP*, p. 59.
26. V. Karn, 'Priorities for local authority mortgage lending, a case study of Birmingham', Research Memorandum No. 52 (Centre for Urban and Regional Studies, University of Birmingham, 1976) p. 45.
27. *HPTV*, I, p. 59, and *HPTV*, III, p. 106.
28. *HPTV*, III, p. 118.
29. See M. J. Boddy, 'The structure of mortgage finance: building societies and the British social formation', *Transactions, Institute of British Geographers Transactions*, n. s., vol. I, No. 1, 1976, and references in Chapter 5 (note 21) for evidence relating to Newcastle, Leeds and Birmingham.
30. *Private Housing and the Working Class*, Final Report Series, No. 3 (Benwell Community Project, 1978) presents an extended discussion of owner-occupation with particular reference to inner-city areas.

31. D. Harvey 'The political economy of urbanisation in advanced capitalist societies: the case of the United States', in G. Gappert and H. Rose (eds), *The Social Economy of Cities* (Sage, 1976); and 'Government policies, financial institutions and neighbourhood change', in M. Harloe (ed.), *Captive Cities* (Wiley, 1977).
32. *Guardian*, 25 October 1975.
33. *Private Housing and the Working Class*, p. 88.

Chapter 9

1. *HPTV*, II, p. 5.
2. *HPTV*, I, pp. 211 and 213.
3. D. C. Stafford, *National Westminster Bank Quarterly Review*, November 1976, p. 11.
4. *Facts and Figures*, 8 (BSA, October 1976).
5. Housing Centre Trust, *Housing Finance Review: Evidence to the Secretary of State for the Environment* (1975).
6. London Boroughs Association, *Evidence for the Review of Housing Finance* (n.d).
7. *HPGP*, p. 49.
8. London Boroughs Association, *Evidence*; *HPTV*, I, p. 235.
9. *HPTV*, II, p. 13.
10. *Royal Commission on the Distribution of Income and Wealth*, Cmnd. 6171 (HMSO, 1975) p. 7.
11. For a more detailed discussion of the nature of capital gains see M. Ball, 'Owner occupation', in *Housing and Class in Britain* (Political Economy of Housing Workshop, 1976); D. Saunders, 'Domestic property and social class', *International Journal of Urban and Regional Research*, vol. 2, No. 2, 1978.
12. *HPTV*, II, p. 116.
13. Ibid, p. 114.
14. Shelter, *Reform of Housing Finance*, p. 25.
15. *HPTV*, II, p. 18.
16. Ibid, p. 4.
17. *Private Housing and the Working Class*, Final Report Series, No. 3 (Benwell Community Project, 1978) p. 105.
18. For example, the Building Societies (Reorganisation and National-isation) Bill, presented by John Ryman, MP, 22 December 1976.
19. *Hansard*, cols 222–4, 14 March 1978.
20. British Property Federation, *Policy for Housing* (1975) paras. 5.10. and 5.12.
21. Royal Institution of Chartered Surveyors, *Housing: the chartered surveyors' report*, (November 1975) para. 8.4.2.
22. Department of the Environment, 'Proposed government savings

bonus and loan scheme for first time buyers', consultative memorandum, August 1977.

23. *Roof*, vol. 4, No. 1, 1979. Editorial.
24. *Co-operation between Building Societies and Local Authorities* (BSA, 1978), p. 38.
25. V. Karn, 'Pity the poor home owners', *Roof*, 4 January 1979.
26. Ibid, p. 14.
27. *HPTV*, I, p. 58.
28. See *The Poverty of the Improvement Programme* (revised edition) (Community Development Project Political Economy Collective, 1977).
29. *Private Housing and the Working Class*, pp. 92–108.
30. See M. Boddy and F. Gray, 'Filtering theory and the legitimation of inequality', *Policy and Politics*, 7.1, 1979.
31. *Private Housing and the Working Class*, p. 110.
32. See *Whatever Happened to Council Housing* (Community Development Project Information and Intelligence Unit, 1976).
33. A. Murie, 'The sale of council houses: a study in social policy', Occasional Paper No. 35 (Centre for Urban and Regional Studies, Birmingham University); R. Forrest and A. Murie, 'Social segregation, housing need and the sale of council houses', Research Memorandum No. 53 (Centre for Urban and Regional Studies, Birmingham University, July 1976); V. Karn, 'How can we liberate council tenants?', *New Society*, 29 March 1979.
34. Murie, 'The sale of council houses', p. 155. Murie also quotes (p. 162) the Housing Management Sub-Committee of the Central Housing Advisory Committee report, 'Council Housing: purposes, procedures and priorities' (HMSO, 1969) as saying (p. 25): 'We think it is relevant to record that while there are over 150 professional staff in the Ministry of Housing and Local Government concerned with housing and construction, there is only *one* who is concerned with *housing management*.'
35. J. Greve, 'Voluntary housing in Scandinavia', Occasional Paper, No. 21 (Centre for Urban and Regional Studies, Birmingham University, 1971).
36. See Murie, 'The sale of council houses', for a discussion of this argument.

Bibliography

A list of abbreviations appears on p. 148.

Building society history and home-ownership

Bellman, H., *Bricks and Mortals* (Hutchinson, 1949).

Bellman, H., 'Building societies: some economic aspects', *Economic Journal*, vol. 43, March 1933.

Bellman, H., *The Building Society Movement* (Methuen, 1927).

Bellman, H., 'The building trades', in *Britain in Recovery*, produced and published by the British Association for the Advancement of Science, 1938.

Bellman, H., *Capital, Confidence and the Community* (Heffers, 1938).

Bellman, H., *The Silent Revolution* (Methuen, 1928).

Bellman, H., *The Thrifty Three-Millions* (Methuen, 1935).

Bowley, M., *Housing and the State 1919–1944* (Allen and Unwin, 1945).

Brabrook, E. W., *Building Societies* (1906).

Brabrook, E. W., and Scratchley, A., *The Law of Building Societies*, 2nd ed. (1882).

Branson, N., and Heinemann, M., 'Homes, landlords and building societies', in *Britain in the Nineteen-Thirties* (Panther, 1973).

Cleary, E. J., *The Building Society Movement* (Elek, 1965).

Gauldie, E. *Cruel Habitations: a History of Working Class Housing 1780–1918* (Allen and Unwin, 1974).

Gosden, P. H. J. H., 'Building societies', in *Self-help: Voluntary Associations in Nineteenth Century Britain* (Batsford, 1973).

Hobson, O. R., *A Hundred Years of the Halifax* (1953).

James, J. H., *A Treatise on Benefit Housing Societies* (1846).

Leeds Permanent Building Society, *A Survey of One Hundred Years* (LPBS, 1948). A history of the society 1848–1948.

Ludlow, J. M., 'Building societies', *Economic Review*, vol. 3, No. 1, 1893.

Mansbridge, A., *Brick on Brick* (CPBS, 1934). A history of the Cooperative Building Society.

Masterman, N. C., *John Malcolm Ludlow: the builder of Christian Socialism* (Cambridge University Press, 1963).

Pawley, M., *Home Ownership* (Architectural Press, 1978).

Price, S. J., *Building Societies: their origin and history* (Franey, 1958).

Price, S. J., *From Queen to Queen* (TPBS, 1954). A history of the Temperance Permanent Building Society.

Royal Commission on Friendly and Benefit Building Societies, First report with minutes of evidence, Parliamentary Papers, vol. XXV (HMSO, 1871); Second report, Parliamentary Papers, vol. XXVI (HMSO, 1872); Fourth report, Parliamentary Papers, vol. XXIII (HMSO, 1874).

Royal Commission on the Housing of the Working Classes, with minutes of evidence, Parliamentary Papers, vol. XXX (HMSO, 1884–5).

Royal Commission on Labour, Parliamentary Papers, vol. XXXIX, part 1 (HMSO, 1893–4).

Scratchley, A., *A Treatise on Benefit Building Societies* (1849).

Times, The, 'British homes: the building society movement', reproduced from the Building Societies number of *The Times*, 31 May 1938.

Valance, A., *Very Private Enterprise* (1956). An account of the Liberator Building Society collapse.

Watkins, E. S., 'Building societies', in G. D. H. Cole (ed.), *Studies in Capital and Investment* (Gollancz, 1935).

Building societies and owner-occupation

Artis, M. J., Kiernan, E. and Whitley, J. D., 'The effects of building society behaviour on housing investment', in M. Parkin and A. R. Nobay (eds), *Contemporary Issues in Economics* (Manchester University Press, 1975).

Ashmore, G., 'The owner occupied housing market', Research Memorandum No. 41 (Centre for Urban and Regional Studies, University of Birmingham, 1975).

Ashworth, H., *Building Society Work Explained*, 14th ed. (Franey, for the Building Societies Institute, 1973).

Ball, M., 'Owner occupation', in *Housing and Class in Britain* (Conference of Socialist Economists Housing Workshop, 1976).

Bank of England Quarterly Bulletin, 'Financial intermediaries: building societies', March 1971.

Barbolet, R. H., 'Housing-classes and the socio-ecological system', Working Paper No. 4 (Centre for Environmental Studies, 1969).

Boddy, M. J., 'Building societies and owner occupation', in *Housing and Class in Britain* (CSE Housing Workshop, 1976).

Boddy, M. J., 'Political economy of housing: mortgage-financed owner occupation in Britain', *Antipode*, vol. 8, No. 1, March 1976.

Boddy, M. J., 'The structure of mortgage finance: building societies in the British social formation', *Transactions, Institute of British Geographers*, n.s., vol. 1, No. 1, 1976.

Boléat, M., 'Das haus that Jacques built', *The Bankers Magazine*, August 1976.

Boléat, M., *The Building Societies Association* (BSA, 1979).

Boorman, J. T. and Peterson, M. O., 'Instability of savings flows and mortgage lending by financial intermediaries', *Scottish Economic Journal*, October 1973.

Buchanan, C. and Partners, *The Prospect for Housing*, for the Nationwide Building Society (1971).

Building Societies (Reorganisation and Nationalisation) Bill (presented by Mr John Ryman, MP), 22 December 1976.

Building Societies Association, *Guide to Building Society Finance* (BSA, 1974).

Building Societies Association, *Evidence Submitted to the National Board for Prices and Incomes June–August 1966* (BSA, 1966).

Building Societies Association, *Co-operation between Building Societies and Local Authorities* (BSA, 1978).

Building Societies Association, *Evidence Submitted by the Building Societies Association to the Committee to Review the Functioning of Financial Institutions* (BSA, 1978).

Building Societies Association, *The Housing Policy Review and the Building Societies* (BSA, 1978). Evidence submitted by the BSA to the Housing Finance Review, comments by the BSA on *Housing Policy – a Consultative Document*, and papers and proceedings of a BSA conference on the Housing Policy Review, December 1977.

Building Societies Institute, *Building Society Branches*, 3rd ed. BS Administration Booklet 5 (Franey, for BSI, 1970).

Building Societies Institute, *Building Society Management*, 5th ed., BS Administration Booklet 1 (Franey, for BSI, 1970).

Building Societies Institute, *The Influence of Building Societies on the Present and Future Patterns of Society*, Report of a Summer School (1964).

Building Societies Institute, *The Investment Department*, 10th ed., BS Administration Booklet 2 (Franey, for BSI, 1974).

Building Societies Institute, *The Mortgage Department*, 8th ed., BS Administration Booklet 3 (Franey, for BSI, 1972).

Centre for Urban and Regional Studies Housing Monitoring Team, 'The structure and functioning of building societies: a head office view', Research Memorandum No. 64 (Centre for Urban and Regional Studies, University of Birmingham, 1978).

Clark, S., 'The last resort? How councils make home loans', *Roof*, October 1976.

Clayton, G. *et al.*, 'The portfolio and debt behaviour of British building societies', Series 16A (Société Universitaire Européenne de Recherches Financière, 1975).

Community Development Project (Benwell), 'Private housing and the working class', Final Report Series, No. 3 (Benwell Community Project, 1978).

Community Development Project (Birmingham) and Karn, V. A., *Local Authority Mortgages in Saltley?* (Birmingham CDP, 1975).

Community Development Project (Saltley), 'Investment mortgages in Saltley' (a report to the Director of Fair Trading under the 1974 Consumer Credit Act and to the Secretary of State for the Environment), June 1975.

Duncan, S. S., 'Self-help: the allocation of mortgages and the formation of housing sub-markets', *Area*, vol. 8, No. 4, 1976.

Evans, A. W., *The Five Per Cent Sample Survey of Building Society Mortgages*, Central Statistical Office Studies in Official Statistics No. 26 (HMSO, 1975).

Ford, J., 'The role of the building society manager in the urban stratification system: autonomy versus constraint', *Urban Studies*, No. 12, 1975.

Foster, J., 'The demand for building society shares and deposits 1961–73', Discussion Papers in Economics, No. 9 (Department of Social and Economic Research, University of Glasgow, 1975).

Foster, J., 'The redistributive effects of the composite income tax arrangement and building society behaviour', Discussion Papers in Economics, No. 5 (Department of Social and Economic Research, University of Glasgow, 1974).

Ghosh, D., *The Economics of Building Societies* (Saxon House, 1974).

Ghosh, D. and Parkin, J., 'A theoretical and empirical analysis of portfolio, debt and interest behaviour of building societies', (Manchester School, September 1972).

Gough, T. J., 'Determinants of fluctuations in private housing investment', *Applied Economics*, June 1972.

Gough, T. J., 'Phases of British private housebuilding and the supply of mortgage credit', *Applied Economics*, September 1975.

Green, G., 'Property exchange in Saltley', in *Housing and Class in Britain* (CSE Housing Workshop, 1976).

Greer, R., *Building Societies?*, Fabian pamphlet (Fabian Society, December 1974).

Hadjimatheou, G., *Housing and Mortgage Markets: the UK experience* (Saxon House, 1976).

Harrison, M. L., 'The local authorities building societies support scheme in Leeds', Housing Research Paper, No. 1 (Department of Social Policy and Administration, University of Leeds, February 1977).

Harrison, M. L., 'Local authority mortgages in Leeds after local government reorganisation' (survey of 200 mortgages post April 1974), Housing

Research Paper, No. 2 (Department of Social Policy and Administration, University of Leeds, 1977).

Ineichen, B., 'Home ownership and manual workers' life-styles', *Sociological Review*, n.s., vol. 20, August 1972, pp. 391–412.

Ineichen, B., 'Home ownership: a neglected social revolution?', *Town and Country Planning*, vol. 41, No. 9, 1973.

Karn, V. A., 'Priorities for local authority mortgage lending: a case study of Birmingham', Research Memorandum No. 52 (Centre for Urban and Regional Studies, University of Birmingham, May 1976).

Karn, V. A., 'Pity the poor home owners', *Roof*, vol. 4, No. 1, January 1979.

Kemeny, J., 'Urban home-ownership in Sweden', *Urban Studies*, vol. 15, No. 3, 1978.

Lambert, C., 'Building societies, surveyors and the older areas of Birmingham', Working Paper No. 38 (Centre for Urban and Regional Studies, Birmingham University, 1976).

Lee, G., *The Services of a Building Society* (Hodder and Stoughton, 1964).

Llewellyn, D. T., 'Do building societies take deposits away from banks?', *Lloyds Bank Review*, No. 131, January 1979.

McIntosh, N., 'Mortgage support scheme holds the lending lines', *Roof*, vol. 3, No. 2, March 1978.

Mills, J., *Building Society Law (Wurtzburg and Mills)*, 14th ed. (Sweet and Maxwell, 1976).

Modligiani, F. and Lessard, D., *New Mortgage Designs for Stable Housing in an Inflationary Environment*, Conference Series, No. 14 (Federal Reserve Bank of Boston, 1975).

Oherlihy, C. St J. and Spencer, J. E., 'Building societies' behaviour 1955–70', *National Institute Economic Review*, vol. 61, August 1972.

Organisation for Economic Cooperation and Development (OECD), Committee on Financial Markets, *Flexibility in Housing Finance* (OECD, 1975).

Organisation for Economic Cooperation and Development (OECD), Committee on Financial Markets, *Housing Finance: present problems* (OECD, 1974).

Pollock, R., 'Supply of residential construction: a cross examination of recent housing behaviour', *Land Economics*, February 1973.

Revell, J., 'UK building societies', *Economic Research Papers*, University College of North Wales, 1973.

Revell, J., 'UK building societies', Report 3, Annex 1 of OECD, *Housing Finance: Present Problems* (OECD, 1974).

Rose, H., 'Building societies and the changing capital market', The Bellman Lecture (Abbey National Building Society, 1974).

Saunders, P., 'Domestic property and social class', *International Journal of Urban and Regional Research*, vol. 2, No. 2, June 1978.

Shelter Housing Aid Centre (SHAC), *Mortgages in London*, Pamphlet no. 2 (Shelter, 1973).

Smith, L. B., *The Postwar Canadian Housing and Residential Mortgage Markets and the Role of the Government* (Toronto University Press, 1974).

Stone, M. E., 'The housing crisis, mortgage lending and class struggle', *Antipode*, vol. 7, No. 2, 1975.

Struyk, R. S. and Marshall, S., 'The determinants of household home ownership', *Urban Studies*, vol. 11, No. 3, 1974.

Tunnard, J. and Whately, C. *Rights Guide for Home Owners* (Child Poverty Action Group, 1977).

Vickers, L. E., *Buying a House* (Penguin, 1976).

Whitehead, C., *The UK Housing Market* (Saxon House, 1974).

Whitely, J. D., 'Mortgages: the case for index-linking', *National Institute Economic Review*, November 1974.

Williams, P., 'The role of financial institutions and estate agents in the private housing market: a general introduction', Working Paper No. 39 (Centre for Urban and Regional Studies, University of Birmingham, 1976).

Williams, P., 'The role of institutions in the inner London housing market: the case of Islington', *Transactions, Institute of British Geographers*, n.s., vol. 1, No. 1, 1976.

Williams, P., 'Building societies and the inner city', *Transactions, Institute of British Geographers*, n.s., vol. 3, No. 1, 1978.

Wistow, G., 'Managing housing policy – the implementation of policy in the owner occupied sector', *Local Government Studies*, vol. 4, No. 3, October 1978.

Housing in general

Ambrose, P. J., 'The land market and the housing system', Urban and Regional Studies Working Paper, No. 3 (University of Sussex, October, 1976).

Berry, F., *Housing: the Great British Failure* (Charles Knight, 1974).

Boddy, M., and Gray, F., 'Filtering theory, housing policy and the legitimation of inequality', *Policy and Politics*, vol. 7, No. 1, January 1979.

Bow Group, *Towards Freedom in Housing* (Bow Group, 1975).

British Property Federation, *Policy for Housing* (BPF, December 1975).

Central Office of Information, *British Banking and Other Financial Institutions*, Reference Pamphlet No. 123 (HMSO, 1974).

Central Office of Information, *Housing in Britain*, 3rd ed., Reference Pamphlet No. 41 (HMSO, 1975).

Charles, S., *Housing Economics* (Macmillan, 1977).

Clarke, S. and Ginsburg, N., 'The political economy of housing', *Political Economy and the Housing Question* (CSE Housing Group, 1975).

Committee on the Working of the Monetary System ('The Radcliffe Report'),

Cmnd. 827 (HMSO, 1959), and Memoranda of Evidence, vol. 2, part IV (HMSO, 1960).

Community Development Project, *Profits Against Houses*, submitted as evidence to the Housing Finance Review (CDP Information and Intelligence Unit, 1976).

Community Development Project, *Whatever Happened to Council Housing?* (CDP Information and Intelligence Unit, 1976).

Community Development Project (North Tyneside), 'North Shields working class politics and housing 1900–1977', *Final Report*, vol. 1 (North Tyneside CDP, 1978).

Community Development Project (Southwark) and Joint Docklands Action Group, *Alternative Forms of Tenure: preferences and costs* (CDP, 1975).

Conference of Socialist Economists Housing Group, *Political Economy and the Housing Question* (CSE, 1975).

Conference of Socialist Economists Housing Group, *Housing and Class in Britain*, (CSE, 1976).

Cullingworth, J. B., *Essays on Housing Policy – the British Scene* (Allen and Unwin, 1979).

Department of the Environment, *Housing Land Availability in the South East – a consultant's study*, produced by the Economist Intelligence Unit Ltd in association with Halpern and Partners (HMSO, 1975).

Donnison, D., *The Government of Housing* (Penguin, 1967).

Duclaud-Williams, R. H., *The Politics of Housing in Britain and France* (Heinemann, 1978).

Economists Advisory Group, *Personal Savings and Wealth in Britain*, by E. V. Morgan (*Financial Times*, 1974).

Fair Deal for Housing, Cmnd. 4728 (HMSO, 1971).

Forrest, R. and Murie, A., 'Social segregation, housing need and the sale of council houses', Research Memorandum No. 43 (Centre for Urban and Regional Studies, University of Birmingham, 1976).

Harloe, M., Issacharoff, R. and Minns, R., *The Organisation of Housing* (Heinemann, 1974).

Harvey, D., 'Class-monopoly rent, finance capital and the urban revolution', *Regional Studies*, vol. 8, Nos. 3–4, 1974.

Harvey, D., 'The political economy of urbanisation in advanced capitalist societies: the case of the U.S.', in G. Gappert and H. Rose (eds), *The Social Economy of Cities* (Sage, 1976).

Harvey, D., 'Government policies, financial institutions and neighbourhood change', in M. Harloe (ed.), *Captive Cities* (Wiley, 1977).

Headey, B., *Housing Policy in the Developed Economy* (Croom Helm, 1978).

Hillebrandt, P. M., *Economic Theory and the Construction Industry* (Macmillan, 1974).

Holmans, A. E., 'A forecast of the effective demand for housing in Britain', *Social Trends*, No. 1, 1970.

Housing Centre Trust, *Housing Finance Review: evidence to the Secretary of State for the Environment* (HCT, November 1975).

Housing Policy: a consultative document, Cmnd. 6851, (HMSO, 1977). Government Green Paper, accompanied by *Technical Volume*, Parts I, II, III (1977).

Hughes, G. A., *Inflation and Housing* (Housing Research Foundation, 1974).

Institute of Fiscal Studies, 'Housing finance', IFS Publication No. 12 (IFS, 1975).

Labour Party, *Banking and Insurance Green Paper*, report of a Labour Party Study Group (LP, 1973).

Labour Party National Executive Committee's Housing Sub-Committee, *Labour Party Evidence to the Review of Housing Finance* (LP, March 1976).

London Boroughs Association, *Evidence Submitted by the Housing and Works Committee of the LBA to the Review of Housing Finance by the Secretary of State for the Environment* (London Boroughs Association, 1975).

McPherson, C. B., *The Political Theory of Possessive Individualism* (Oxford University Press, 1962).

McRae, H. and Cairncross, F. *Capital City: London as a financial centre* (Eyre Methuen, 1974).

Madge, J., *The Housing Experience of Newly Married Couples* (Centre for Studies in Social Policy, 1976).

Murie, A., 'Household movement and housing choice', Occasional Paper No. 28 (Centre for Urban and Regional Studies, University of Birmingham, 1974).

Murie, A., 'The sale of council houses', Occasional Paper No. 35 (Centre for Urban and Regional Studies, University of Birmingham, 1976).

Murie, A., Niner, P. and Watson, C., *Housing Policy and the Housing System* (Allen and Unwin, 1976).

National Board for Prices and Incomes, 'Rates of interest on building society mortgages', *Report* No. 22, Cmnd. 3136 (HMSO, 1966).

National Economic Development Office, *Finance for Investment* (NEDO, May 1975).

National House-Building Council, *Housing Finance Review: memorandum of evidence by the NHBC* (NHBC, n.d.).

Needleman, L., *The Economics of Housing* (Staples Press, 1966).

Nevitt, A. A., *Housing, Taxation and Subsidies* (Thomas Nelson, 1966).

Niner, P., 'Local authority housing: policy and practice', Occasional Paper No. 31 (Centre for Urban and Regional Studies, University of Birmingham, 1975).

Odling-Smee, J., 'The impact of the fiscal system on different tenure patterns', in *Housing Finance*, Publication No. 12 (Institute of Fiscal Studies, 1975).

Orren, K., *Corporate Power and Social Change* (Johns Hopkins University Press, 1974).

Revell, J., 'Building societies', in J. Revell, *The British Financial System* (Macmillan, 1973).

Revell, J., 'Housing Finance', *Three Banks Review*, July 1977.

Royal Institution of Chartered Surveyors, *Housing: the chartered surveyors' report* (RICS, November 1976).

Shelter, *Reform of Housing Finance*, Shelter's evidence to the Housing Finance Review (Shelter, 1975).

Smith, S., *Guide to Housing* (Housing Centre, 1977).

Stafford, D., *The Economics of Housing Policy* (Croom Helm, 1977).

Stafford, D., 'Government and the housing situation', *National Westminster Bank Quarterly Review*, November 1976.

Widening the Choice: the next steps in housing (Government White Paper), Cmnd. 5280 (HMSO, 1973).

Statistics and information sources

Annual Returns Form AR 11. Statutory return from all societies to the Registry of Friendly Societies in prescribed form. Includes assets, income and expenditure and an analysis of lending and investment.

Bank of England Statistical Abstract. Includes building society holdings of Government debt, and flow of funds accounts in which the societies are distinguished.

Building Society Affairs (BSA). Approximately quarterly. Chairman's comment, short explanatory articles on aspects of building-society operations from the building-society point of view.

Building Societies Association (14 Park Street, Mayfair, London W1Y 4AL).

BSA Bulletin (BSA). Quarterly. Formerly *Facts and Figures* to No. 15, July 1978. A comprehensive presentation of statistics on building societies and owner-occupied housing. Tables include building-society progress, savings, mortgages, distribution of loans, house-prices, house-building. Includes a regular commentary on building societies and the housing market, and supplementary articles and tables.

Building Societies Gazette (Franey and Co). Quarterly, first published January 1869. 'An independent journal devoted to the principles of thrift and home-ownership.'

Building Societies Institute, Fanhams Hall, Ware, Hertfordshire. Produces *Building Societies Institute Journal* every two months.

Building Societies Yearbook (Franey and Co). Annual. Includes historical tables on the building societies and of interest rates, annual review and report of the BSA, and the most recent balance sheet of all building societies, together with postal addresses and list of directors and executives.

Building Societies' Who's Who (Franey and Co). Occasional from 1949. Includes biographical notes of building-society directors and executives. Includes partial list of individuals' company directorships and other interests.

Chief Registrar of Friendly Societies Annual Report: Building Societies (HMSO). Not published 1939–51 inclusive. Prior to 1915 report included in Parliamentary Papers and since then the relevant BS section has been 'Part D' (1915–39), 'Part 5' (1946–66) and 'Part 2' (1967–to date).

Companies Registration Office (Companies House, 55–71 City Road, London EC1Y 1BB). Files on individual companies open to public inspection. Include annual reports and accounts; memoranda of association; major shareholdings; directors and their other directorships; loans received, including those from building societies, listing amount and form of security offered.

Compendium of Building Society Statistics (BSA). Compilation of statistics relating to the activities of building societies including building society financial statistics, 1955–77; Registry of Friendly Societies statistics on building societies, 1890–1977; rates of interest; house-prices.

Economic Trends (Central Statistical Office: HMSO). Monthly. Time series of house-building, building-society receipts and lending and house-prices. *Economic Trends Annual Supplement* has figures back to 1945.

Factual Background (Bristol and West Building Society). A quarterly review of statistics and other data produced by the Research Department of the Bristol and West Building Society. Includes tables on building societies, personal savings and credit, and housing.

Family Expenditure Survey (Department of Employment: HMSO). Annual. Household expenditure figures, including housing by tenure.

Financial Statistics (Central Statistical Office: HMSO). Monthly. Tables relating to financial institutions, personal-sector savings and investment, and interest rates, as well as building-society investment and lending statistics.

General Household Survey (Office of Population Censuses and Surveys: HMSO). Annual since 1971. A comprehensive analysis of housing stock, household characteristics, tenure, amenities, house-building, housing finance and investment.

Homes (Abbey National Building Society). Quarterly. Housing and housing finance statistics and commentary.

Housing and Construction Statistics (Department of the Environment: HMSO). Quarterly. The major official source of statistics on all aspects of housing and housing finance.

Housing in Great Britain (S. M. Farthing and M. C. Fleming, Heinemann, 1974). Royal Statistical Society/Social Science Research Council review of UK statistical sources.

Inland Revenue Statistics (Board of the Inland Revenue: HMSO). Annual.

Includes estimates of personal wealth which identify separately building-society investment and dwellings.

Newsletter of the International Union of Building Societies and Savings Associations (BSA). Quarterly, from the BSA.

Occasional Bulletin (Nationwide Building Society). Quarterly, October 1970 onwards. Previously published under the society's former name, Cooperative Permanent BS, since 1952. Contains quarterly figures on regional house-prices based on mortgage approvals and other statistics.

Planned Savings. Monthly. Contains annual survey of building-society lending policy, and frequent articles on mortgages and investment in the building societies.

Registry of Building Societies (17 North Audley Street, London W1Y 2AP). Files on individual societies open to public inspection by prior appointment. Contents include societies' annual return to the Registrar (AR 11 forms); annual reports; directors names; details of transfers of engagements, unions, mergers, changes of name.

Roof (Shelter's housing magazine). First published October 1975, bi-monthly from January 1976. Articles and statistics on building societies, housing finance and policy.

Royal Commission on the Distribution of Income and Wealth ('The Diamond Commission'), Report No. 1, Cmnd. 6171 (HMSO, 1975); Report No. 4, Cmnd. 6626 (HMSO, 1976); and Report No. 5, Cmnd. 6999 (HMSO, 1977). Statistics on the importance of building-society investment, home-ownership and imputed rental income to the distribution of income and wealth. Report No. 5 devotes a chapter specifically to housing.

Social Trends (Central Statistical Office: HMSO). Annual. Includes tables on the housing stock, households' rent and mortgage costs, housing improvement and construction, and public spending on housing.

The Times 1000 (*The Times*). Annual summary of leading companies and financial institutions, including building societies.

Index